A NEW CENTURY
OF SEX KILLERS

D0320492

A NEW CENTURY OF SEX KILLERS

Brian Marriner

PAN BOOKS

First published 1992 by True Crime Library

This edition published 2005 by Pan Books
an imprint of Pan Macmillan Ltd
Pan Macmillan, 20 New Wharf Road, London N1 9RR
Basingstoke and Oxford
Associated companies throughout the world
www.panmacmillan.com

ISBN 0 330 42105 0

1 3 5 7 9 8 6 4 2

A CIP catalogue record for this book is available from
the British Library.

Printed and bound in Great Britain by
Mackays of Chatham plc, Chatham, Kent

To my son, Steven,
for the encouragement.
And for Mike James,
for the inspiration.

ABOUT THE AUTHOR

Until his death in 1999 Brian Marriner was one of Britain's leading true crime authors whose work is published all over the world. An expert in criminology and forensic science he was a regular contributor to the top non-fiction crime magazines *True Detective*, *True Crime Monthly* and *Master Detective* and has written editions of *Murder Casebook*. His book *Forensic Clues to Murder* was described by Colin Wilson as "the definitive text on forensic medicine, which is destined to become a modern classic."
What distinguishes Brian Marriner's work is his uncanny knack of probing the motives and thinking behind the crimes, while introducing the most gruesome elements with calm scientific interest.

Contents

Foreword
by Colin Wilson

John Addington Symonds's classic *Renaissance in Italy* contains an account of one of the most appalling tyrants known to history – Ibrahim ibn Ahmed, a ninth-century prince of Africa and Sicily. We would probably say simply that the man was an insane sadist. Symonds tells how on one occasion he murdered sixty youths "originally selected for his pleasure" by burning them alive in a furnace or suffocating them in the steam chamber of his bath. Eight of his brothers and his own son were murdered in his presence:

> But his fiercest fury was directed against women. He seems to have been darkly jealous of the perpetuation of the human race. Wives and concubines were strangled, sawn asunder and buried alive if they showed signs of pregnancy. His female children were murdered as soon as they saw the light; sixteen of them whom his mother managed to conceal and rear at her own peril were massacred upon the spot when Ibrahim discovered whom they claimed as a father.

There then follows an extremely curious passage:

Contemporary Arab chroniclers, pondering upon the fierce and gloomy passions of this man, arrived at the conclusion that he was the subject of a strange disease, a portentous secretion of black bile producing the melancholy which impelled him to atrocious crimes.

As to Symonds himself, he tried to explain Ibrahim's crimes by inventing a new word – haematomania, which simply means blood-lust.

But then we have to remember that Symonds was writing around 1870, and that at this time no one understood the nature of sex crime. What seems stranger still is the very idea was unknown. Only a few years earlier, in 1867, a clerk named Frederick Baker approached a group of children near the town of Alton in Hampshire, England, and persuaded an eight-year-old girl named Fanny Adams to go with him for a walk. A few hours later her disembowelled body was found in a hop garden, literally torn to pieces. Baker's diary had an entry: "Killed a young girl today. It was fine and hot."

In reporting this story, and Fred Baker's subsequent execution, the *Illustrated Police News* explained that the killer was the son of an alcoholic and was suffering from "mania". The fact that the child's genitals were missing was not mentioned.

In discussing the case in my *Criminal History of Mankind*, I point out that even the account in the *Illustrated Police News* offers us a number of interesting clues to the psychology of the killer. When the child's mother encountered Baker soon after the abduction and asked him what had happened to her daughter Baker seemed perfectly calm, and assured her that Fanny had gone off to buy sweets. She saw no blood on his clothing. That would be impossible unless Baker had stripped himself naked before killing her child. And that suggests premeditation, as does his unperturbed manner – a man who has just surrendered to an overwhelming passion would feel shaken and guilty. So Baker had thought it out in advance. In fact few sex killers commit their crimes "out of the blue"; most of them have been brooding on rape for a long time, and many have a collection of pornography. Frederick Baker was a paedophile, and he had probably been indulging in sadistic daydreams, including decapitation – Fanny's head was the first part of her to be found – for months or years before he finally nerved himself to put his fantasies into practice.

Just over twenty years later, what I have called "the age of sex crime" was launched by the unknown maniac known as Jack the Ripper. As everyone now knows, he killed five women in the Whitechapel area of London between August and November 1888, usually disembowelling them, and taking away certain inner organs. But one of the oddest aspects of the Ripper murders is that the Victorians did not recognise them as sex crimes. Sir Melville Macnaghten, Commissioner of Police soon after the murders, described the Ripper as "sexually insane." Yet what he meant was almost certainly that the Ripper was a "religious maniac" who hated prostitutes because of their immorality. In fact this was one of the most popular theories at the time – that he was a puritan driven to insanity by his hatred of immoral women.

Eleven years after the Ripper murders, in 1899, there appeared in England an edition of a strange German work called *Psychopathia Sexualis* by a German doctor named Richard von Krafft-Ebing, which achieved instant wide circulation. This was the first major clinical work on "sexual perversion", and it devoted its final chapter to a consideration of the problem of sex crime. This, says Krafft-Ebing, is on the rise, particularly the rape of children under the age of fourteen. And this comment itself offers an important insight into the rise of sex crime. In the nineteenth century there was so much poverty that any "gentleman" with five shillings in his pocket could pick up a working-class girl and take her to the nearest rooming house. "Walter", the anonymous author of the Victorian sexual classic *My Secret Life*, describes dozens of such encounters, in many cases with girls who were virgins when he met them. This meant that it would have been pointless to commit rape on a teenage girl, when she would probably consent to intercourse for a few shillings. But children were still "forbidden". This explains why, in the mid-nineteenth century, 90 per cent of rapes that came to court were committed on children. It was not until the early twentieth century, when women began to work in factories and offices, and they ceased to be available to casual Don Juans like Walter – became "forbidden" too – that they began to figure increasingly in the rape statistics.

But it is interesting to note that the few sex murders mentioned by Krafft-Ebing were all committed by idiots or "degenerates"; people with a history of alcoholism and mental illness. In fact, he cites far more cases of exhibitionism than of murder. And he obviously finds this just as difficult to explain, except in terms of insanity and "degeneracy". He explains that modesty is an ingrained characteristic in all civilized societies, and that therefore anyone who offends public decency by exposing himself must be mentally defective or degenerate.

Now obviously the doctor is overlooking an important alternative: that a perfectly normal person may have such a high level of sex drive and be so frustrated, that his "civilized" inhibitions disappear, and he goes out and exposes himself to a schoolgirl, or makes an attempt to assault her sexually. Why did he overlook anything so obvious? The answer is, quite simply, because he was born in 1840, and grew up in a society in which sex crime was a rarity, except among drunks or degenerates.

It is not surprising that Dr Krafft-Ebing failed to understand the real nature of the problem. Even today, with roughly a century of sex crime behind us, we are only just beginning to grasp what happened. And what happened is very odd indeed. In previous centuries there was very little sex crime in our modern sense of the word. *The Newgate Calendar* (1774) is one of the most comprehensive accounts of crime in England in the eighteenth century, and there are only three or four "sex crimes" in the whole book – a lord who kidnapped and raped a Quakeress, a teacher who had sexual intercourse with a ten-year-old servant girl, and so on. The great majority of the crimes involve robbery. And that was because, in the eighteenth century, most people were so poor that their main problem was simply keeping body and soul together. Moreover, sex was so freely available that rape would have been superfluous.

One of the great social revolutions of the eighteenth century occurred in 1740, when a novel called *Pamela* appeared on the bookstalls in London. It was written by a printer named Samuel Richardson, and told the story of a pretty servant girl whose young master makes strenuous efforts to take her virginity, and ends by marrying her. *Pamela* was the first novel in our modern sense of the word. Dozens – in fact, hundreds – of novels had been written and published before then, but they were mostly old-fashioned tales of travel and adventure. *Pamela* was more like a soap opera, a novel with which every reader could "identify". And within a year or two, novels had become the great popular entertainment of the age. And many of them, like *Pamela*, contained a strong element of voyeuristic sex.

Seven years after the publication of *Pamela*, a penniless young adventurer named John Cleland wrote a sex-novel called *Memoirs of a Woman of Pleasure* – better known as *Fanny Hill* – the first pornographic novel. It tells the story of how a young country girl comes to London, takes a job as a maidservant in a place which she is too innocent to recognize as a brothel, is introduced to the delights of sex by a lesbian, then loses her virginity to a young gentleman who subsequently deserts her; after that she makes a living by selling her body. The government was so shocked by Cleland's novel that he was offered a life pension on condition he wrote no more, and he lived happily ever after. And it was another fifty years or so before pornography really "caught on" – largely as a result of the underground popularity of the novels of the Marquis de Sade. By the year 1830 – shortly before the accession of Queen Victoria – England was flooded by pornographic novels (many printed in Amsterdam) with titles like *The Lustful Turk* and *The Bedfellows*. And devotees of pornography (like Keats's biographer Lord Houghton) would have noticed an interesting difference between *Fanny Hill* and *The Bedfellows*. *Fanny Hill* was quite unashamedly ribald and Rabelaisian; this new pornography was somehow furtive. For example a typical story might describe how a ten-year-old girl peeps in through the pantry window and sees the butler masturbating; curious to learn more, she takes the first opportunity to ask him what he was doing, and after swearing her to silence, he tells her about the birds and the bees... And in a day or so, he climbs into her little bed and "makes a woman of her". Sex was ceasing to be a hearty pleasure that could be described in the kind of cheerfully bawdy language Shakespeare would have used, and had become a matter of *imagination*. And there was something curiously overheated and feverish about the Victorian sexual imagination. Victorian pornography is full of incest and seduction of minors and men peeping through holes in lavatory doors. It was at about this time that an engineer discovered "superheated steam", and it would not be inaccurate to say that Victorian pornographers discovered "superheated sex".

That is what Krafft-Ebing failed to understand: that a perfectly normal person could become so obsessed with sexual desire that he might become a kind of sexual criminal. And it is true that during Krafft-Ebing's lifetime this was still by no means obvious. The case of Frederick Baker – already discussed – was one of the first notable sex crimes to take place in England, and Krafft-Ebbing included it in a later edition of *Psychopathia Sexualis*. But Baker was obviously mentally unstable. So was Eusebius Pieydagnelle, a French butcher's assistant who became so obsessed with blood that he finally went on a killing rampage, stabbing seven people to death and experiencing orgasm as he did so. So too was Jesse Pomeroy, an American teenager with a sadistic streak who murdered two children in Boston. As was the Italian Vincenz Verzeni, who could only achieve orgasm while throttling women. And so was the Frenchman Louis Menesclou, who lured a four-year-old girl to his room in Paris, then raped and dismembered her. So was the French Jack the Ripper, Joseph Vacher, who roamed around the countryside in the 1890s, committing murder and rape whenever he got the opportunity – a frightening anticipation of the modern "serial killer." When Krafft-Ebing died in 1902 it was by no means obvious that the sex killer might be, in many respects, a fairly normal individual.

But as the new century progressed, it became increasingly obvious. Even as early as 1895, a Sunday school teacher named Theodore Durrant lured two girls into a Baptist church in San Francisco, and raped them after killing them. A man named Hadley rented a house in San Francisco, lured a teenage babysitter to it, and left her naked body in the bed for weeks – he was never caught. In 1913 a teenager named Mary Phagan was murdered in a factory basement in Atlanta, Georgia; Leo Frank, the Jewish manager of the factory, was accused of the crime, and lynched. Many years later it was established that the actual killer was the black caretaker. The most interesting thing about the Frank case is that it created such a world-wide sensation, demonstrating that sex crime was still a rarity.

But it was during and after the First World War that the age of sex crime really began. In a village near Budapest, a man named Bela Kiss lured women to his cottage and killed them for their money and possessions, concealing the naked bodies in oil drums. Kiss was a handsome Don Juan, much admired by women; he was also a "satyr", a man with such a craving for sex that he often made love to several prostitutes a day. He used the money from his murders to hire more prostitutes. "Satyrism" may or may not be abnormal, but it is certainly fairly common (in 1981 the novelist Georges Simenon admitted in his *Intimate Memoirs* that he had been a lifelong satyr, and that he had made love to some ten thousand women, mostly prostitutes). A number of German sex killers, including Fritz Haarmann, Karl Denke, Georg Grossmann, Adolf Seefeld and the "Düsseldorf vampire" Peter Kürten, operated during and after the First World War, and made the concept of serial murder – which had caused such universal panic in the days of Jack the Ripper – familiar to police forces all over Europe. Meanwhile in the United States, Earle Nelson, known as "the Gorilla Murderer", wandered around from Seattle to Buffalo leaving a trail of raped and strangled bodies, while a violent rebel named Carl

Panzram killed at random because he found life so awful that he felt he was doing his victims a favour by helping them out if it.

And now, as we approach the end of the twentieth century, sex crime has become – as Brian Marriner remarks – a growth industry. We do not fully understand the reasons for it, but one is fairly obvious. The level of sexual promiscuity has always been high in slums. In the Whitechapel of Jack the Ripper – where the average number to a room was seven – incest was common, and children played "mothers and fathers" as a matter of course. A friend of Lord Salisbury was walking down a slum court in London when he saw a boy and girl of about ten attempting sexual intercourse on the pavement. He pulled the boy off the girl, and received the indignant rebuke: "Why do you take hold of me? There's a dozen of them at it down there." Many years later a zoologist named John Calhoun tried the experiment of overcrowding rats in cages, and found to his astonishment that, beyond a certain degree of overcrowding, he was breeding "criminal rats" who roamed about in gangs committing cannibalism and rape. This obviously explains what is happening in a modern city like New York, where, a few years ago, a gang of teenagers raped and sodomized a female jogger in Central Park, leaving her with serious permanent injuries. In our overpopulated world, we are witnessing the human version of the "overcrowded rat syndrome" on a terrifying scale.

One of the major problems for policemen investigating rape is that the sex criminal is not easy to track down by normal methods of scientific crime detection. He strikes casually and, unlike a burglar, seldom leaves behind clues in the form of fingerprints. This is why Jack the Ripper was never caught; this is why Joseph Vacher evaded the French police for three years; this is why the Yorkshire

Ripper was able to remain at large for more than five years, until he was finally caught by chance. But the case of Colin Pitchfork undoubtedly marks a major turning-point in the history of crime detection. The discovery of "genetic fingerprinting" means that – unless he takes the precaution of wearing a condom – every rapist now leaves behind his "fingerprint" inside his victim. And even if he wears a condom, a single spot of his blood, or a fragment of his skin under the victim's nails is enough to reveal his identity. Just as the discovery of fingerprints in the 1880s changed the history of crime detection, so the discovery of the genetic fingerprint potentially makes sex crime the easiest type of crime to detect. But this would require a considerable act of courage on the part of governments. In the early days of fingerprinting the government of Argentina proposed that it would be a simple matter to have a national fingerprint register, by taking the prints of every baby when it was born. But the idea caused such a storm that it was soon dropped, and no government has dared to revive it since. Yet it is, on the whole, a simple and practical idea that would dramatically reduce the crime rate. If it became a matter of course for every sexual offender to be "genetically fingerprinted", the same would apply to the sex-crime rate. And if *everyone* was genetically fingerprinted at birth, premeditated sex crime – of the type committed by the likes of Ted Bundy, John Duffy and Michael Fairley ("The Fox") – would virtually disappear, for the rapist would know in advance that he was leaving his signature behind.

This is no place to examine the new problems posed by the "serial killer" – Brian Marriner has done it adequately and powerfully in this volume. It is enough to point out that new techniques like "psychological profiling" – as used in the John Duffy case – and the widespread use of police computers, are proving to be as successful as "Bertillonage" and fingerprinting in the last decade of the nineteenth century. After a century of sex crime, the odds are once again beginning to switch against the criminal and in favour of the police. So although the cases in this book are gruesome and horrific, there can be no doubt that its ultimate message is one of optimism: that in the present climate of scientific progress, sex crime is one day destined to become as obsolete as stage-coach robbery or cattle rustling.

Colin Wilson

Introduction
A New Century of Sex Killers

In the first edition of *A Century of Sex Killers* I made no secret of the fact that writing a book which detailed the most sordid and depraved acts of which human beings are capable was not a pleasant experience. Immersing myself in the minds of some of the most infamous sex killers in history was neither a healthy occupation nor an enjoyable one. And yet, as I maintained at the time, I believed it to be a necessary duty. The book had to be written. Sex murder was then a growing crime. It was an issue that needed to be addressed.

Today the situation has not improved. In fact it is considerably worse. Sex crimes now seem to be almost epidemic; moreover, they are becoming more gruesome by the day. It is the responsibility of every civilised adult to come to terms with this fact and understand what it means. We can no longer bury our heads in the sand and hope the problem will go away. We need to confront the terror and work out why it is happening.

My basic thesis remains unchanged from the earlier book. I still believe that sex killers speak to us in a kind of code, and beg us to try and comprehend their words and interpret their actions. They want to be identified and caught. William Heirens's cry "For Heaven's sake, catch me before I kill again" is untypical of the sex killer, but only because of its eloquence. Most other rapists and murderers make the same plea but, alas, they speak only through the blood and pain of their crimes. If we are to have a chance of understanding what they are saying we have to study their terrible deeds and delve into their twisted thought processes and warped motivations. Again we should stress that we do not do this to satisfy some academic or intellectual interest, nor to try and derive some prurient pleasure from imagining their crimes. We do it simply as an act of self-preservation. Only when sex killers are understood can their menace be stopped and their ghastly crimes, which are now sweeping across almost every nation, brought to a halt.

We should not be alarmist. Sex killings are still a rarity. But they are not so rare that we can be complacent about them. In the earlier edition of this book in 1992 I pointed out the alarming statistics relating to sex crimes. Today the figures are no more reassuring. The increase has not slackened, and what is more the severity and horror of the attacks now seems to be rising too. In the last five years we have seen the most terrifying gargoyles emerging from the depths: Andrei Chikatilo, who raped and murdered at least fifty-five people in the Russian Republic; Jeffrey Dahmer, "The Milwaukee Cannibal"; Robert Black; Colin Ireland; Aileen Wuornos. And this is to say nothing of the ghastly events that took place in the home of Fred and Rosemary West at 25 Cromwell Street, Gloucester, England. These are extremes, of course. But they are the sort of extremes that few of us could ever have imagined, even in our worst nightmares, just a few years ago. One hardly dares contemplate what will come next. What further horrors can man perpetrate?

Sex crimes are not new. Sex has always been a potent force and a powerful motive for violence, especially when coupled with jealousy and pride. It has led to tragedies since time began. But whilst sex crimes certainly happened in the past they were, in the centuries before our own, always a case apart. They were rarities, freaks. The twentieth century has changed all that. It has brought us something that is both qualitatively and quantitatively different.

It began, perhaps, with Jack the Ripper who terrorised London's Whitechapel district in the late summer of 1888. Significantly, however, though Jack killed five prostitutes with hideous savagery, his crimes were relatively modest by today's standards. Moreover, at the time his murders and mutilations were not even thought of as sex crimes. They were viewed as the crazed antics of a man who was "morally insane" and, quite possibly, possessed. He was such a horrific aberration that only demonic forces could explain him.

My personal feeling is that it is Reginald Christie rather than Jack the Ripper whom we should claim as the man who truly ushered in the modern age of the sex killer, the era when the sex killer emerged as a social reality. Reggie Christie killed at least six women in his London home in the 1950s, and though no one ever doubted that he was evil, talk of the devil was never mentioned. Christie's motives were too transparent for that. His crimes were neither frenzied nor manic. Instead the killer employed a cool, twisted logic to satisfy his gruesome predilections namely, to murder his victims and then have sex with their corpses. His crimes were as passionless as they were perverted and, perhaps for this reason, the Christie case still has the power to horrify and shock. Christie was soon followed by Heath, Cummins, Manuel and Byrne and the long line of sex killers down to the present day which includes such appalling examples as the Yorkshire Ripper, Dean Corll, John Wayne Gacy, Ted Bundy, Heidnik, Nilsen and Jeffrey Dahmer.

Today we tend to think of America as the land of the sex killer, with Britain following the trend. But in fact it has become an international problem. Polish police have arrested a man suspected of the sexually motivated killing of no less than twenty-three people in towns across their country. In Spain Francisco Escalero has confessed to the killing of eleven. Italy has the "Monster of Florence" and Australia its "back-pack" killer. Jack Unterweger is Austrian, Nikolai Dzumagaliev is Russian, Avzal Simons is from South America. The epidemic has no boundaries. So why is it happening?

In 1824 Thomas De Quincey published his celebrated essay *Murder Considered As One of the Fine Arts*. This, he announced, was a paper to be read out to the "Society for the Encouragement of Murder" and very amusing it was too. But whilst the essay is often regarded as nothing more than gallows-humour one should remember that De Quincey was using irony to point out an unpleasant truth. Let us suppose that such a "Society" existed, for example. How would it go about encouraging sex murder? The answer is obvious. It would advocate doing precisely what we do today: exploit and package sex as a commercial product. To "do dirt on sex", as D. H. Lawrence would have said. It is quite possible that pornographic books and videos have done more to incite sex crimes and contribute to the huge escalation in rape attacks than any other single factor. The reader should be struck by the many cases in this book in which the killer was found to possess an extensive library of pornographic magazines and video films. Let us look at a typical case.

Robert Poulin was a Canadian youth, aged eighteen. In 1975 he lured a neighbour's seventeen-year-old daughter into his Ottawa home, manacled her to the bed, raped and sodomized her, then stabbed her to death. He set fire to the house, then went to his school armed with a shotgun and began shooting fellow-students at random. He injured seven of them before turning the gun on himself and blowing his head off. When the police searched his home they found a large collection of pornographic magazines and a blow-up rubber doll. His diary read: "I've thought of committing suicide, but I don't want to die before I've had the pleasure of fucking some girl." He recounts how he had puchased the doll by mail-order. Then a later passage reads: "Doll arrived. Big disappointment." It was a sad, pathetic case of a youth with absurd, enhanced expectations about sex. The reality was such a total disappointment.

The sex hunger that Poulin endured is plain to see. Perhaps because of the undue emphasis placed on sex by the justly maligned media, young men like Robert Poulin are led to expect more than reality can deliver. Perhaps they kill merely out of a sense of frustration.

Hunger was the title of a remarkable novel by the Nobel-winning author, Knut Hamsun. Written in 1890, the book is a vivid impressionistic study of the alienation that is now common in modern society. For Hamsun hunger is not merely the want of food. Hunger is deprivation, the starving of an appetite or a need which, if it gets out of control, leads to antisocial behaviour. The need can take many forms. One can, for example, hunger for sexual or financial gratification and these both can lead to crime and violence. Perhaps more interestingly, however, Hamsun suggested that there are also hungers of a more esoteric kind These too have their impact on the criminal. For instance there is the hunger for recognition, for fame, to be *known*. We all experience this sort of hunger from time to time. In the criminal it seems to loom abnormally large. So too with the curious need for feeling at peace with oneself, for feeling that one "belongs".

For an example of the first type of hunger think of Colin Ireland. In a year-long reign of terror he murdered five London homosexuals in the most grotesque way. And the reason? He simply wanted to find fame as a killer. Of the second, recall the case of Christie. You may remember his bizarre confession describing the feelings he had as he gazed down on the body of Muriel Eady, whom he had just strangled and raped: "Once again I experienced that quiet, peaceful thrill. I had no regrets." Here we can clearly identify the mechanism of hunger at work. For Christie only the act of killing, followed by sex, gave any meaning to his torpid sense of reality. Only murder gave him peace, his appetite could be satiated in no other way. In a sense it is almost pointless to condemn him. His hunger was a fact of his psychology, a manifestation – albeit a deviant and destructive one – of a universal feeling that all of us share. It can be neither condemned nor condoned. It simply is. Unfortunately, just as existential hunger can lead some individuals to great things, to marvellous discoveries, innovations and inventions, in other individuals it is switched to the negative pole.

Of course, one could argue that hunger need not always be satisfied. Many people crave money, sex, love, fame, "belonging" and never have their craving fulfilled. But increasingly, it seems, this is being tolerated less and less. Perpetual hunger in the sense that Hamsun used the word is not something modern man will put up with. As a consequence we are witnessing the emergence of a new type of criminal. This is the criminal that I have called Reactive Man. Reactive Man refuses to accept life as he finds it. The old-style criminal wanted to steal an apple from the orchard; Reactive Man wants to burn the orchard down. He is the scavenger, the looter living in the wreck of civilisation. Freedom – the problem of what to do with it – is his disease. Boredom is his natural state. He feels stifled and trapped, viewing violence as the only means of escaping from the strait-jacket of his mundane life. He is the consummate criminal, and his life is a chain-reaction which can only end with his death or imprisonment for life.

Reactive Man reacts against what he feels to be the restraints and repressions of our society. He is never in the wrong, he is never sorry. And he is breeding fast – faster than we can build cages to house him. He is the stranger among us, never of us. Many labels could be hung on him (and indeed are) but none tells us very much. Rebel, Psychopath, Terrorist. All are shorthand symbols for a state of mind. And that state of mind is hate. Freud said that, if a baby had the power, it would destroy the world from the rage born of the frustration of its infantile desires. Perhaps Reactive Man is the same. Perhaps he is simply immature. But, if he is, he certainly doesn't think so. As a rule he feels superior to the rest of us. Cleverer, braver, stronger, much more "grown up" than anyone else.

That attitude of superiority comes across strongly in the Moors Murders case. Ian Brady corrupted Myra Hindley with his mix of sex and de Sade. Both came to feel that other people were no more than insects, morons, maggots, cabbages. They *deserved* to be killed. Brady and Hindley felt entitled to murder them.

Peter Sutcliffe murdered thirteen women in his five-year reign as the Yorkshire Ripper. When he was finally captured the police found in his lorry a card, lettered by hand and reading: "In this truck is a man whose latent genius, if unleashed, would rock the nations..." Straight away the problem can be seen in his logic: how can any man consider that the murder of thirteen defenceless women constitutes an act of genius? Sutcliffe, however, clearly thought that he had the right to kill them. His contempt for his victims and glory in himself was an example of the frantic ego-assertion which characterises so many of today's killers.

So what are we to do? Should we continue throwing our undesirables into prison? It doesn't seem to work – and why should we expect it to? It is impossible not to think of the sex-criminal as being sick, as intrinsically lacking in normal psychological vitamins. His whole life is an act of hunger. To treat him we would first have to know what he hungers for. Punishment is a useless expedient, like caging a starving wild animal demented by hunger and expecting it to reform.

So what is it that the sex-killer wants? The more one looks into the subject, the more one finds that this is a question that is impossible to answer. Consider, for example, the alarming case of the Californian "Sunset Boulevard" killer, Douglas Daniel Clark.

In the summer of 1980, thirty-four-year-old Douglas Clark and his girlfriend Carol Bundy, thirty-seven, took to driving along Sunset Boulevard picking up girls. Once inside the car Clark would force them to perform oral sex on him, whilst his plump girlfriend looked on in glee. At the moment of climax Clark would shoot his victims in the head. He murdered five girls in this way, their ages ranging from fifteen to twenty-four. But this was not the extent of his appetite. After the murders he decapitated his victims. Clark kept their heads in the freezer at the home he shared with Carol Bundy. In the evening they would take out the heads, and after Carol Bundy had played with them and made up their faces "like Barbie dolls", as she expressed it, Clark would copulate with them. Arrested, tried and convicted, Clark was sentenced to death for the killings; his girlfriend received a life sentence. But no one, either during the court case or after it, could comprehend the motives or find any reasonable explanation for the behaviour of the monstrous couple.

The one thing that the Clark case made clear, however, was that both Clark and Bundy had no regard at all for the unfortunate women they had killed. It was an example of the basic "throwaway" attitude common to many sex killers, the total lack of identification with the victims, who remained objects for amusement even after their death. In England we see the same callousness in the terrible killing of Suzanne Capper. In December 1992 this sixteen-year-old girl was subjected to brutal torture, abuse and humiliation by a group of individuals she had looked on as her friends. They finally left her for dead by the side of a road, having set fire to her with the cries of "Burn, baby, burn". She died shortly afterwards. How could they have behaved in that way? How could they have been so monstrous?

It is easy to hide behind psychiatry and dismiss these killers as being in some way sick, as of course they are. But sickness does not explain it all. We must also accept some of the blame ourselves. We bore these killers. We nurtured them and shaped them. The sex killers amongst us come from our society not from another planet. They are somebody's daughter or somebody's son. They are our responsibility. It is time we faced up to it: they are our dragons whom we must slay – or perish ourselves.

There are no easy solutions to the problem. Locking sex killers away in prison is the worst possible answer, since a lengthy confinement only serves to incubate the perverse desires which will be displayed once again when the prisoner is released. Neither is castration the answer. Where it has been practised in the USA and elsewhere the castrated offenders have been known to commit further sex attacks. There is only one punishment that guarantees no re-offence, and that is the death penalty – and I hope we never go down that rocky road again. Surely it would be far better to find out why the sex killers act as they do and then maybe, just maybe, we will be able to show them how to curb their appetites and satiate their gruesome hunger by other, less horrific means. It is with this in mind that I have written this new volume.

This compendium of sex killers is by no means comprehensive. No one book could house all the demons in our midst. But the major cases are here.

Brian Marriner
May 1995

Chapter One
THE GERMAN SEX KILLERS

It may seem presumptuous for an English writer, coming from a nation which has produced both Jack the Ripper and Reginald Christie, to open a study of sex killers with an account of the German experience. But the fact is, Germany started the modern trend for serial sex killings and it still has the unenviable record of having reared more sex killers than any other European state. Moreover, it is not just "ordinary" sex killers that Germany has produced. They have been fiends and ghouls, necrophiles and cannibals.

One is reminded of **Kuno Hofmann**, the necrophile who terrorised northern West Germany in the early seventies. At first his activities were restricted to removing corpses from their resting places and defiling them in certain ways – decapitating and mutilating them, eating parts of them and attempting intercourse. Then he found his first live victims. On 6th May 1972, in the village of Lindelburg, a teenage couple were shot dead in their car. There was evidence that the murderer had drunk some of the dead woman's blood and had lingered over her corpse, examining her genitals. It was four days later that Hofmann was apprehended and confessed to the crime.

Hofmann, of course, was an aberration. Judged to be criminally insane, his case was never even brought to trial. Instead he was committed for life to a psychiatric institution. Nonetheless, the callousness, brutality and sheer loathsomeness of his crime has echoes elsewhere in Germany's criminal history. Indeed, one might even speculate that there is something in the German national character that lends itself to such behaviour. Perhaps there is a dark impulse buried deep within the German psyche, an impulse which found its fullest and most gruesome expression in Nazism but which is also manifest in the sex murders – the *Lustmorde* – of its history.

Fritz Haarmann, the homosexual "Butcher of Hanover", who murdered about fifty young men in the years following the First World War, is another ghoul who could be used to illustrate the viciousness and the cold-bloodedness of which the German sex killer is capable. Haarmann killed his victims by biting through their wind-pipes, then sold their bodies for meat, after sodomizing them. He had a keen commercial instinct – selling his victims' clothing, for example – and took a gruesome pride in his achievements. Arrested in May 1924, he cheerfully confessed to the killings and expressed surprise when he was only charged with twenty-seven. Of these he denied only three, in one case disdainfully claiming that the alleged victim was not pretty enough to merit his interest. Shown a photograph of the murdered man, he protested: "I have my taste, after all. I could never have chosen such an ugly creature as the photograph depicts."

At his trial Haarmann insisted on conducting his own defence and remained nonchalant throughout the entire proceedings, at one point complaining that there were too many women in the courtroom. When found guilty he told the court, "I want to be executed on the market-place. On my tombstone must be put this inscription: 'Here Lies Mass-Murderer Haarmann'." The court acceded to neither request, and Haarmann was duly decapitated within the walls of Hanover Prison.

Haarmann was executed just as Nazism was beginning to envelop the country with the boast that the new order and the new Nazi morality would bring an end to deviant killers like him. But it singularly failed to do so. Indeed, if anything the country's brutal sex murders increased in frequency and horror. This caused the Party considerable embarrassment and annoyance, and a good many crimes of the era were hushed up and not reported in the press in the hope that they would not be noticed.

Adolf Seefeld was born in 1871. He was charged with the murder of a young boy in 1908, but the evidence was too thin to convict him. Subsequently, Seefeld would spend some twenty-three years in jail for sexual offences against boys before finally being executed for a killing spree that resulted in the deaths of at least a dozen victims.

Seefeld was a sad and seedy character. A travelling clock-and-watch repairer by profession, in reality he lived the life of a tramp, often sleeping out in the open. He gained a reputation of sorts as a kind of warlock among simple country folk, and was believed to be capable of putting spells on sheep and cattle. Initially, he confined his homosexual inclinations to molestation and assault on his young victims. It was only later that he began killing in earnest.

Seefeld had a rare *modus operandi*: he killed his victims by poisoning them with liquids which he concocted from wild plants and fungi. The bodies of the twelve young boys that were found between 1933 and 1935 were all discovered in attitudes of peaceful repose. Equally strange was the fact that there was no apparent evidence of sexual assault. It would appear that for Adolf Seefeld homosexual practices palled, and he found murder to be an even better thrill.

Among his victims were eleven-year-old Kurz Gnirk, murdered on 16th April 1933; Ernest Tesdorf, ten, killed

2nd November 1933; William Metzdorf, seven, and ten-year-old Alfred Praetorious who were killed as a "double event" on 22nd November 1933. Then came Hans Korn, eleven, on 16th January 1934; two boys – Thomas and Newman – were found on 16th February 1934; another two boys, Edgar Dietrich, six, and Arthur Dinn, four, were found together in a forest on 16th October 1934; and a boy called Zimmermann was murdered on 23rd February 1935.

Seefeld was arrested after the murder of the last boy, Zimmermann, and his trial took place a year later. It was barely reported in the Nazi press and the full horror of his crimes was never fully made known. But he was found guilty and duly executed on 23rd May 1936. Seefeld's case is notable in that it fits the usual profile of the sex killer, with the intervals of peace between murders decreasing as if spiralling into a final frenzy.

Bruno Lüdke was another mass-killer whose crimes the Nazi regime tried to hush up. Unlike Haarmann and Seefeld, Lüdke's chosen victims were women rather than young boys. But he was no less gruesome in his methods. His usual method of killing was stabbing or strangling. He would then have sex with the corpse.

Born in 1909, Lüdke was a mental defective with a history of torturing animals, and the psychiatric background of a full-blown sadist. He began killing when he was just eighteen and it was only thanks to the turmoil of pre-war and wartime Germany that he evaded capture for so long. In fact, relatively early in his criminal career Lüdke had been apprehended and convicted of sexual assault. As a consequence he was sterilized, apparently on the orders of SS Chief Heinrich Himmler. But the operation did nothing to curb his sexual appetite or his taste for killing.

On 29th January 1943 the body of 51-year-old Frieda Rösner was found in a gravel pit on the outskirts of Berlin. She had been strangled. Near her body lay the small pile of firewood she had been collecting. The ensuing inquiry into her murder was headed by Kriminalkommisar Franz, a policeman with a high reputation for solving cases. He had all the known criminals in the area surrounding the village of Köpenick – close to where the body had been found – rounded up and brought into the Berlin police headquarters. Lüdke was among them. He was questioned and asked if he had known the murdered woman. He admitted that he did and had last seen her in the woods. Lüdke was then accused directly of committing the murder, at which point he sprang at the throat of his police questioner and had to be restrained by force.

Eventually he did admit the crime, pointing out that under Paragraph 51 of the Nazi criminal code mental defectives could not be indicted for murder. He also went on to confess to the murders of eighty-four other women throughout Germany since 1928.

It seems unlikely that Lüdke's actual total of victims was as high as he claimed, even though the information he provided was accurate about the circumstances of each case. There is speculation that various local police chiefs were only too glad to blame him for all Germany's unsolved crimes – he was a choice scapegoat – and Lüdke was happy to fall in with their plans. But if he did this out of a belief that as a mental defective he could not be punished, he would live to regret it. Faced with both a political embarrassment and a legal dilemma, the Nazis quickly found an easy solution. Lüdke was sent to a hospital in Vienna, where he was used as a guinea-pig for experimental drugs. He died following a lethal injection on 8th April 1944.

Paul Orgorzov's reign of terror was much briefer than Lüdke's, but it was no less of a problem for the Nazis. Operating between 1939 and 1941, he became known as the "S Bahn Killer" because of his habit of murdering women on trains or near the railway lines. A sadist, he raped his victims after bludgeoning them to death. He was tried on 24th July 1941, aged twenty-eight. It was a short, one-day trial, the Nazis being anxious to keep the case under wraps – Orgorzov was a known Party member. He was found guilty of the murders of eight women, mostly around the Berlin area, and was speedily executed within two days of the verdict.

The end of the war provided no let-up in the terrors that stalked the country. **Rudolf Pleil** liked to refer to himself as *der beste Totmacher* – the best death-maker – and boasted of having murdered fifty women. He was a small, chubby man, with a friendly face, and began his killing spree in 1945 using a variety of weapons in his attacks: stones, knives, hammers and hatchets. He had started his criminal career as a burglar and began attacking women merely to rob them. But the urge to rape his unconscious victims proved irresistible and, after rape, murder soon followed. Pleil truly enjoyed his gruesome work, taking a perverse pleasure in mutilating his victims' bodies afterwards.

Following his arrest, Pleil began to write letters to the authorities offering his services as a public executioner. Now and again he would also confess to another murder. It was widely supposed that he did this just to get himself an outing from the prison, but his confessions could not be ignored. He wrote to one mayor suggesting that he look in the town's well: subsequently a strangled body was recovered from it. Pleil described himself in letters as "quite a lad." "Every man has his passion," he said, "I prefer killing people." Rudolf Pleil committed suicide in his cell in February 1958, before he could be brought to trial.

Two years later and another killer-rapist was before the German courts. **Heinrich Pommerencke**, twenty-three, would receive six life terms of imprisonment, which amounted to some 140 years in jail, for six rape-murders and twenty rapes.

Pommerencke was a small youth whom girls tended to ignore, and it was perhaps this which induced a sense of sexual inferiority in him – although he boasted that he seduced his first girl at the age of ten. Born in Mecklenburg, close to Rostock, he began raping girls at the age of fifteen, waiting outside dance-halls to accost them. After his capture he told police that he had committed his first murder after going to see the Hollywood epic *The Ten Commandments*. The scenes of harlots dancing around the Golden Calf filled him with disgust and with a certainty that women were the source of all the world's evils. He decided to teach them a lesson, he said. Immediately after the film he attacked and raped an eighteen-year-old girl in a local park, cutting her throat when he had finished with her. Although he claimed at his trial that he never intended to kill any of his victims but simply to render them incapable of putting up any resistance, the evidence speaks otherwise. It reveals an insane lust to kill. He once pushed one of his victims, twenty-one-year-old Dagmar Klimek, out of a speeding train, then pulled the emergency cord and jumped out after her and stabbed her to death. A week later, on 8th June 1959, he strangled sixteen-year-old Rita Waltersbacher. Found guilty of six murders, Pommerencke told the court that he had wanted to kill seven women, as he felt that seven was a lucky number. He also blamed sex-films for his rape-attacks, claiming that they made him feel so tense inside that "I had to do something to a woman."

If Pommerencke was an example of the sexually inadequate male, **Dieter Beck** was the exact opposite. A handsome man with a succession of girlfriends, charming and well-spoken, he had no problem in getting women into bed. But although a sexual success in the town of Rehme, West Germany, he grew tired of pliant females and began hunting girls who would fight back. During the "swinging sixties" he raped and murdered three women: Ingrid Kanike in 1961, Ursula Fritz in 1965, and Annaliese Herschel in 1968. At his trial a stream of former girlfriends followed one another into the witness box to testify to his sweet nature, though some recalled that he did have a penchant for fondling their necks during intercourse. In June 1969 he was found guilty of the three murders and sentenced to three life terms.

Klaus Grabowski, another German child-killer, had the rare distinction of being murdered in court by the mother of one of his victims. Her actions cannot be condoned, but they can be understood. Especially in the light of Grabowski's long history of sex attacks.

In 1970 he was convicted of child molestation and given a light prison sentence, with a recommendation that he should receive psychiatric treatment. In those days his sexual perversions with children were relatively innocent and consisted of removing their clothing and tickling their genitals – there was never any hint of violence in his offences. Subsequently, however, this was to change. In January 1975 he lured a child into his flat and tried to remove her clothing. Panicking when the child began to scream, he attempted to strangle her, but recovered enough sanity to stop his attack and revive the girl with cold water. He then sent her home. Arrested for the attack, he found the courts this time were not so lenient. They sentenced Grabowski to be detained for a lengthy period in an institution for sexual psychopaths.

But when he agreed to be castrated he won an early release.

Castration is supposed to remove the sexual impulse: it did not have this effect with Grabowski – proof that the sex drive is located in the head rather than the loins. He continued to lure little girls to his room with candy, and then sexually assault them. By January 1980 Grabowski was living in a two-room flat on the Wahmstrasse. He was now aged thirty-four.

On the morning of 5th May 1980 seven-year-old Anna Bachmeier vanished while out playing. Police were called to search for the missing child, and when they realized that Grabowski lived only a street away from the Bachmeier home they took him in for questioning. They discovered that he had been receiving hormone injections to restore his virility, and a girlfriend confirmed that the injections worked. More importantly, a witness was found who remembered having seen Grabowski talking to a little girl at the relevant time. Grabowski finally admitted that he had killed the child. He had strangled her and buried her body just outside the town. He took the police to the site of the grave.

Grabowski's trial began on 3rd March 1981, with the defence demanding that the charge should be reduced to manslaughter on the grounds that the murder had not been a sex murder, or premeditated – Grabowski had strangled her in panic – and that he had voluntarily allowed himself to be castrated. (The question of why he had removed the girl's tights, which he used to strangle her, was not raised.) As the trial progressed the general feeling was that the killer would receive a light sentence.

On 6th March Klaus Grabowski took his place in the dock as usual, and Marie Anne Bachmeier, the mother of the murdered girl, crossed the courtroom swiftly and shot him with a Beretta pistol. Grabowski fell dead, and the mother dropped the pistol and waited to be arrested.

She was later put on trial for manslaughter, and though she had a good deal of public sympathy behind her and a defence appeal which raised a large amount of money on her behalf, Frau Bachmeier was sentenced to six years' imprisonment.

Fritz Honka was the caretaker of an apartment block in the seedy St Pauli district of Hamburg. The tenants had long been complaining of the stench that seemed to engulf the building, but it wasn't until firefighters broke into his attic apartment on 17th June 1975 that they discovered the reason why. Hidden behind the wooden panelling on the walls of the flat the firemen found the remains of four elderly prostitutes. They had all disappeared from local bars four years previously.

Honka confessed to the murders, and said that he had strangled the women because they had refused to perform oral sex with him. He had cut their bodies up with a knife in his kitchen sink. He had also doused them liberally with deodorant when the smell of their decomposition grew too strong. Police learned that he had tried to have sex with the corpses more than once.

Honka, who had been previously charged with assault on two local women, was found guilty and sentenced to life in prison.

Robert Wilhelm Stullgens was another sex killer with an obsession for fellatio. On 12th June 1980 the inhabitants of a block of flats at 12 Trussmannstrasse, Düsseldorf, asked the police to investigate the apartment belonging to Margaret and Wilhelm Deck. The family had not been seen for two days and their neighbours were worried. The police duly arrived and broke into the apartment. There they discovered the naked body of Frau Deck and also the bodies of her two children, Thomas, two, and baby Christian, just six weeks old.

All had been strangled. The husband, Herr Deck, was missing.

The police conducted door-to-door inquiries, and as a result of information from another neighbour broke into a flat occupied by a man named Stullgens. He was not at home, but in his flat was the body of Wilhelm Deck. He had been stabbed in the back.

Police records revealed that Stullgens had been released from prison only five months previously, having completed a sentence for rape. He had raped a young mother in a park, and attempted to rape her child. Stullgens was traced to Essen, where he had fled to seek refuge with his mother. He was arrested and taken back to Düsseldorf, where he confessed to the murder of the Deck family. He told police that he had seen Margaret Deck in the basement of the block of flats and had felt an urgent need to have sex with her. But he was able to control his compulsion enough to concoct a devilish plan. He waited for the husband to return home from work, then asked him to come up to his flat to help him move some furniture. Once inside Stullgens's flat, the husband was stabbed to death. Stullgens then took the dead man's keys and let himself into the Deck flat, where he forced Margaret Deck to strip naked and perform oral sex on him before he killed her and the two children. Stullgens was sentenced to life imprisonment.

It is with the Stullgens case that we will close our overview of German sex-killers. We have not tackled them comprehensively – that would take a book in itself – but we have at least been able to get a flavour of the type. We have also ended on a city which is now irredeemably linked to another killer; a unique gargoyle, at once the most horrifying and the most puzzling of all sex killers: Peter Kürten.

Chapter Two
PETER KÜRTEN
"A KING OF SEXUAL DELINQUENTS"

The terror of Peter Kürten, a man whose appearance gave the impression of nothing more sinister than a bank manager or a civil servant, is unrivalled even amongst the grisly company of other sex killers. The address where he lived, 71 Mettmännerstrasse, has entered criminal folklore along with such other notorious addresses as 10 Rillington Place and 39 Hilldrop Crescent. No study of the sex killer would be complete without an examination of Kürten, described at his trial as "a king of sexual delinquents". This German monster is of special interest because in most cases we know very little about the inner workings of the killer's mind. With Kürten we know almost too much, thanks to the investigative work of Karl Berg, MD. Dr Berg spent the year between Kürten's arrest and execution talking to him and examining him. The resulting book, *The Sadist* (1945), is a penetrating insight into the motives and reactions of a man who stands almost alone in the annals of twentieth-century murder: truly a man who could be termed a "monster".

Dr Berg, Professor of Forensic Medicine at Düsseldorf University and Medico-Legal Officer of the Düsseldorf Criminal Court, was personally involved in the police investigation of the "Düsseldorf Murders" as well as the subsequent clinical examination of the perpetrator. His insight into Kürten's motivation was therefore unique and

Dr Berg's later book became the first detailed study of the mind of a multiple killer, and it began with these words: "The epidemic of sexual outrages and murder which took place in the town of Düsseldorf between the months of February and November in the year 1929, caused a wave of horror and indignation to sweep throughout Germany and the whole world." That is as good an introduction to the effect Kürten produced as any. Dr Berg also reveals that the murders were variously reported in the press as the "Ripper Murders," the "Vampire Murders" and the "Werewolf Murders".

It is important to understand the social background to the Kürten case, and the typical German murder of the time. Prior to Kürten, the three worst German murderers were George Grossmann, Karl Denke and Fritz Haarmann. We have already described the crimes of Haarmann, and those of the other two in the trio were no less odious. Indeed, they were frighteningly similar. All were operating during the famine years following the First World War, when meat was scarce. Denke, like Haarmann, killed young men and sold their flesh – in his case pickling it first. With typical Germanic thoroughness he kept a record of the name, date and weight of each carcass as it was pickled. Grossmann was a similar ghoul, though this time it was women who were the victims. He killed scores of girls before selling their flesh as meat.

It was these three who set the stage for the appearance of the super-monster who would succeed them, and just five years later he made his début. The first attack, in February 1929, was the culmination of a long and grisly apprenticeship.

Peter Kürten was born on 26th May 1883, the son of a violent drunkard. One of a family of thirteen, he knew poverty early on, and was brought up in an atmosphere of overcharged sex – he had to sleep with his sisters, and listen to and also watch his parents having sexual relations. Kürten claimed that one of his sisters attempted to seduce him, though this was unproved. What is certain, however, is that his father was sentenced to three years' imprisonment for incest with Peter's thirteen-year-old sister. The Kürtens shared their house with a dog catcher who taught the young boy how to masturbate animals. This too may have contributed to Peter Kürten's later deviancy. "My youth was a martyrdom," he told Berg.

Kürten's grandfather had served prison terms for theft and there was a long history of feeble-mindedness in the family on his father's side. Because of this it could be said that Kürten is proof of the hereditary factor in developing criminals, or conversely the belief of sociology that it is the environment that makes the criminal. Certainly his lengthy spells in prison did nothing to help him, and served only to incubate his perverse desires.

According to his later confession Kürten committed his first murder when he was just nine years old. While playing on a raft on the river Rhine he pushed a playmate over the side and into the water. When another friend jumped in and tried to rescue the boy Kürten dragged him under the raft and he drowned too. Four years later Kürten began practising bestiality with sheep, pigs and goats. His first ejaculation coincided with him stabbing a sheep while he had intercourse with it. He discovered that the sight of blood gave him intense pleasure and from that moment on the link between sex and blood became firmly fixed in his mind.

At sixteen he ran away from home, stealing money to travel to Coblenz, where he lived with a prostitute with masochistic tendencies who encouraged him to torture her. It was also in Coblenz where he was arrested for theft and went to prison for the first time. It was to be the first of seventeen sentences that were to take twenty-seven years of his life. That first sentence was one of four in harsh conditions, and Kürten would later tell his judges: "When I came out of prison I think I was a little crazy.... it was too heavy a punishment, in my opinion. I was too young for it." He served his first sentence at the Berger Gate, where he came under the influence of hardened criminals. He had himself tattooed – a typical act of prison culture. He was always to complain of having been over-punished for trivial offences.

When he was released in 1899 he started to live with another prostitute. She was twice his age but, like his first partner, she was a woman inclined to masochism. It was during this year, according to Kürten's own confession, that he committed his first adult murder. He said he strangled a girl while having sex with her in the forest. However, there is no police record of this incident.

Kürten spent the years between 1900 and 1904 in prison, serving two sentences – one for minor fraud, the other for trying to shoot a girl. It was during these periods in jail that Kürten began to dream of taking his revenge on the unjust society which had imprisoned him. He told Dr Berg:

> The long sentences I served when still quite young had a very bad effect on me. I did not masturbate. I got my climax of enjoyment when I imagined something horrible in my cell in the evenings. For instance, slitting up somebody's stomach and how the public would be horrified. The thought of wounding was my peculiar lust, and in that way I got my ejaculation... That went on for years. If I hadn't had that I would have hanged myself.

Kürten even used to break prison rules deliberately, so that he would be put in a solitary punishment cell where he could indulge his fantasies more freely.

After prison he was called up as a conscript to the Army, but soon deserted. It was at this point that he began his acts of arson, setting fire to barns and hayricks, hoping that tramps might be sleeping in the hay. He told Dr Berg, "I got sexual excitement from watching my fires, but I did not ejaculate."

In 1905 he received seven years' imprisonment for thirty-four thefts and twelve burglaries. He served his sentence in Münster Prison where, he said, "I had cell madness." He once rolled himself in a bundle of silk claiming he was a silkworm. It does not take a psychiatrist to work out the terrifying symbolism of this occurrence. If Kürten was a chrysalis now, he was already beginning his horrific metamorphosis. It would only be a matter of time before the true demon killer would emerge.

Kürten boasted that at Münster he was able to poison some convicts in the prison hospital, a claim that has never been substantiated. But it was certainly here where he refined his dreams of revenge. Imprisonment can break the weak – the majority of first-time convicts never reoffend – but with certain exceptional individuals it serves only to compress the psyche, to harden them. Kürten came out of prison in 1912 a cold and sinister man, determined to have his revenge on society.

He was soon back in jail, having received a one-year term for the sexual maltreatment of a servant girl, and also for discharging a firearm in a restaurant during an episode when he tried to accost another woman. He was released again on 25th May 1913 and according to his own account – Kürten was able to recall details from his past in amazing depth – it was then that he experienced a delicious new thrill in killing.

Kürten was now making his living as a burglar, and one evening he broke into a pub in the Wolfstrasse, Köln-Mulheim, when the family were out at a fair. In one of the bedrooms he found thirteen-year-old Christine Klein asleep.

In his own words to the court which tried him:

> I was hunting round the bedroom by the light of a pocket lamp... I saw a girl of about nine years in bed. I flung myself on this girl in a state of great agitation and strangled her, and when she was lying there quiet I took out my sharp little pocket-knife and cut the child's throat... First I had only the intention of stealing, but when I saw the child there came on me, beside the other excitement, the remembrance of my terrible sufferings and humiliations during my years of imprisonment... The remembrance of those brutal punishments, which in my opinion were often unjust, combined with the strong sexual passions which I have inherited from my father, made me absolutely crazy.

He said the act of killing made him feel "free" for the first time. The child had in fact been strangled, had her throat cut, and her sexual organs penetrated with fingers. By pure chance Kürten left his handkerchief behind which, by coincidence, bore the same initials as the girl's father, Peter Klein, who became the prime suspect in this terrible crime.

That same year Kürten attacked four others, though none of them fatally. Two women he attempted to strangle and a young couple he knocked into unconsciousness with a hatchet, gaining sexual excitement from seeing the blood. He also set fire to another hay wagon.

Kürten spent the next eight years – 1913 to 1921 – in prison, where he endured more "terrible sufferings", thus increasing his mad desire for revenge. It had become a vicious circle: increased punishment led to increased revenge.

In 1921 Kürten went back to his old town of Altenberg, telling everyone that he had been a POW in Russia. At this time he attempted to strangle a war widow. He also met his future wife. A peasant woman, three years his senior but looking considerably older, she too had served time in prison. Ten years earlier she had been arrested for shooting a lover who had jilted her. As a consequence she was jailed for five years. It was a punishment which she took in good heart. Indeed, she even extended it, stoically accepting all life's burdens as further punishment for her crime. She was later to say: "I have taken all things as a punishment for my old life."

Why Kürten was so attracted to her is difficult to understand, but she was to become his sheet-anchor, the one fixed solid rock in his existence. He never ill-treated her, but showed her only the greatest respect. She was the only individual for whom Kürten felt any sense of affection, later saying that he felt more guilt over betraying her in his acts of infidelity than for any of his acts of murder. It may be that Kürten regarded her as a soul-mate; after all, she too had suffered in prison. When Kürten proposed marriage she initially refused him; only when he threatened to murder her did she consent to a wedding.

For the next two years, following the marriage in 1923, Kürten lived a normal life as a married man in Altenberg, having a good job and becoming active in trade-union circles. He was twice accused of sadistic maltreatment of servant-girls, but managed to wriggle off the charges. The cases never came to court.

In 1925 the Kürtens moved to Düsseldorf and settled into their new home at 71 Mettmännerstrasse. Here Kürten took to walking the streets, fantasizing about blowing up the city with dynamite. He also began his sadistic attacks. Initially they were widely spaced in time, as if in rehearsal for the main event. Then they became more frequent and violent. It is the typical pattern of the sexual psychopath. In the first year there were three attempted strangulations of women, the following year, one. In 1927 there were five cases of arson and one attempted strangulation. The next year saw eleven arson attacks. Within the first few weeks of 1929 there were six more arson attacks on barns and haystacks and then, on 3rd February 1929, came the first murderous attack on a woman. Düsseldorf's "Reign of Terror" had begun.

Frau Apollonia Kühn was walking through the streets of the city when a man came up behind her, grabbed her tunic and stabbed her twenty-four times with a pair of scissors. Dr Berg noted that the wounds had been inflicted in rapid succession, as if her assailant had been in some kind of frenzy. Frau Kühn's injuries were horrific, but miraculously she survived.

A week later, however, the body of a not so lucky victim was discovered. We have some confusion over the date of this first murder. Dr Berg gives 9th February and numbers the case 46. Case 45 (Kühn) and 47 (Scheer) are also recorded as February crimes. But Margaret Wagner, in her book *The Monster of Düsseldorf* (1932), gives 8th March as the date of the first killing – a date followed by other writers. But as Dr Berg appeared as an expert witness at the trial of Kürten, I am inclined to accept his dating.

On 9th February 1929 the body of eight-year-old Rosa Ohliger was found near Düsseldorf's Vinzenz Church. She had been strangled and then stabbed thirteen times in the chest. The killer had subsequently doused her with paraffin in an attempt to set her on fire. The post-mortem examination revealed that the girl had injuries to her genitals and her hymen was torn. Ejaculation had not taken place within her vagina, Dr Berg noted, but the killer had inserted into it a finger smeared with semen. Semen was also found on the girl's knickers.

The two separate crimes, the stabbing of Frau Kühn and the murder of the child, were not linked by the police at the time. Neither was the next attack, committed three days later.

On 13th February Rudolf Sheer, a 45-year-old mechanic, was on his way home on the road to Flinger. He was somewhat the worse for drink when Kürten pounced. Kürten stabbed the mechanic repeatedly, mostly in the head. Sheer died almost instantly. The police were bewildered by the crime. There had been no robbery, and the killing appeared to be motiveless. With the benefit of hindsight, however, Dr Berg tells us that the three crimes had the following factors in common: each had been a sudden attack in an isolated spot; each attack had been made at dusk; in each case a stabbing instrument had been used; and they all shared the common factor of appearing to be motiveless.

The police were baffled by these attacks. They had not a clue as to what madman might have committed them. But then, on 29th April, a lunatic by the name of Stausberg was arrested for attacking two women. He confessed not only to these assaults but also to the murders. The police thought they had their man, and indeed that is the way it seemed, for the Düsseldorf killings came to an abrupt stop. But it wasn't to last.

There was a long lull, but then in August 1929 a spate of attacks and murders reawakened the fears of the local people. On the evening of 21st August a Frau Mantel was stabbed in the back. Later that same evening two others, Anna Goldhausen and a man called Gustav Kornblum were both stabbed in similar fashion. Miraculously all three survived. Then, on 24th August, a double murder stunned the city. The bodies of two girls, five-year-old Gertrude Hamacher and fifteen-year-old Louise Lenzen, were found strangled and stabbed in an allotment close to their homes. Their throats had been cut in an apparently motiveless act of murder and neither had been sexually assaulted.

Twelve hours later Gertrude Schulte, a 26-year-old domestic servant, set off to visit a local fair. On the way she was approached by a man calling himself Fritz Baumgart. He accompanied her to the nearby woods and then, once under the cover of the trees, he pushed himself up against her and attempted to have sex. Fräulein Schulte refused his advances. "I'd rather die," she said. "Well, die then," declared "Baumgart" coldly. He stabbed her several times, so violently that the tip of the knife-blade broke off inside her spine. Again the stabbing was in a rapid pattern, but this time Kürten's victim survived and was able to give the police a good description of her attacker.

It was at this point that the police began to think that they were looking for two killers, since it hardly seemed likely that the same man who had killed two girls on Saturday evening would be seeking further victims on the Sunday.

In September came three more attacks on women, in one case the girl being thrown into a nearby river after attempted strangulation. But it was another murder, in late September, which caused a sensation. It signalled the start of a spate of hammer attacks. Ida Reuter, a servant-girl, set out for a Sunday walk and never returned home. The next day, 24th September, she was found in a meadow near the Rhine at Düsseldorf. The body lay with legs apart and the genitals exposed – as if deliberately. Sperm was found in her vagina, and her knickers were missing. The cause of death was a series of vicious hammer-blows to the head. Police now suspected that *three* killers might be operating in Düsseldorf. It was not a wild thought. Killers of this type were thought never to change their *modus operandi*. The stabber could not be the hammer-attacker, they thought.

On 12th October, at 6.30 a.m., missing servant-girl Elizabeth Dorrier was found unconscious and gravely injured near the river Düssel. She died the following day without ever regaining consciousness. She had been battered about the head with a hammer, and her vagina was injured, indicating a sexual motive for the killing. Her hat and coat were missing.

On 25th October came a double hammer-battering in two separate parts of the city. Frau Meurer, thirty-four, was knocked unconscious by a man with a hammer, and Frau Wanders, a prostitute, was also knocked out with four blows from a hammer. Then, on 7th November, a five-year-old girl, Gertrude Albermann, went missing from her home. Two days later her body was found near a factory yard, lying among nettles and brick rubble. She had been strangled and stabbed thirty-six times. She lay face downwards with her legs apart. Her knickers had been torn, and there were injuries to her vagina and anus.

By now the city was verging on the edge of hysteria, with newspapers headlining each new "Vampire Murder". The panic increased when Kürten, imitating Jack the Ripper (whom he greatly admired), began sending letters to the police and the newspapers indicating where the body of another victim might be found. He drew a little map. Police searched a meadow and dug up the body of Maria Hahn, a servant-girl. She had been dead since August, and police unearthed her body on 14th November. It was completely naked, and bore twenty stab wounds – three to the temple, seven to the neck and ten in the breast. The girl had been completely mutilated. Dr Berg noted "coitus per anum". Thousands of morbid spectators flocked to the spot where the body had been found.

The panic in Düsseldorf led to Germany's greatest detective, Detective Chief Inspector Gennat, being assigned to the case. He had an excellent reputation as a meticulous man-hunter, having once followed up no less than 800 clues to track down a murderer. His first act was to hold a press conference at which he told reporters that the present case was unique in the history of criminology, and that the original Jack the Ripper was a mere beginner compared to his new disciple. But he prophesied that the killer would make a mistake and be caught, as he had "a yearning for publicity".

Inspector Gennat tried to organize the local police, who were now in a very dispirited state. They were convinced that they were hunting no less than four separate killers: a stabber; a strangler; a hammer-killer and a homosexual killer who killed men only. So great was the interest aroused by the case that the crime writer Edgar Wallace booked into a Düsseldorf hotel to be close to the action.

One of Inspector Gennat's first efforts to identify the mass-killer was to arrange for a tailor's dummy, dressed in the clothing of Elizabeth Dorrier, to be taken around the dance-halls of Düsseldorf. He hoped that someone might recognize her and remember the girl's companion on the day of her death. He then began to coordinate an intensive house-to-house inquiry, hoping that he would find some more clues. Most of all, however, he waited for the killer to strike again. He felt sure that somehow the fiend would give himself away. Extraordinarily, however, no new murders occurred.

Unknown to the police and citizens of Düsseldorf, the killing spree had already come to an end. There had been eight murders in ten months, and fourteen attacks, but now the murders stopped. The attacks would continue for another six months, including the attempted strangulation of one woman in February 1930; two in March and three in April. These were followed by attacks on several girls and a hammer attack on Charlotte Ulrich in that same month. Then, in May, came the attempted strangulation of Maria Büdlick – or "Butlies" – and finally the attempted murder of Gertrude Bell.

It was the attempted strangulation of Maria Büdlick on 14th May 1930 which was to lead to Kürten's arrest. He had at last made the mistake prophesied by Inspector Gennat. Maria Büdlick was a servant-girl who had come from Cologne to Düsseldorf looking for a job. When she arrived at the railway station she was accosted by a strange man who tried to persuade her to go with him. Kürten intervened, angrily denouncing the man as a "pervert" and offering the girl his protection. The girl trusted him. He seemed a soft-spoken and gentle-mannered man.

Kürten took the girl to his apartment at 71 Mettmännerstrasse for some refreshment. He gave her a drink of milk and a sandwich and offered to take her to a hotel. He took her for a walk through the woods, the Grafenbergerwald, telling her that the hostel lay in the "Wolf's Glen" on the other side. It was once they were in the forest that Fräulein Büdlick realized she had made a mistake. Her escort turned on her and attacked her. He tried to rape her, all the while squeezing his hands around the unfortunate woman's neck. But then, for some reason that no one knows – the one single piece of information that prevents us from fully understanding the Kürten case – he stopped. Kürten never completed the attack. Instead he released his intended victim and asked her if she could remember where he lived. Wisely Maria Büdlick said no, so he let her go.

Later the girl wrote an account of the incident in a letter to a friend. It arrived at the wrong address, and was handed over to the police. They traced Fräulein Büdlick, and on 21st May 1930 she led the investigators to the Mettmännerstrasse. She was unable to remember the number of the house but walking down the street she thought she recognised the building and led the officers inside. The killer saw the detectives talking to his landlady in the foyer and he fled.

Precisely why Kürten decided to give up at this point is uncertain. The police could have charged him with the attempted rape of Maria Büdlick, but could hardly have proved the murders against him. Still, whatever the reason, Kürten suffered some form of spiritual collapse and decided that the game was over. That night when his wife returned home in the early hours from the restaurant where she worked – Kürten usually met her outside to protect her from the "monster" – he confessed everything to her and prepared himself for the end.

At first his wife did not believe him, and he was forced to relate various details of his murders to convince her that he was telling the truth. Frau Kürten was horror-struck; she had had no idea, not even a vague suspicion. Once the news had sunk in she suggested a suicide pact would be the best solution, but Kürten persuaded her to do the sensible thing and turn him in, thus collecting a share of the sizeable reward that was now on offer. He then took her out for a last meal.

Frau Kürten was so upset that she found it quite impossible to eat. Her husband, however, had no such problem. He ate up his meal and then tucked into her portion. Kürten's appetite never deserted him at any point in his life.

On 24th May Frau Kürten went to the police. On that same afternoon, outside St Rochus church, she met her husband in the company of four armed policemen. Kürten smiled reassuringly and submitted without any struggle.

Nobody could believe Kürten was the killer. His wife had known nothing of his double life. Their sex life, she said, had been normal and active. "He frequently had sexual intercourse with me, even against my will. In the last two years he has been extremely keen on it," she told the police. Kürten's workmates were no less surprised. His employers described him as a "good worker", and to the neighbours he appeared to be a respectable man. They remembered that at the time of the murder of little Rosa Ohliger he had said that whoever did it ought to be handed over to the people to be torn to pieces.

For the police it was the end of a long and complicated investigation. No fewer than 2,650 clues had been followed up; 200 people had falsely confessed to the murders; 250 accusations a day were received at police headquarters; 13,000 letters a day had poured in to Düsseldorf police; 9,000 people had been questioned, and a card-index file of 70,000 entries had been compiled. The same problems were later to be encountered by the police hunting the Yorkshire Ripper: they found themselves buried under a mountain of paperwork.

Peter Kürten immediately made a full confession to the murders, although he was later to withdraw it. But Gertrude Schulte picked him out of an identity parade. He appeared in court to be charged in June 1930, and was remanded in custody until his trial in April 1931. This was the year that Dr Berg spent examining him.

Dr Berg found Kürten to be "frank and ironic". He had a pocket edition of the criminologist's classic Lombroso, and used the hereditary factor as an excuse for his murders – that and the revenge-fantasies which prison had incubated in him. He told Dr Berg that he had become interested in his own perverse desires, and said: "As regards the motives I gave for my actions... I had begun to think things over because of the criminal inspector who was so very interested in the psychological aspects of the case But I must own up that in spite of this, I really always was in the frame of mind when I had the desire – or perhaps you would call it the urge – to kill somebody. The more people the better, and yes, if I had the means of doing so, I would have killed whole masses of people – brought about catastrophes. Every evening when my wife was at work I went prowling about for a victim... The sex urge was always strong in me, particularly during the last years. But it was increased by the deeds themselves. That was why I had to go out again and again to look for another victim."

When asked how he managed to have normal sexual intercourse with his wife, he replied that it had been with great difficulty. He said he had to fill his head with sadistic fantasies before he could succeed. He said in the course of another interview, "The main thing with me was to see blood. . . I felt sexually excited."

He confirmed that the act of stabbing brought about an ejaculation, saying:

> It was thus as I lay on the Albermann child, my member still in the child's vagina, while I con- tinued to stab her breast... I had no satisfaction during the sexual act, only later on during the throttling. I became stiff again, and when, as I stabbed her throat, the blood gushed from the wound, I drank the blood from the wound and ejaculated. I probably drank too much blood, because I vomited.

Speaking again of his wife – Kürten was delighted to learn that she had received some of the reward money – he said:"I always got on well with my wife. I did not love her for any sensual motives whatsoever. It was respect for her noble character."

The Hahn case had elements of necrophilia:the naked body had been sexually assaulted, both vaginally and anally; leaves and soil were found in the anus. Kürten admitted that after he had killed and buried her he decided to alter the location of the grave. He dug her up, kissing and fondling the corpse. He said he had wanted to crucify her body to a tree "to stir up some excitement", but it was too heavy. He reburied it, and later often visited the grave. He claimed he was able to ejaculate simply by fingering the earth that covered it.

The revelations of Kürten to Dr Berg still have the power to terrify. He emphasized that he always ejaculated when he heard the sound of gushing blood, and said that once while out looking for a victim in the Hofgarten he decapitated a sleeping swan. "In the spring of 1930 I noticed a swan sleeping at the edge of the lake... I cut its throat. The blood spurted up and I drank from the stump and ejaculated."

When he committed arson, or a murder, Kürten would mingle with the crowds that gathered, and achieved orgasm by the uproar provoked in the spectators. Yet he insisted to Dr Berg, "I am not mad." He told Dr Berg about his fantasies of blowing up bridges and poisoning wells, of blowing up Düsseldorf with dynamite. Or how he would save Düsseldorf from the "monster" and be hailed by a grateful public with torch-light processions. At first he attempted to convince Dr Berg that he killed "for revenge on society", but later admitted the sexual motive for his crimes. He told Dr Berg, "When Professor X was here for the first time, he brought his lady assistant with him, and she had such a lovely white neck that I would have loved to strangle it."

He also revealed that in his years in prison he had gained sexual pleasure from the written word. "I always read the murder stories in the newspapers. They excited me sexually... I have read Jack the Ripper several times."

Peter Kürten's trial began on 13th April 1931 in the drill-hall at Düsseldorf police headquarters. Grisly exhibits produced in court included the skulls of some of his victims, and the weapons he used to kill – plus the spade used to bury Maria Hahn. In accordance with the German custom, the trial took place before three judges and a jury. Kürten stood in the dock smartly dressed, his hair neatly combed, his pleasant-looking face attentive. He was now almost forty-eight, and had spent over twenty years of his life in prison.

The indictment against him included nine murders and seven attempted murders. Dr Jansen, for the prosecution, asked several times for the press to be excluded because of the unsavoury nature of the evidence, but the judges refused. The presiding judge, Dr Rose, allowed Kürten to tell his life story from the dock. "I was born in 1883... as a child I suffered much from my father's drunken brutality," he began.

Later the judges began to ask questions:

Judge: "Why did you write those letters to the press and police?"

Kürten: "I hoped to achieve a sadistic satisfaction from them, and succeeded in doing so."

Judge: "What made you change the instrument of murder [from knife to hammer]?"

Kürten: "I hoped to get more enjoyment from it... but this did not quite give me the satisfaction I wanted."

Kürten was civil and soft-spoken in the dock, anxious to communicate his thoughts.

In a later testimony he said, "In prison I began to think a great deal about revenging myself on society. I did myself a great deal of damage through reading blood-and-thunder stories; for instance I read the tale of Jack the Ripper several times. When I came to think of what I had read in prison, I thought what pleasure it would give me to do things of that kind once I got out again." He spoke of his "sexual tension", and of the great pleasure he derived from the shock and indignation his crimes caused. He also admitted that he had deliberately changed his choice of weapons "to bring about the theory that there were several murderers at work".

Professor Berg gave evidence, describing Kürten as "king of the sexual delinquents". Kürten, he said, could not be categorized. He had no *modus operandi*. Sometimes he robbed his victims, sometimes not. He attacked men, women and children, displayed every sexual aberration, yet lived a normal life as a husband to his wife, who never once suspected the grim truth about him. He was not weak-minded but strong-minded, and had an incredible memory of crimes committed over two decades. He was a pyromaniac, had delusions of grandeur, megalomania and sexual mania. Kürten differed from the normal sadist in that he pursued *different methods of violence* alternatively. Instead of following a set *modus operandi*, he deliberately changed his methods to fool the police – and succeeded. He had a great ability to lie and deceive, possessed great presence of mind and an ability to bluff.

Kürten had been a professional burglar in his earlier years, said the Professor, and had simply extended his field of activity to murder, using his developed skills to avoid detection and capture. He was a vain and cunning criminal. His excuse of revenge against an unjust society was simply a mask for his sadistic sex drive. Years of solitude in prison cells had developed in him the power of auto-suggestion: "the ability to achieve orgasm purely by his indulgence in sexual fantasies". "Was he mad?" Shaking his head sadly, Dr Berg said, "Kürten is perfectly sane."

The defence was one of insanity at the time of the murders. Professor Rather gave psychiatric evidence for the defence, Professor Sioli for the prosecution.

Kürten's wife was also called to give evidence. She said: "I never connected my husband with the Düsseldorf murders. I never saw any marks on his clothes, because he was always so particular about cleaning them himself. He always slept soundly. Taken all round, he was good-tempered and kind-hearted. He often told me about the bad treatment he had had in prison, of being taken in fetters through the town when he was only a boy."

Dr Hertel, the magistrate who had interrogated Kürten initially and taken down his confession, told the court, "Kürten was an inexplicable riddle. What was Kürten's spiritual state before and during the acts? Why did Kürten make his confession to his wife?... Kürten must have guessed that his hour had come. A deep spiritual depression forced him to lay bare his secret... I had the immediate impression he would retract his confessions... He retracted everything... The fight with Kürten lasted two months, the fight for the truth with a skilful, strong and intelligent adversary. In the end there came to be a certain bond between myself and the accused... His confession came entirely of his own free will. He bowed to the majesty of the law... He admitted premeditation in every case to his crimes."

Dr Jansen, the prosecutor, asked Professor Sioli: "Kürten has told us that if danger of arrest threatened, even in the midst of his passion he could stop the attack and flee. Is not that a proof that impulse was not irresistible?" Professor Sioli replied, "It is a proof."

Dr Wehner, the young defence lawyer, asked : "Another expert called Kürten the king of sexual delinquents because he unites nearly all the sexual perversions in one person. Can that not change your opinion?"

Professor Sioli: "I cannot see in Kürten's case any borderland case of premeditation."

Dr Wehner: "That is the dreadful thing – that the man Kürten is a riddle to me – that I cannot solve it! Haarmann only killed men. Landru only women. Grossmann women. But Kürten killed men, women, children and animals – he killed everything he found!"

Professor Sioli: "And was at the same time a very clever man and quite a nice one."(There was laughter in court at this sally.)

One witness, a girl who was assaulted by Kürten when she was sixteen, told the court how one day he stood in front of a waxwork display of murderers and burglars, and said, "One day I shall be as famous as they are." This desire to become known has motivated many modern crimes – particularly the assassination of famous men – but the drive is present in most of us, even amongst hangmen. In his autobiography *My Experiences as an Executioner* the English executioner James Berry tells us that he was inspired to apply for the post of hangman after reading about his predecessor, Marwood, in a newspaper. "To travel and become famous like him!"

Kürten's final remarks are of some interest. He declared that the real reason he confessed to his wife was because "there comes a time in the life of every criminal when he can go no further. And that spiritual collapse is what I experienced."

Eventually the prosecutor stood up to make his final speech. He summed up the case: "The 48-year-old Kürten has spent more than twenty years in prison. His sadistic desires developed to a dreadful intensity when allowed full play in his imagination... But he has no reason for making imprisonment in itself the cause for his tendencies. When he came into the cells reserved for prisoners undergoing special punishment, it has been acknowledged that he deliberately brought this about to indulge his dream-desires in a more undisturbed way...

"Unappeasable sadist and egocentric indulger in delusions of grandeur, Kürten had nine victims to his account, butchered in the most gruesome manner only to satisfy his own appetites. He tortured his victims more and more bestially before he killed them as he became increasingly harder to satisfy. He began to consider killing whole sections of the population. Kürten absolutely deserves the title of 'king of Sexual Delinquents'.

"In the opinion of expert psychiatrists, Kürten was fully responsible for his actions. He only murdered in his leisure hours when he knew himself to be free from the supervision of his wife. If he had murdered according to the dark urge or under some compulsion, he would never have chosen his times so carefully. As for the theory of expiation – that he sought a victim to appease his wronged sense of justice for evil done to himself – that was not a delusion but a creation of his own imagination... to defend his own actions to himself. Kürten believed he had the right to indulge himself at will at the expense of his victims. The true motive for all his criminal actions was sexual satisfaction. Kürten is a pyromaniac, a sadist, a fetishist and a masochist... A man of high intelligence and penetrating mind, he is absolutely and entirely responsible for all his actions... I demand for Peter Kürten the penalty of death nine times...."

Kürten's counsel made no attempt to hide his client's guilt, but he did question the prosecution's assumptions as to his motives and state of mind. "I too am convinced of Kürten's guilt," he said. "But a soul of this kind cannot be dissected, cannot be analysed like an ordinary psyche. Kürten is a psychological riddle."

The jury was out for an hour and a half, returning with guilty verdicts on all the charges. Kürten was sentenced to death nine times. He refused to appeal against the sentence, telling Dr Berg, "It would be the pleasure of all pleasures to hear my own blood gushing into the basket when my head is cut off." He also revealed, "I could never have stopped my attacks. If I were outside again today I couldn't guarantee that something of the kind might not happen again. I haven't felt any pricks of conscience up to now. I could not act differently."

Kürten was eventually persuaded to apply for a pardon, which was duly refused. However, it was widely believed that in the end he would not be executed as the government of the day was in the process of considering the abolition of capital punishment. All the same, the execution was arranged.

Kürten, born a Catholic, left letters to the relatives of his victims expressing regret, but it is unlikely that he could have felt genuine remorse. Following his conviction, he was bombarded with love-letters, and received hundreds of requests for his autograph.

On the morning of 2nd July 1931, at Klingelpütz Prison in Cologne, Kürten was executed by guillotine. He had enjoyed the condemned man's last meal so much – Wiener Schnitzel, chips and white wine – that he asked for it again. He remained cheerful to the last.

During his trial Kürten had expressed the hope that the full details of his crimes would not be published in the newspapers, as he himself had been morally damaged by reading such accounts. This is a telling point, and one which begs the question: if you believe that pornography and violent literature can influence a potential killer, why write about Kürten?

The answer, quite simply, is that the study of murder and the science of criminology is an attempt to find a *pattern* in what otherwise might be regarded as senseless and wanton slaughter. And an actual murder case can tell us more about the motivation of a man stripped down to his basic drives than any novel. Sir Leslie Stephens, himself a judge, wrote a long time ago, "The highwayman is often more interesting to the historians of society than the learned judge who hangs him." Lombroso was the first man to attempt to find a pattern in the chaos of crime, even if his methods have long since been discredited. Conan Doyle's Sherlock Holmes personified this when he said to Watson, "If only we could lift the roofs from all the houses in London, what incredible twists and turns we would see, what *patterns...*"

The first thing to emerge from a study of Kürten is the grim effect of lengthy imprisonment on the human psyche. Albert Camus was remarkably perceptive when he wrote in *The Rebel*: "Twenty-seven years in prison do not, in fact, produce a very conciliatory form of intelligence. A lengthy confinement makes a man either a weakling or a killer... In prison, dreams have no limits and reality is no curb. Intelligence in chains loses in lucidity what it gains in intensity." He was talking about the Marquis de Sade, a man whose savage intelligence remained unbroken throughout his years in the Bastille, and who poured out his sick fantasies in words – millions of them.

From personal experience I know that prison is a place where men are either broken or made harder. Imprisonment has the effect of compressing the soul, and there seems to be an optimum amount of imprisonment the individual can take. Just so much educates; too much erodes. Kürten spent his time in prison dreaming of revenge, of "compensatory justice": that is, getting his own back on his tormentors by in turn tormenting the innocent. It was a twisted thought, of course, but behind it one can see a kind of warped logic.

Pierre Lacenaire, the convict writer-philosopher, is an interesting example of this. He was executed in Paris in January 1836 at the age of thirty-four. In his *Memoirs* he tells us of his suicidal state of mind at the time of his crime, his despair of society. But rather than kill himself he decided to "have the blood of society". He thus killed a woman and her son. Lacenaire was the archetypal "loner"; an intelligent man, he despaired of the social injustice he saw all around him, and retreated into the defeatism of crime. He claimed he wanted to "cancel his relations with society", and the triangular blade of the guillotine granted his wish. The annals of crime are full of such types. Peter Kürten, disgusting and horrific as he was, was just another one of their number.

Chapter Three
LOVERS OF THE DEAD

It is impossible to write a book of this nature in chronological order – which is the ideal. Now and again, in order to make an important point, it is necessary to group together several cases which are separated geographically and by time. In this chapter I intend to examine the link between sex murder and necrophilia – a crucial link which will be seen time and time again with other accounts in this book. Necrophilia is one of the most problematic areas to explore because it is almost impossible for the average human being to understand it. With a little effort and some imagination it is possible for most of us to enter the mind of the murderer, the rapist, the robber or the assassin. We can make some informed guesses as to their motivations and desires. We can get an idea of what makes them tick. But the necrophile is different. How can we even imagine the desire to have sex with the dead, the necrophile's erotic attraction towards corpses?

The case-histories of the perpetrators make the mind reel. It is a crime which appears to defy reason, negating every normal human impulse.

So what lies behind it?

The most obvious and the most frequently used explanation is that the necrophile is a man who cannot face a living, mature woman. When we look at the actual case histories, however, we find that this rarely applies. Reginald Christie was a sexual inadequate, known as "Reggie No-Dick" and "Can't Do It Christie" in his youth. Ed Gein also had serious sexual problems and would have found sex with the living hugely traumatic. But these are the exceptions. The vast majority of recorded necrophile killers have been able to maintain perfectly normal sexual relations outside their crimes. Sergeant Bernard, for example, was an extremely virile man who kept his wife and mistress busy. Peter Kürten satisfied the prostitutes with whom he lived, and had his wife complain that he was sexually insatiable. Dennis Nilsen had a very active homosexual love life. Yet these too seemed to prefer sex with the dead than with living partners that were readily available. The question we have to ask is why.

Necrophilia has a long history. Taboo though it is, sex with the dead has been practised all through the ages. Today, in all civilized societies, it is regarded as a criminal offence and carries stiff penalties. But the very fact that it is on the law books demonstrates that the practice exists. Fortunately, however, the necrophile is rarely driven to murder. Most reported cases of necrophilia involve morgue attendants and the like who have defiled the already dead bodies in their charge. The Los Angeles psychiatrist Paul de River in the book *The Sexual Criminal* (1956) gives an account of a typical case. The individual concerned is an unmarried man, aged forty-three:

> At the age of eleven, while a grave-digger in Milan, Italy, I began masturbating, and when alone would do so by touching the bodies of dead, young, good-looking women. Later, I began inserting my penis into the dead girls. I came to America... where I secured a job

washing bodies in a mortuary. Here I resumed
my practice of having intercourse with dead girls,
sometimes in the caskets or on the table where
the bodies are washed.

Distasteful and disturbing as this case is, it is not
actually distressing. Compared to the likes of Joachim Kroll
it is positively innocent. But one wonders if this was
how Kroll began. Not, perhaps, with the rather pathetic
account above – which strikes one as a perversion that
was as likely to have arisen out of boredom and a twisted
sense of mischief as anything else – but maybe with other
similar though more morbid cases.

Dr de River gives the case-history of another morgue
attendant, a 21-year-old American, whose necrophiliac
impulses were altogether more sinister and more intense
than in the first example. Referring to the patient only
by the initials D.W., de River relates how, at the age
of eighteen he had fallen in love with a girl. D.W. had
intercourse with her just once, before she died of
tuberculosis. Her death shattered him, at the funeral he
wanted to jump into the grave with her. Later he said,
"Whenever I masturbated I visualized having intercourse
with my dead sweetheart." D.W. abandoned his plans to
enter medical school, and instead enrolled at a school of
undertaking. He worked hard at his new profession, and
duly graduated. But the presence of dead females excited
him, and he began masturbating over them, then violating
the corpses. In a two-year period he violated hundreds of
female corpses ranging from infants to elderly women.

As time went by D.W.'s perversion developed and grew
into a compulsion that became ever more violent and
sordid. De River relates one episode that is particularly
unpleasant:

> . . . on one occasion he was so impressed with the corpse of a young girl fifteen years of age that when alone with her the first night after death, he drank some of her blood. This made him so sexually excited that he put a rubber tube into her urethra and with his mouth sucked the urine from her bladder... he felt more and more the urge to go further... to chew part of her body. He was unable to resist the desire, and turning the body upon its face, he bit into the flesh of the buttocks...   He then crawled upon the cadaver and performed an act of sodomy on the corpse.

Clearly D.W.'s compulsion was now escalating to unpleasant heights. But would he have ever crossed the line completely? Suppose he lost his job in the mortuary. Would he then roam the streets, searching out lonely women and creating corpses on his own?

It is hard to dismiss this possibility but in fact expert opinion suggests that this terrifying transition, from scavenger to predator, is not one that is likely to be made. D.W. had a compulsion towards sex with the dead, but he did not have a compulsion for death itself. In this he was altogether different to the ghouls with whom we are concerned.

Necrophilia is, by definition, an erotic attraction to corpses. For the murdering necrophile, however, this is an altogether inadequate explanation. Much better would be the definition put forward by the German criminologist H. von Hentig. He treats it for what it is: *anti-life*. Necrophilia, he writes, is "the desire to tear apart living structures". Von Hentig cites the case of a man who stabbed thirty-six cows and mares to death, and then cut off various parts of their bodies. We could cite Peter

Kürten who tore out dog's intestines or the American mass murderer Herbert Mullin, who did the same with the girls he killed. Vascher disembowelled his victims, Ed Gein cut them up and hung them to cure like animal carcasses...

Of this murdererous necrophilia one of the earliest cases we have details about is that of **Sergeant François Bertrand**, a young French soldier born in 1822, who was arrested in Paris in 1849 for a series of sex crimes. As a child he was unusually strong, with more than a hint of sadism in his character. He smashed things frequently, and at the age of eight was already masturbating. He joined the Army and became a good soldier. By the age of twenty-four he was beginning to treat animals in a sadistic manner, killing dogs and tearing out their intestines with his bare hands. He became a necrophile at twenty-five, describing it in detail in his confession.

> At midday I went for a walk with a friend. It happened that we came to the garrison cemetery, and seeing a half-filled grave I made an excuse to my friend and left him, to return to the grave later. Under the stress of a terrific excitement I began to dig up the grave with a spade, forgetting that it was clear daylight and that I might be seen. When the corpse – a woman's – was exposed I was seized with an insane frenzy and, in the absence of any other instrument, I began to beat the corpse with the spade. While doing so I made such a noise that a workman engaged near the cemetery came to the gate. When I caught sight of him I lay down beside the corpse and kept quiet for a while. Then, while the workman was away to get the police, I threw some earth on the corpse

and left the cemetery by climbing over the wall. Then, trembling and bathed in cold perspiration and completely dazed, I sat for hours in a small spinney. When I recovered from this paralysis I felt as though my whole body had been pounded to a pulp, and I felt weak in the head.

Later he dug up the corpse with his hands and tore open the abdomen.

Bertrand continued to commit acts of this nature, once digging up fifteen corpses in one night before he found one which satisfied him, and even swimming rivers to indulge his perversion. Of one corpse, that of a sixteen-year-old girl, he said, "I did everything to her that a passionate lover does to his mistress." He added, "All my enjoyment with living women is as nothing compared to it." He was eventually caught by an elaborate booby-trap: he tripped over a string attached to the trigger of a rifle and was shot and wounded. Following his trial he received a sentence of one year's imprisonment, and disappeared from the annals of crime.

In 1871 **Vincenz Verzeni**, twenty-three, committed two murders with necrophilia in mind. One was of a fourteen-year-old girl, the other a 28-year-old woman. He attacked them in the fields, strangling them and tearing out their intestines and genitals with his hands. Under interrogation he admitted experiencing sexual pleasure when choking a woman. Whether he actually achieved penetration with his victims' corpses, however, is open to question.

There was no doubt, however, with **Joseph Vacher**, who terrorised France a few years before Jack the Ripper inflicted his terror on London. Vacher was tried in 1897, and sent to the guillotine on 31st August 1898, his severed head afterwards being examined by experts seeking some clue to his twisted personality. Born in 1869, his whole life expressed resentment of society. (He was later to blame all his troubles on being bitten by a mad dog at the age of eight.) His background was average for the period: one of fifteen children in a peasant family, from a very early age he suffered from acute boredom, as if life was permanently grey. He entered a monastery at one point, as if seeking some meaning to life, but was expelled after making sexual advances to other novices. During national service in the army he attempted to commit suicide when a young girl rejected his proposal of marriage. The bullet failed to kill him and just left him with facial paralysis on the right side. For this he was committed to a mental hospital, being discharged as "cured" in April 1894.

It was then that he began to kill; leading the life of a tramp and wandering the countryside in search of victims. In May 1894 he killed twenty-year-old Eugénie Delhomme, his first known victim. After strangling her, he cut her throat, severed her right breast and trampled on her belly, after which he had intercourse with the body. In the following three and a half years Vacher murdered at least seven women and four youths, most of whom he disembowelled.

For five months following his arrest he was studied by a team of alienists headed by Professor A. Lacassagne. It was perhaps the first time in history in which a scientific attempt was made to probe the mind of a killer. Joseph Vacher confessed to the murders with the following statement: "Yes, it is I who committed all the crimes with which I am charged – and I committed them all in moments of frenzy." He had to be carried semi-conscious to the guillotine.

There is a strong element of the necrophile in the case of **Bela Kiss**, a Hungarian with a penchant for preserving the bodies of his victims, as a butterfly-collector preserves his specimens. In 1916 soldiers searching for petrol at his farm outside Budapest found more than twenty petrol drums, each containing the strangled corpse of a woman pickled in alcohol. Kiss used to advertise in the newspapers regularly for female companions, and although press reports at the time attributed the motive for the murders to the theft of their belongings, the puzzle remains: why keep the bodies? Incidentally, Kiss was never arrested. It is believed that he switched identity papers with a dead soldier, and later emigrated to America.

The case of Peter Kürten has already been discussed and we have seen how he found death an immense sexual turn-on. **Edmund Emil Kemper**, the American "Co-ed killer", shared a similar perversion. His self-confessed catalogue of crimes was truly terrifying, including murder, necrophilia and cannibalism involving at least eight victims, amongst whom was his mother. Kemper not only attempted intercourse with his victims' corpses, he also admitted sexual excitement in the act of decapitation. His crimes will be reported in more detail later in this book.

Joachim Kroll, who became known as "The Ruhr Hunter", was a German cannibal killer and necrophile who between 1959 and 1976 terrorized the Ruhr area of West Germany, and had a large police task-force hunting him. His method was to strangle and rape his victims, and then remove portions of their flesh to be taken home and eaten later. It was the reported murder of Manuela Knodt, sixteen, which began the scare. Her body was found near the village of Bredeney, close to Essen, in the summer of 1959. A virgin prior to the attack, she had been strangled and raped. Slices of flesh were missing from her thighs and buttocks.

On 23rd April 1962 Petra Grese, thirteen, was found dead in a forest near Walsum. This time both buttocks and the left forearm and hand were missing. On 4th June – just a couple of months later – Monika Tafel, thirteen, was found dead near Walsum. She had been on her way to school when she had been abducted. She too had been strangled and raped, and missing this time were large steaks of flesh cut from her buttocks and thighs. On 22nd December 1966 five-year-old Ilona Harke was strangled in a park in Wuppertal. She had been raped and flesh had been removed from her buttocks and shoulders.

Kroll was nearly caught a number of times, but it wasn't until ten years later that he was finally apprehended. Four-year-old Marion Ketter had been playing with friends in the Duisburg suburb of Laar when a small, balding middle-aged man persuaded her to go off with him. After Marion's mother reported the child's abduction the police conducted door-to-door inquiries. At one apartment block a tenant told them that his neighbour, lavatory attendant Joachim Kroll, had told him not to use the top-floor toilet as it was blocked-up. When the man asked: "With what?" Kroll had replied, "With guts."

A plumber was called to investigate the toilet. It was indeed blocked up with guts – the plumber found the internal organs of a small child, including the lungs. When police searched Kroll's apartment they found parcels of human flesh in plastic bags in the deep-freeze and bubbling away in a saucepan on the stove was a stew, with a child's hand prominent among the carrots.

Kroll was a mild little man, and obviously mentally retarded. When questioned at the police station (he actually believed he would be allowed to go home afterwards) he confessed to dozens of rape-murders, dating back to February 1955. His flat was full of electrical sex-gadgets and rubber sex-dolls. Kroll said he liked to strangle the dolls as he masturbated. He talked quite freely about his perverse desires, saying that he was too shy to have sex with a conscious woman, which explained his habit of rendering his victims unconscious or dead before raping them.

During his subsequent confession he revealed how, at the age twenty-two, he had begun killing for sex. The first murder was in February 1955, when he had attacked a 19-year-old girl, raping her after knocking her unconscious. In June he struck once more, again raping his victim whilst she lay unconscious. The murder, mutilation and defiling of Manuela Knodt, Petra Grese, and Monika Tafel had thus occurred fairly late in his career.

Hans van Zon was a mass-murderer who appeared to kill totally without motive. He lived in a fantasy world, almost entirely within his own head, and killed without rhyme or reason. It could thus be argued that he cannot be considered a necrophile – he was more a fantasist. But isn't it significant that his fantasy involved necrophilia?

Van Zon was born in 1942 in Utrecht, Holland, and grew up as a typical mother's boy. He appeared introverted to others, never joining in playground games and the like. At sixteen he left home and went to live in Amsterdam, describing himself as a "student," and lived by petty crime. He borrowed money – which he never returned – to buy himself expensive clothes, and he capitalized on his good looks by having many love-affairs, some with men.

In July 1964 he committed his first murder. Out with a girl named Elly Hager-Segov for the evening, he suddenly felt an urge to kill her. It was an urge he didn't try to resist. Claiming to have missed the last train home, he persuaded her to let him spend the night in her room, where they made love. When she refused to make love a second time he strangled her, stripped her naked, cut her throat and then continued with his love-making.

In 1965, he killed a homosexual film-director, Claude Berkeley, in Amsterdam. In April of the same year he killed his then current girlfriend, Coby van der Voort, by persuading her to try a sex stimulant. It was in fact a knock-out drug, and once she was unconscious he clubbed her to death with a length of lead-piping, undressed her, stabbed her with a knife and tried to have intercourse with the body.

Van Zon made the mistake of boasting about the murder in the hearing of ex-convict Oude Nol, who blackmailed him into committing more murders, this time for gain. He killed a shop-keeper in May 1967, and a farmer in August. But when he attempted to murder a rich widow whom Oude Nol had once courted he failed to do the job properly. She recovered and went to the police. Van Zon was arrested and got life imprisonment. Oude Nol, incidentally, received seven years.

In all the above cases the compulsion to kill far exceeds any compulsion for sexual gratification with the victim. Indeed, the sex act with the corpse, gory though it often is, seems almost to be an afterthought. A conclusion to the proceedings. And indeed this might be exactly what it is. The necrophile killers, having demonstrated their supreme power over their victims by taking their lives, subsequently confirm and perhaps even consecrate the victory by defiling the corpse. They are doing much the same thing that Myra Hindley did when she allowed Ian Brady to take photographs of her kneeling on the grave of John Kilbride. Both are weird and sinister ritualistic acts, without which, in the killer's eyes, the murder remains somehow incomplete.

This final indiginity which the necrophile killer inflicts on his victim is unquestionably obscene and barbaric. Curiously, however, it is not necessarily hostile. Though some of the cases we have mentioned describe brutal and vicious assaults on the corpse, dismembering and mutilating it and removing chunks of flesh, there are also occasions when the defilement is almost tender.

One is reminded of the case of Dennis Nilsen, the former policeman who was tried in 1983 for the sex murders of fifteen young men, killed in his London homes, then cut up and flushed down the drains. He often had sex with the corpses, masturbating over their remains in a symbolic gesture of farewell. By all accounts, this was done with some affection. He treated the corpses as friends, a fact that was also demonstrated by the way he kept one dead body sat in an armchair for a few days because, "it was nice to have somebody to come home to". So too did **Ed Gein**, the infamous American ghoul who provided the inspiration for Alfred Hitchcock's *Psycho*. Though Gein cut up his victims and hung them to cure like animal carcasses he also, in his own perverse way, treasured their remains.

Ed Gein was a bachelor, aged fifty-one, when he was arrested in 1957 for the murder of Bernice Worden, owner of the local general store at Plainfield, Wisconsin, USA. Gein was a farmer whose early upbringing by a puritanical mother had made sex a taboo subject. He resorted to digging up female corpses to examine and experiment on, in at least one case taking the body home to have intercourse with it. He dug up the corpses of a dozen or so middle-aged women, keeping the sexual organs – putting their vulvas in a box – and returning the rest of the body to the grave. He said he couldn't stand the thought of worms getting to them, as the sexual organs seemed to be "like living things". This, of course, was an absurd thing to say, especially after the police had raided his home and found the dead store-keeper decapitated and hanging up by her heels like an animal carcass, a refrigerator full of human remains, a grisly collection of shrunken heads, human skin being made into items like belts and wallets and a preserved human breast. "Living things" was the one thing that Ed Gein was not big on. But he still treasured the vulvas.

The literature of the criminologist and the psychiatrist is full of cases of sadism and necrophilia. Freud, Krafft-Ebing, Hirschfeld and de River have all produced compilations of case-histories detailing every imaginable sexual perversion, and yet there is still no satisfactory explanation for necrophilia. In this brief study we have noted various clues that might help to explain things. They don't really prepare us, however, for that most famous necrophile of all, Reginald Christie.

Chapter Four
REGGIE "NO-DICK" CHRISTIE

John Reginald Halliday Christie was an unappetizing character. A thin man, bald and physically weak, he was a neurotic and unpleasant individual. Born on 8th April 1898, he was brought up in Halifax, West Yorkshire, one of a family of seven children.

Even as a child Christie displayed the incipient hypochondria that would plague his adult life. He missed school on many occasions because of imaginary illnesses. Like John Haigh, the so-called "Acid-Bath murderer" of the forties who was brought up a few miles away in Wakefield, Christie sang in the local choir. But he was not a popular boy. At school he was known as a cissy; later on because of his lack of sexual prowess he was dubbed "Reggie No-Dick". There is no cruelty quite so pointed as that of children.

After leaving school he got a job with West Yorkshire Police in Halifax but was soon sacked for pilfering. He was also sacked for petty theft by his subsequent employers at a carpet mill. Many murderers display early signs of thievery, reminding one of De Quincey's jocular dictum: "If once a man indulges himself in murder, very soon he comes to think little of robbing; and from robbing he comes next to drinking and Sabbath-breaking; and from there to incivility and procrastination." Christie was certainly among their number.

Later he became a projectionist at the Gem Cinema in Halifax. Perhaps the flickering fantasies he watched night after night stimulated his murderous impulse, although he was later to say that the most important event in his childhood was viewing a dead body – that of his grandfather – when he was eight. This may be of prime importance, given the necrophiliac aspect to the case.

He was called up for service in the First World War and was injured in France by an exploding mustard-gas shell. He was gassed twice and blinded for some months, after which he spoke in a low, apologetic tone and wore glasses, apparently for his short-sightedness. He was married in May 1920, the marriage fortunately being childless. He had a succession of jobs: variously, cinema operator, clerk and postman. In April 1921 he was sentenced to three months' imprisonment for stealing postal orders. In 1923 he was bound over for obtaining money by false pretences, and in that same year he went to London, leaving his wife behind in Sheffield. Free from marital encumbrance, he drifted from job to job, and in September 1924 was given nine months' hard labour for theft at Uxbridge. After this he seems to have settled down, holding a clerical job for five years. But in 1929 his basically criminal character surfaced again, when he received six months' hard labour for attacking a woman with a cricket bat. In 1933 he again went to prison for stealing a car.

His abandoned wife visited him in prison, and on his release went to live with him in London, the ten years' separation apparently forgiven and forgotten. It was in 1938 that the couple rented the three-roomed ground-floor flat at 10 Rillington Place, an address which was to become notorious in criminal history. Within the next few years several women were to be murdered in that house...

Christie became a War Reserve policeman in 1939, and used his authority as a "special" during those wartime years to its fullest possible extent. He became officious, rude and petty-minded. Perhaps the cloak of authority gave him a feeling of power; certainly it led to his first murder. He was based at Harrow Road Police Station, and called at a snack-bar to inquire about a man wanted for theft. There he met Ruth Fuerst, twenty-nine, a tall Austrian girl who had come to England in 1939 as a student nurse. Since Christie was vague about the date of her murder – or even if she was his first victim – she must be presumed to have been killed at some time in late 1943. She was last seen alive on 24th August 1943.

The 45-year-old Christie, in his dark blue uniform and peaked cap, invited Miss Fuerst back to 10 Rillington Place for a cup of tea, his wife being away visiting relatives in Sheffield. Her remains, recovered some ten years later, gave no indication as to the cause of death. But we have her killer's statement about it to police.

> She was very tall, almost as tall as me and I was 5ft 9in. She undressed and wanted me to have intercourse with her. I got a telegram while she was there saying that my wife was on her way home... I got on the bed and had intercourse with her. While I was having intercourse with her I strangled her with a piece of rope. I remember urine and excreta coming away from her.
> She was completely naked... She had a leopard skin coat and I wrapped this around her... I put her under the floorboards. I had to do that because of my wife coming back... next day my wife went out. While she was out I picked the body up from under the floorboards and dug a

hole in the garden, and in the evening, when it was dark, I put the body down the hole and covered it up quickly with earth.

Christie was sacked as a War Reserve constable because a soldier complained about his association with his wife. He then got a job with Ultra Radio in Acton, west London and there met small, plump Miss Muriel Eady, thirty-two. She and her boyfriend used to visit the Christies at Rillington Place, but one day she arrived alone. She complained of catarrh, and Christie said he could help her because of his "medical knowledge" – which was elementary first-aid training.

Christie's readiness to help Miss Eady indicates that he had already developed his ingenious method of gassing victims and it is certainly not beyond the bounds of possibility that he had used it before in crimes we know nothing about. But, according to the record, Muriel Eady was the first to use the "breathing machine".

Muriel placed her head over the square glass jar, in the metal lid of which Christie had punched two holes. Connected to these holes were rubber tubes, one leading to a mixture of Friar's Balsam, herbs and other inhalants. These provided some relief from her congestion. But they also served another more sinister purpose. These heady vapours disguised the smell of what was coming from the other tube. The second tube was connected directly to the gas tap.

Once Miss Eady was unconscious Christie strangled her with a stocking and had intercourse with her corpse. In his confession Christie said, "I gazed down at her body and felt a quiet, peaceful thrill. I had no regrets..." She too was buried in the garden. The date of her death was shortly after 7th October 1944, the day when she was last seen alive.

A New Century of Sex Killers

Christie never said what he did with his victims' corpses. But it is not hard to guess what went on in his twisted mind. With his victims either comatose or dead, "Reggie No-Dick" was transformed into a virile he-man. He could now indulge in his necrophiliac sexual rites, possibly masturbating over the corpse of his victims – as did another, later necrophiliac, Dennis Nilsen.

There may have been women who survived his gassing experiments, or participated willingly, or victims we do not know about, because after killing two women in 1943 and 1944 he did not kill again until five years later, when he murdered Beryl Evans and her daughter.

One of the mysteries of the case, and one which complicates the narrative, is the matter of Timothy Evans. In August 1949 Evans and his young wife Beryl, who lived with their baby daughter in the flat above the Christies, had a violent quarrel. Christie was later to claim that he found Mrs Evans lying in front of the gas fire, having attempted suicide, and that he revived her. The following day, he said, she again wanted to kill herself, begged him to help her, and offered him sexual intercourse in return. He had intercourse with her, strangling her with a stocking as he did so.

It was suggested that Christie offered to perform an abortion on Mrs Evans, who was pregnant at the time of her death, and killed her while she was inhaling his special gas mixture to render her unconscious. Evans mentioned the question of abortion to the police in his confession. He claimed his wife had been trying to abort herself with a syringe and tablets. Christie, he said, had approached him and offered to perform a safe abortion, claiming to have studied to be a doctor before the war and showing Evans various medical books. His statement went on: "On the Monday evening [7th November] my wife said that Mr Christie had made arrangements for the first thing

86

Tuesday morning. I didn't argue with her." In another statement he added, "when I came home in the evening [Tuesday] he was waiting for me at the bottom of the stairs. He said: 'It's bad news. It didn't work.'" Christie claimed her stomach had been 'septic poisoned'. Evans described how he found his wife lying dead on the bed. "I could see she was dead and she was bleeding from the nose and lower part." He said he and Christie carried the body downstairs, Christie saying he would get rid of it later. Christie emphasized that Evans would be suspected of her murder, while he himself, as a former policeman, would be free of any suspicion. As for the baby, Geraldine, Christie said he had arranged for a couple to adopt her. The facts are that the bodies of Mrs Evans and her daughter were both found in the wash-house.

On Monday 14th November 1949, Evans went on the run, having sold his furniture for £40. But after a week or so he walked into a police station in Wales, and made a statement confessing to the murder of his wife. He said he had put her body down a drain – even though it was found in the wash-house. Evidently Evans was quite ignorant of the fact that his daughter was also dead. At one point he did accuse Christie of being the real murderer, but when told that the body of his daughter had also been found he withdrew the accusation. Evans was of low intelligence, which possibly explains why he did not immediately inform on Christie when he found his wife strangled. Perhaps he did murder his child – he was alleged to have confided to a prison warder that he killed her because "her crying got on my nerves."

Evans was tried for the murder of his daughter at the Old Bailey in January 1950. One of the chief prosecution witnesses against him was Christie. Evans's counsel attacked his testimony, bringing out his past convictions and suggesting that Christie was the real murderer, and that having killed Mrs Evans in a failed abortion attempt he had to kill the child too. Evans went into the witness-box to claim that Christie had killed his wife in the process of aborting her and had helped him carry the body downstairs. The prosecuting counsel asked him: "Can you suggest why Mr Christie should have strangled your wife?" Evans replied lamely, "Well, he was at home all day..."

For his part, Christie, the virtuous ex-policeman, replied from the witness box that he knew nothing of any abortion, and said that at the time of the murder "I was in bed a lot of the time with the illness I had, which is enteritis and fibrositis in my back." His doctor confirmed this, and said he doubted if Christie could have carried a body downstairs: "At the time I was seeing him he could hardly get off the chair sometimes; I had to help him up." On Friday 13th January 1950 Evans was found guilty and sentenced to death. Christie was in court and burst into tears as he heard the news. Evans was taken down from the dock. He was hanged on 9th March.

After Christie's eventual detection as a strangler of females himself, there was a public outcry for a review of the case against the long-dead Evans with Ludovic Kennedy writing a fine book on the case which challenged the verdict with one compelling question to the readers: did they believe "That Evans and Christie, quite unknown to one another, were both strangling females in the same house in the same sort of way?" A review was eventually carried out by Mr Scott Henderson, and in his Report, published just before Christie was executed, he declared that there had been no miscarriage of justice in the Evans case.

This verdict could never be accepted, and due almost solely to Ludovic Kennedy, the government of the day were forced to order a judicial review of the case of Evans in public, headed by Mr Justice Brabin. The hearing took place during the winter of 1965-6, at the end of which the judge came to the astonishing conclusion that "it was more probable than not" that Evans did kill his wife – but not his daughter. As Christie's confession to the murder of Mrs Evans was now on record (Christie had described in detail how he made a pretence of aborting her and gassed her using a length of rubber tubing; how she struggled, and he hit her about the face, whipped out what he called "my strangling rope" and strangled her, and then had intercourse with her corpse), Justice Brabin's decision was inexplicable. Yet, it achieved what was needed. Since it was for the murder of his daughter that Evans had been hanged, he was entitled to a free pardon. This was granted by the Queen on 18th October 1966 and Evans's remains were removed from Pentonville Prison to be reburied in consecrated ground.

After this detour into the Evans case – essential to grasp fully the extent of Christie's hypocrisy and glib manner – we return to the killer himself back in the early 1950s. Having had his brief moment of glory as a witness in the Evans trial (he kept newspaper accounts of the trial in his wallet), life went on as normal for Mr and Mrs Christie. Christie had helped hang a man for his own murders, yet seems to have felt no lasting remorse, though he was frequently visiting his doctor with a string of complaints which included insomnia, headaches, diarrhoea, flatulence, amnesia, back-ache and fibrositis. After the war he had secured a clerical position with the Post Office Savings Bank, but when his past convictions came out he was sacked and forced to seek another job. He was now a clerk with British Road Services. The year was 1952 and Christie, aged fifty-four, was in a state of decline both mentally and physically. Earlier that year he had been advised to go into a mental hospital for treatment for an anxiety neurosis, but he refused. On 6th December he gave up his job at British Road Services. The decline had become a terminal breakdown.

Rillington Place had now become a slum area. In the Christies' building four Jamaican families had moved into flats on the first and second floors. They were noisy, troublesome neighbours and Reginald Christie complained about them more than once. But it was to no avail. Ethel Christie in particular was very upset by their behaviour and it was taking its toll on her health. It was thus that she became her husband's next victim. As he put it: "She was becoming very frightened from these blacks... and she got very depressed. On 14th December [Sunday] I was awakened at about 8.15. I think it was my wife moving about in bed. I sat up and saw that she appeared to be convulsive, her face was blue and she was choking... I did what I could to restore her breathing, but it was hopeless... I couldn't bear to see her, so I got a stocking and tied it around her neck to put her to sleep. I placed her under the floorboards. I thought that was the best way to lay her to rest."

What is interesting about this episode is that Christie's behaviour after the death of his wife bore a remarkable similarity to that of Timothy Evans after the death of *his* wife. Both sold their wives' wedding rings, and both sold the household furniture *to the same dealer*.

Christie sold his furniture on 6th January 1953, keeping only a mattress and blankets, a table and chairs and some crockery and cutlery. For ten weeks of bitter cold he lived in the back room with only his mongrel dog and cat for company. Every day he poured disinfectant down the drains and around the house to disguise the smell of his wife's decomposing remains. In fact, the atmospheric conditions in the house led to a process of dehydration and there was very little odour.

Sunk in apathy and despair, literally at the end of his tether, Christie had become divorced from reality and was experiencing what psychiatrists term "disassociation". That is, he was not really conscious of what he was doing, but viewed his own actions as if he was a spectator. Unemployed, with no wife to care for him and only £2.14s a week dole money to live on, Christie might well have committed suicide. Instead, with what was left of his dwindling reserves of sexual energy, he murdered three prostitutes.

They were Kathleen Maloney, twenty-six; Rita Nelson, twenty-five, who was six months pregnant – both killed towards the end of January; and the last victim, Hectorina MacLennan, twenty-six, killed about 6th March. All were stuffed into an alcove which had formerly been used to store coal, and Christie had wallpapered over this to conceal it and make the wall appear continuous. MacLennan was naked save for a brassière, which appeared to be hooked on to a nail, holding her upright in a squatting position with her head bowed. The other two were partly clothed and wrapped in blankets. All three prostitutes had VD, all had been strangled with a ligature, all three had a cloth between their legs, tied like a diaper. Mrs Christie too had been diapered. Intercourse had taken place with all three prostitutes at about the time of death.

It was Christie's last fling; in a sense he was living posthumously. On Friday 13th March he illegally sub-let his three rooms to a couple, taking three months' rent in advance. He then took his dog to a vet to be destroyed, and walked out of 10 Rillington Place for the last time on 20th March 1953, carrying his few possessions in a cheap suitcase. He spent that first night at a doss-house in King's Cross. He was drifting now, rootless...

The new tenants enjoyed an occupancy of just one day before the landlord visited and threw them out. The landlord then invited one of his tenants, a Mr Beresford Brown, who was living in Evans's old room, to use the kitchen in Christie's quarters. It was the unfortunate Mr Brown who, wanting to put up a bracket on the wall to hold a radio, discovered the hollow spot. Pulling back the wallpaper, he uncovered Christie's cache of bodies.

The police were quickly summoned, and senior detectives watched as Dr Camps, the Home Office pathologist, supervised the removal of the bodies, after they had been photographed *in situ*.

The house was now thoroughly searched, and later that night the body of Mrs Christie was discovered under the floorboards. Next the garden was dug up. Bones were uncovered which made up two complete female skeletons – a human femur was propping up the garden fence. These were the remains of Ruth Fuerst and Muriel Eady. In the yard the police found a tobacco tin containing four sets of pubic hair.

By the next day the newspapers had gone wild with bold headlines about the "House of Horror". A photograph of Reginald Christie was published in all the newspapers with the usual euphemism that police believed he could "help them in their enquiries". Despite an intensive police hunt nationwide Christie eluded the police for almost a week, wandering around London in a daze. At 9.10 a.m. on Tuesday 31st March PC Tom Ledger was patrolling the embankment near Putney Bridge. He saw what he took to be a tramp leaning on the embankment wall, staring out across the river. The man was scruffy, unshaven and hungry-looking. Once he had removed his hat at the constable's request, the PC recognized him instantly by his bald dome as being Christie. The officer arrested him and took him to Putney police station. Standing by that embankment, Christie must have looked a forlorn figure. He was in a state of spiritual suspension; an inner moral collapse had left him utterly devastated.

Christie was to make a series of statements, at both Putney and Notting Hill police stations. He admitted the "mercy killing" of his wife, and later the murders of the three prostitutes. But he did not confess to gassing or strangling them, or to having intercourse with them, although the forensic evidence was positive on all three points. This was a peculiar trait of Christie's, a kind of mealy-mouthed puritan streak. He did not like to talk about anything "dirty", and thought masturbation was wicked. And so in all his statements he attempted to keep out all references to those things which he could not face. Every murder had been an accident, following a struggle. It had been the victim's fault...

Kathleen Maloney had forced her way into his house, demanding money and threatening to create a scene. Rita Nelson had Irish blood – she started fighting. MacLennan struggled. Ruth Fuerst tried to force him to leave his wife. Mrs Evans had asked him to help her kill herself.

In his interviews with the police he was vague and wandering, by turns apologetic and weeping, defensive and angry. Of the murder of Maloney, he said he had known her previously. She had watched as Christie photographed another prostitute in the nude. On the night of her murder she had been very drunk. She asked Christie for money. He took her to Rillington Place and sat her in a deck chair. Above her head hung a length of rubber tubing sealed by a bulldog clamp. Christie loosened the clamp and she became drowsy. Christie said, "There was a piece of rope. . . hanging from the chair. I don't remember what happened but I must have gone haywire. The next thing I remember she was lying still in the chair with the rope around her neck." He told of removing her knickers and having intercourse with her, then placing a diaper between her legs. "I left her there... after that I believe I had a cup of tea." He was always drinking tea; a strong brew kept him refreshed during his murders.

Rita Nelson came next. She had come to London three months pregnant and had made an appointment to be admitted to a hospital for unmarried mothers. She never kept that appointment. It may have been that Christie persuaded her that he could give her an abortion and introduced her to his gassing device. He said she struggled – so he had to strangle her. Then he had intercourse with her, diapered her, and put her in the alcove with Maloney. After which, presumably, he had a cup of tea...

Miss MacLennan was looking for lodgings with her boyfriend. Christie let them look around his rooms at Rillington Place and even allowed them to sleep overnight. Then he made sure of getting her alone in the house while her boyfriend was at the Labour Exchange. "I took her into the kitchen and poured out a drink for her... when I undid the clasp to release the gas she spotted me. She became uneasy and got up to leave. But I was determined she should not escape, and I followed her into the hall. I seized hold of her neck and applied just sufficient pressure to make her limp. I took her into the kitchen and I decided that it was essential to use the gas again. I made love to her, then put her back in the chair. I killed her." She went into the alcove with some difficulty: it was now full.

After being charged with the murder of his wife, Christie was remanded to Brixton Prison. On 15th April he was also charged with the murders of the three women in the alcove. By now his defence counsel had informed him that the only possible defence was one of insanity. He was interviewed in prison several times by a defence psychologist, Dr Hobson. At first he denied killing Mrs Evans. It was not until 27th April that he admitted killing her – but not the baby, Geraldine. He remarked to the prison chaplain:"The more the merrier!" He had now confessed to the murders of seven women.

By now the case was attracting the same kind of feverish national interest as would the Moors Murders ten years later, and already sick jokes were circulating – the traditional British response to any tragedy or catastrophe, as if to counteract the horror. A typical joke was: "Poor Christie: six women in the house and nobody to make him a cup of tea."

On 18th May Mrs Evans and her baby were exhumed and their bodies examined. Three leading pathologists took part in the post-mortem, and one of them, Dr Keith Simpson, tells us in his book *Forty Years of Murder* that although Christie claimed ownership of the infamous collection of pubic hairs with the words: "The pubic hair in the tin found at 10 Rillington Place came from the three women in the alcove and from my wife" – in fact none of the clumps of hair matched any of the victims. There were also other discrepancies in Christie's story. Mrs Evans had not been gassed, although Christie said he had used gas on her. Dr Simpson is of the opinion that Christie's confession to the murder of Mrs Evans was false, and made to bolster his defence of insanity. Evidence that points again at Evans as the killer of his wife.

On remand in prison Christie put on weight and took part in games. He seemed to be in his element. He found he was good at chess and was called "Chris the chess champion" by other prisoners, to whom he boasted of his murders, confiding that his aim had been to commit twelve. Doctors who interviewed him in prison described him as being "insignificant and unattractive, and full of snivelling hypocrisy." He often spoke of himself in the third person and described the murders as "these regrettable happenings". But although Christie probably did suffer some kind of amnesia regarding the details of the murders – his self-love could not let him admit to himself that he was a strangler, a necrophile and probably a child-killer – he was, in other respects, very much in control of himself. It is perhaps significant that he boasted to other prisoners: "I could always get Evans to do whatever I wanted." Christie's IQ was found to register 128, compared to Evans's 68.

The trial of Christie for the murder of his wife began on Monday 22nd June 1953 in the No 1 Court at the Old Bailey, before Mr Justice Finnemore. The Attorney-General, Sir Lionel Heald, prosecuted, while Mr Derek Curtis-Bennett QC led for the defence.

Although Christie had admitted to this murder, the prosecution still had to present its evidence. Witnesses were called to testify to the effect that Mrs Christie had last been seen alive on 13th December 1952. Her body, the court heard, was found beneath the floorboards in the front room. Pathologists testified that death was due to strangulation – and so it went on. However, the Attorney-General, aware of the public unease about the execution of Evans, now tried to show Christie was lying when he said he had killed Mrs Evans.

On the second day of the trial Mr Curtis-Bennett rose for the defence. He brought to the attention of the jury details of all seven murders to which Christie had confessed, even though he was only being tried for one. Mr Curtis-Bennett said that he would not deny for a moment that Christie had killed his wife. Indeed, the jury would hear from Christie's own lips how he had killed her and others. The defence was simply that Christie was mad, so mad that under the M'Naghten Rules he did not know that what he was doing was wrong. "Now," Mr

Curtis-Bennett concluded, "this man at this moment will go into the witness box and tell his terrifying story..."

Christie walked jerkily from the dock to the witness box, and once there stood staring blankly for half a minute. He appeared to be weeping. Led gently by his counsel, the meek-looking man with the bald head and spectacles told slowly and hesitantly of killing seven women. He was taken through the murders in detail, one by one. Asked whether he had committed any murders between 1944 and 1949, Christie replied, "I don't know." "You mean you might have done?" queried Curtis-Bennett. "I might have done. I don't know whether I did or not," Christie responded.

The judge then asked him why, in the first statement to the police on 31st March, he had omitted to mention the murders of Fuerst, Eady and Mrs Evans. Referring to the murder of Mrs Evans, Christie replied, "Well, the case I just dismissed from my mind and never gave it a second thought." The judge reminded him that he had testified at the trial of Timothy Evans – had he forgotten that?

"Yes, sir, it had gone clean out of my mind."

Dr Hobson was called for the defence. He said Christie suffered from hysteria, and it was highly probable that at the time of the crime he did not know that what he was doing was wrong. "He has an abnormal memory... I believe these tricks of memory, or avoidance of getting down to disturbing topics, is to preserve his own self-respect, rather than to avoid incriminating himself."

The prosecution called two doctors in rebuttal, Drs Matheson and Curran. Dr Matheson described Christie as "a man of weak character. He is immature and certainly in his sex-life... I would call him a man with a hysterical personality..."

Dr Curran expressed the opinion that Christie was an "inadequate personality with hysterical features... a very extraordinary and abnormal man." He said he did not believe Christie's alleged loss of memory was genuine. "He has, like many other criminals and murderers, a remarkable capacity for dismissing the unpleasant from his mind... He is a man with a remarkable capacity for self-deception."

In his final speech for the defence Mr Curtis-Bennett stressed that Christie must have been insane to have committed such terrifying acts, and then he pondered aloud: "One wonders about the probability of there being two stranglers living in the tiny premises..."

The jury retired at 4.05 p.m. on the fourth day of the trial and returned at 5.25 that same afternoon with a verdict of guilty. Mr Justice Finnemore donned the black cap, and pronounced the sentence of death. Christie was resigned to his fate in the condemned cell, and in a funny sort of way was happy to be facing oblivion. On the morning of 15th July 1953 Albert Pierrepoint hanged him by the neck until he was dead – just as he had done to Timothy Evans three and a half years earlier.

Men cannot become monsters simply by committing monstrous acts. But Christie came close. The absence of knickers on the corpses suggests a fetishism; certainly he was a necrophile. It is suggested that he would have gone on killing compulsively if not apprehended when he was, but on the evidence it seems that Christie had already entered a mental twilight when he was caught. He was a burnt-out case who had embraced death, as opposed to life, and probably went to the scaffold with a sense of relief.

Chapter Five
THE BRITISH YEARS

Reginald Christie stands alone in Britain's criminal history as a unique fiend. Both his character and his crimes were odious in the extreme. And yet he still occupies only a small place in the unpleasant catalogue of sex killers that have plagued the country during and after the Second World War. Many other killers rival him in the barbarity and horror of their methods, and many have used violence to an extent that the feeble Christie could only dream of.

Gordon Frederick Cummins was a young airman who became known as the "war-time Ripper" because he killed with such a compulsive – and even careless – viciousness. He murdered four women in four days in 1942. It was only by pure chance that he was caught, and one dreads to think what the toll would have been had he eluded capture.

Margaret Frances Lowe, forty-three, was a working prostitute who lived in a cheap lodging-house in Gosfield Street in the West End of London. She had not been seen for a few days, but in the turmoil of war, the movements of one individual were of little concern. It was on Saturday 14th February 1942 that her teenage daughter went to visit her and made the grim discovery. Her mother lay dead, having been strangled with a silk stocking. The naked body had been mutilated with a razor blade. Chief Inspector Greeno of Scotland Yard's famed Murder Squad who led the investigation described his first sight of the corpse "as like seeing a crudely butchered carcass."

As the detective studied the body he became aware of the similarities between this victim and two others that had been discovered that week elsewhere in London. Those women had also been strangled and then savagely mutilated.

The first murder had been that of Evelyn Margaret Hamilton, a forty-year-old school-mistress found dead in an air-raid shelter in Montague Place, Marylebone, two days previously. The second had been Mrs Evelyn Oakley (known as Nita Ward), a 35-year-old prostitute who had been found in her Wardour Street flat just the day before. She had had her throat cut and her stomach had been slit open with a tin-opener.

Once it was realized that they were all the work of one psychopath, a "Murder Incident Room" was established at Tottenham Court Road police station, and detectives were instructed to go out and talk to prostitutes and find out whether any of them had been pestered by a sadist or knew of one. Greeno knew only too well that the opportunist sex killer who selects his victims at random is the most difficult killer of all to catch. Only a tip-off could help, or perhaps a mistake by the killer in the course of yet another murder.

That mistake came shortly after the discovery of the killer's fourth victim, a Mrs Doris Jounnet, at her home in Paddington. A report was then received of another attack on a young lady outside a pub near Piccadilly – the Captain's Cabin. A young airman had put his arm around her and forced kisses upon her. When she resisted he tried to strangle her. Fortunately, a deliveryman interrupted the attack and the airman ran off into the darkness. But he left behind a vital clue: his gas-mask lay on the ground, with his service number stencilled on the inside of the case.

The RAF cooperated in tracing the suspect, and he was identified as being Gordon Frederick Cummins, a married student-pilot aged twenty-eight. When confronted by detectives he claimed to be totally innocent of any wrong-doing, having been in bed in his barracks all night. But the alibi was soon broken, and fingerprint evidence confirmed his guilt.

Cummins had a long record of being a "Billy Liar" character. Although well-educated and coming from a good family, he spoke with a fake Oxford accent and claimed to have the right to use the title "Honourable" before his name because he was the bastard son of an aristocrat. He had been dismissed from several jobs for dishonesty.

He had a short trial at the Old Bailey and was duly hanged at Wandsworth Prison on 25th June 1942 during an air raid.

Neville George Clevely Heath lived a fantasy life too, in fact his was even more of a Walter Mitty world than Cummins's. Born in Guildford, Surrey, in 1917, Heath was a handsome man, tall with fair hair, blue eyes and a firm jaw. And he wasn't unintelligent. In all sorts of ways he had advantages over many of his contemporaries. All the same, however, he soon decided that he wanted a good deal more than the world seemed willing to offer him.

When he left school it was to work as a packer in a London warehouse for £1 a week. He soon rebelled against this drudgery and won a short-service commission in the RAF. The glamour of the uniform of the fighter-pilot fell on him like a senator's cloak, but the RAF could not tolerate him for long. Heath was an inveterate liar, always "shooting a line", and in 1937 he was court martialled for fraud and cashiered. Two months after his ignominious discharge he was put on probation for petty fraud.

During the course of the next decade Heath was continually in trouble. He was living on his wits, mostly off women, and often posed as Lord Dudley, or some other nobleman. In 1938 he was sent to Borstal for robbery and then was once more court martialled, this time by the RASC. At the end of the war he went to South Africa to join their Air Force. He was court martialled there too, for fraud and falsely wearing decorations to which he was not entitled. Heath was the type of man who would award himself the Victoria Cross without a second thought. He was also the prototype sadist.

It was in June 1946 that Heath committed his first murder. He invited Mrs Margery Gardner, whom he had met at the Panama Club in South Kensington, to come to his room at the Pembridge Court Hotel in Notting Hill where he was known as "Colonel Heath". Once in the room, Mrs Gardner was tied up, whipped and butchered.

There can be no doubt that Margery Gardner expected some kind of sexual activity to take place, and activity of a "kinky" nature. She was a masochist, and enjoyed bondage and flagellation. In this context it can be argued that she invited her own death; that she provoked in Heath some dormant psychotic streak, and thus belonged to the sub-section of criminology known as "Victimology". That is to say, she was a victim going around looking for someone to kill her. But one doubts that she ever anticipated the truly gruesome treatment that lay in store.

At 2 p.m. the next day, 21st June 1946, a chambermaid tried to gain entry to Heath's room so she could make the beds. When she received no reply to her knocking, she opened the door with the pass key. The room was in darkness, the heavy curtains still drawn. The maid pulled back the curtains and the light flooded in, illuminating a scene of horror.

Mrs Gardner lay on the bed. She was naked and lying on her back. Her ankles were bound tightly together with a handkerchief. Her face and chin were badly bruised, and her body had been savagely whipped. There was blood everywhere.

Professor Keith Simpson was the pathologist called to the scene. He assumed she would have had to have been gagged to stop her screams being heard by the occupants of the bedrooms on either side. He found a total of seventeen lash marks – two of them on her face – which had left distinctive marks. "Find the whip and you've found your killer," he told waiting detectives. He also deduced that the woman's hands had been bound, although the ligature was now missing. Her breasts had been bitten, the nipples nearly bitten off. Her vagina had been badly torn by an instrument being inserted and then rotated – probably a poker. The injuries had been inflicted before death.

It was not too difficult for Detective Superintendent Thomas Barratt (who was placed in charge of the murder inquiry) to deduce the identity of the likely killer – Heath's fingerprints were everywhere – and he lost no time in issuing a press statement to the effect that he wished to interview Heath in connection with the case. By now, however, the killer was on the run.

Heath was arrested two weeks later. He had been unable to keep quiet about his crimes. Like many other sex killers, he had a compulsion to keep in contact with the police who were investigating the murder. He wrote to Superintendent Barratt, admitting he had booked into the Pembridge Court Hotel, but said he had loaned his key to Mrs Gardner who had used the room to entertain a friend. "I returned," he wrote, "and found her in the condition of which you are aware. I realised I was in an invidious position... and left." Heath also contacted the

Bournemouth police, to offer his help in finding Doreen Marshall, twenty-one, who had recently vanished from her room at the Norfolk Hotel.

Miss Marshall was Heath's second victim. Her body was later found lying in some bushes near the cliffs in Branksome Dene Chine, just one and a half miles from the Tollard Hotel. It was swarming with flies.

She was naked and bloody, having obviously put up a desperate struggle for her life. Her pearl necklace had been broken, and beads from it lay scattered all round. One stocking was found some yards away, another was found high up in some bushes. Forensic examination revealed that the girl had been beaten several times on the back of the head, and then the killer had knelt on her with such force that a rib had fractured, piercing the lung. Her wrists had been bound with the handkerchief later found in Heath's hotel room, and she was gagged. The inside of both hands bore defensive wounds, indicating that she had still been alive and trying to fight off the knife when it was used to perform the terrible mutilation of her body.

Two deep knife cuts across the throat were the immediate cause of death, but a nipple had been bitten off, and the knife had been used to cut a large Y-shaped gash from each nipple leading down to the groin. A rough instrument, possibly a branch, had been used to tear open her vagina and anus, perforating the tissues. It was deduced that Heath must have stripped naked to perform his ritual savagery, since no blood was found on his clothing. He must have washed off the blood in the sea before dressing.

After murdering Doreen Marshall, Heath had stolen a few pounds from her handbag, and removed her jewellery. The following day he pawned her ring, and just half an hour before he walked into the Bournemouth police station – where he was arrested – he sold her watch.

There was never any doubt about Heath's guilt, only his sanity. Anticipating that this would be his defence, Mr Anthony Hawke, the prosecuting counsel during Heath's trial at the Old Bailey, declared that although the acts of murder were of such a nature that they indicated a killer "sexually perverted to the stage of monstrosity," that in itself did not excuse the acts. He said that the letter written by Heath to Superintendent Barratt proved that the killer knew that what he had done was wrong and punishable by law.

This claim was countered by Dr Hubert, an expert witness called by the defence. He said that from his examination of the prisoner he was of the opinion that Heath did not realize that his behaviour was wrong or criminal. He felt justified in inflicting cruelty because that was the only way in which he could obtain sexual satisfaction. Mr Hawke asked him: "Is that your answer, Dr Hubert? That in as much as he wished to satisfy his perverted lust he thought it was right to satisfy it?"

"Yes," replied the doctor.

"And therefore he does not know that what he was doing was wrong?" queried Hawke.

"Yes."

Dr Hubert said that Heath was "morally insane", had a "deficient moral sense" and was a sadist of the worst type. He insisted that Heath was certifiably insane. Mr Hawke pressed him: "Are you saying that a person who does a thing which he wants to do because it suits him at the moment to do it, if that is a crime, is entitled to be called insane and therefore free from responsibility?"

"Yes," answered Dr Hubert, "if the crime and the circumstances are so abnormal that they are unthinkable to a normal person."

Hawke was outraged: "Does that mean that every sexual pervert, in order to indulge his perversion, is entitled to say he is free of any responsibility for the consequences?"

Dr Hubert looked sheepish. "No," he conceded.

Mr Justice Morris, summing-up to the jury, stressed that the law of insanity "is not to become a refuge of those who cannot challenge a charge when it is brought against them." He added, "A perverted impulse cannot be excused on the grounds of insanity."

The jury retired for just one hour before returning with a verdict of guilty. Neville Heath was hanged at Pentonville Prison by Albert Pierrepoint on 16th October 1946. He remained calm and debonair to the end. Just before he went to the scaffold he was asked if he wanted a whisky. He replied in the affirmative, adding, "I think I'll make it a double."

Peter Thomas Anthony Manuel serves as a typical representative of the character born too strong for his environment – or too weak, depending on one's viewpoint. He was a little man of extreme arrogance who was determined to impress himself on the world, even if it meant talking his way to the gallows. He was a classic "in-betweener"; too intelligent for his surroundings, but not talented enough to channel his intelligence into legitimate means of expression. As a result, his only opportunity to demonstrate his "superiority" came when he conducted his own defence at his murder trial; and an impressive performance it was too. The trial judge referred to his defence as being "conducted with a skill that is quite remarkable." But Manuel was found guilty all the same.

Manuel was born in Manhattan, New York, on 15th March 1927. His family returned to the UK when he was six years old and settled first in Coventry. For Manuel it was not a good move. The dark-haired little boy with the American accent did not fit in at his new school and began playing truant. At eleven he was put on probation for shop-breaking, and soon after was put in a remand home for being out of control.

From the age of eleven to eighteen, Manuel spent most of his time in approved schools and borstals where the authorities attempted to crush the boy's innate sense of superiority and rebellion. They failed. In those precious few adolescent years he might have begun writing poetry or honed some other talent; instead he turned to crime to give himself a sense of identity. He broke out of his various approved schools a total of ten times, committing housebreakings and thefts all around the country. In one house he burgled he found a woman sleeping. He stole her purse and then struck her over the head with a hammer. There was no motive for the vicious assault, which might well have caused death. Manuel just wanted to inflict some pain. He was fifteen years old at the time.

When recaptured he was remanded to Leeds Prison for a spell before being returned to a Yorkshire approved school. Just before Christmas 1942 he broke out yet again and this time attacked a woman on a lonely road, indecently assaulting her as well as robbing her. This was his first recorded sex offence. In 1945 Manuel left borstal for the last time, and after a brief spell trying to earn a dishonest penny in Blackpool he rejoined his parents, who were now living in Lanarkshire. Soon afterwards there was an epidemic of housebreaking in the area. Manuel was promptly arrested on fifteen counts of burglary. It was while he was on bail for these charges that he attacked an expectant mother close to a hospital and raped her. He was sentenced to twelve months on the housebreaking charges but eight years for the rape, which he served at the notorious Peterhead Prison.

If ever there was a place designed to break men's hearts and spirits it is Peterhead. But it failed to break Manuel.

He twice attacked warders and emerged just as villainous as he had been when he had entered. On his release he went to live with his parents in their new home in Birkenshaw, a village just outside Glasgow. Manuel worked as a dustman by day, and in the evening tried to write short stories. He also began sketching, showing some talent as an artist. This, however, was only a half-hearted attempt to channel his frustration into creative outlets. He had already decided that his destiny lay in crime. Manuel now had just one aim: to join Glasgow's underworld and become accepted on his own terms. It was not easy to do, however. Experienced safe-breakers laughed at the young man whom they viewed as nothing more than a petty crook with a big mouth.

In July 1955 Manuel was arrested on a charge of assaulting a girl who was taking a short-cut home from a dance. The girl testified that Manuel had seized her, threatening to cut her throat with a knife, and then forced her to a lonely spot and indecently assaulted her. "Afterwards he told me he had been watching TV that night when he had a sudden impulse to cut someone's head off and bury them." His family had attempted to have Manuel certified unfit to plead, but he refused to do so. In fact, he shrugged off all legal help. Instead he conducted his own defence and was very pleased with the consequence. The jury found the charge not proven and he was released. For the first time Manuel had taken on the forces of the law on its own terms and beaten it.

The police, however, were still certain that the twenty-eight-year-old thug was the culprit, and from that time onward they kept him under special observation. They knew he was a bomb waiting to explode. Manuel responded by writing them anonymous letters, by turns offering false information about crimes and insulting various CID officers.

On 2nd January 1956 Anne Kneilands, seventeen, vanished after leaving her home at East Kilbride on her way to a dance. Her body was found two days later on a local golf course. She had been battered to death with extreme ferocity. Although she had not been sexually assaulted, her knickers were missing. Police suspected that Manuel was the killer, but they could not touch him. They had to abide by the rules and wait for sufficient evidence to warrant an arrest. They searched his home and found nothing. Questioned about scratches on his face, he said he had been in a fight in Glasgow. The fact that he was working near the spot where the girl was found was, he said, pure coincidence.

On 17th September 1956 three members of a family were found murdered in a bungalow at High Burnside. Mrs Watt, her sister, Mrs Margaret Brown, and her daughter Vivienne had all been shot with bullets fired from a .38 Webley revolver. The properties adjoining their home had been burgled.

Mrs Watt's husband, William, had been away on a fishing holiday when the tragedy occurred and was stunned by the news when he returned home. He was more shocked still when he found himself arrested for the crime. An ex-policeman, Watt was to spend sixty-seven days in Barlinnie Prison charged with the murders.

Manuel had also been questioned about the killings and his house had been searched. But as no firearms were found, suspicion against him lifted. At the time he was on bail on robbery charges and in due course he too was sent to Barlinnie to serve a sentence of eighteen months. Once he was inside the jail Manuel made a point of contacting Mr Watt, telling him that he knew he was innocent. Manuel claimed to know the identity of the real killer and assured Watt that he would help him to bring the man to justice. He even sent for Mr Watt's solicitor, Mr Laurence Dowdall, and related details of how each room in the bungalow had been left, as it had been told to him by the "real" murderer. When this information was checked out it matched exactly with the facts.

Alerted to this new development, detectives interviewed Manuel in prison. They were now certain that he was the killer but, with no evidence to back this up, there was little they could do. Manuel would not incriminate himself. He persisted in relating details of the crime, but only in the third person. In November 1957, having served his sentence for burglary, Manuel walked out of prison a free man. He was full of confidence. He even went to the newspapers, offering to sell his story.

Eight days later a Newcastle taxi-driver, Sidney Dunn, was murdered in Durham. He had been shot and had his throat cut. He was known to have picked up a fare who spoke with a strong Scottish accent. On 28th December Isabelle Cooke, seventeen, disappeared while on her way to a school dance. Her route would take her close to Manuel's home. A large team of police searched for the girl; items of her clothing were recovered from the river Calder.

It was an incredible situation. For two years the police had known that Manuel was a killer; it was known to the press; hundreds of members of the public were aware of it, yet he was allowed to walk free, although closely watched. People in a large area around Glasgow lived in fear of the unknown killer, keeping their daughters safely locked away at home, escorting them to school, at a time when the police knew full well who he was. Yet they could not touch him. The rule of law forbade it. Manuel displayed an animal cunning and could not be broken under questioning.

On Monday 6th January 1958 Peter Smart, his wife Doris, and their son Michael, eleven, were found dead in their beds at Sheepburn Road, Uddington. They had been shot with a Beretta automatic pistol. They had actually been killed on New Year's Day – only four days after Isabelle Cooke – but their bodies had lain waiting to be discovered. Detective Superintendent Alex Brown, leading the murder inquiry, did not interview Manuel even though he was certain that he was the killer. He felt that silence was the best weapon against him. If he was ignored he might be forced to show his hand. It was noted that he was spending freely, whereas before he had been broke.

Meanwhile William Watt, an innocent man, had come out of prison determined to track down the man who had slaughtered his family. He talked to many people in Glasgow's underworld, and received definite confirmation that Manuel had bought a gun. Eventually a formal meeting took place between Mr Watt, his solicitor, and Manuel. Mr Watt listened grimly as Manuel spoke of things he had "been told"' about the murders, hoping that Manuel would slip up and incriminate himself. He did not.

In the early hours of the morning on Tuesday 14th January 1958 a large team of CID officers arrived at Manuel's home and arrested him. He was still asleep. In the house police found a camera and gloves stolen in burglaries; it was enough to keep him under lock and key. In an effort to force him to confess to the murders, police also arrested his mother and father. Faced with this, Manuel cracked and promised to make a statement on condition that his parents were freed.

He subsequently took detectives to a field in Mount Vernon, saying, "This is the place. In fact I think I'm standing on her now." Police dug and found the almost naked remains of Isabelle Cooke. Manuel also confessed to the two triple murders and the murder of Anne Kneilands. He told his story with a callous detachment which shocked even the hardened detectives. In his statement he referred to the various murders in detail.

Of Anne Kneilands, he described meeting her and offering to walk her home:

> We walked along a curving country road... About halfway along this road I pulled her into a field gate. She struggled, ran away and I chased her. In the wood she started screaming and I hit her on the head with a piece of iron I had picked up.

Of the Watt family he said:

> I entered the house by breaking a front-door panel made of glass. I opened the bedroom door. There were two in bed. I went into the other room and there was a girl in the bed. She woke up and sat up. I hit her on the chin and knocked her out. I tied her hands and went back in the other room. I shot the two people in this room and then heard someone making a noise in the other room. I went back in and the girl had got loose. We struggled and I flung her on the bed and shot her too.

Of Isabelle Cooke:

> I met a girl walking. I grabbed her and dragged her into a field... I tore off her clothes and tied something round her neck and shoulders. I then carried her up a lane into a field and dug a hole with a shovel... I covered her up and went back the way I came.

Of the Smart family:

> I did it about six o'clock on the morning of
> New Year's Day... I went into the bedroom and
> got £18 or £20 in new notes and four or five
> ten-shilling notes... I shot the man first, and then
> the woman, then I shot the boy... I then went
> into the living-room and ate a handful of wee
> biscuits from a tray.

Peter Manuel was to go on trial for eight of his
known murders; the murder of the taxi-driver could
not be dealt with as it had occurred in England. The
trial began on Monday 12th May 1958 before Lord
Cameron in the Justiciary Building in Glasgow. People
queued for fourteen hours for seats, as if they were
attending a première, and in a sense they were. It was to
be a drama in which Manuel was to be the principal actor,
the hero of his own biography. He was dressed for the
part in a smart blazer, with blue trousers, and a grey shirt
and tie. His coarse good looks, with his dark hair hanging
over his eyes, made him appear like an embryonic Elvis
Presley. He was brimming with confidence.

A jury of fifteen – nine men and six women – were
duly sworn in. Manuel pleaded not guilty to all charges
and had a "special defence" (peculiar to Scottish law) to
some of the matters.

His special defence to the money and articles stolen
from a house near the Watt bungalow and found in his
possession was that he had received them from the
original burglar, whom he named. His second special
defence was one of impeachment: he alleged that the
murders had been committed by William Watt. There were
to be some 280 witnesses, and the forensic evidence was
damning. Both murder guns had been recovered from the

Clyde where Manuel said he had dumped them. The trial lasted sixteen days, and the testimony given ran to well over half a million words.

The first day was taken up with the murder of Anne Kneilands. A bullet had been found in the house by its new owner: it came from the same .38 Webley used to kill the Watt family. The man Manuel had named as the burglar had to appear in court to deny the charge.

On the fourth day William Watt testified about the murder of his family and his meeting with Manuel. He said Manuel had shown him a snapshot of Anne Kneilands, which he had then torn into small pieces. Various unsavoury characters testified about the illegal selling of guns in Glasgow, one telling of how Manuel had collected a "package" from his house.

Halfway through the trial Manuel's counsel submitted that his client's confession should be excluded as it had been obtained under duress. Lord Cameron ruled that Manuel's admission had been made without pressure. The confession was allowed into evidence. Police officers testified as to how Manuel had made his admissions to the murders, and had led them to the spot where Isabelle Cooke lay buried. They insisted that Manuel had refused to have a solicitor present when he wrote his statement.

On the tenth day of the trial came the drama. Manuel sacked his counsel and announced that he would be conducting his own defence. It was the high-point of his life. He was now the focus of attention, with the chance to demonstrate his cleverness. He recalled Detective Inspector Tom Goodall of Glasgow CID and subjected him to a gruelling cross-examination. Manuel spoke fluently and without reference to notes. Using the legal terminology to which he had become well used, he tried to trap the inspector into damaging admissions. When Goodall described how Manuel had led officers to the spot where Isabelle Cooke lay buried, Manuel established that it had been dark at the time. "In which hand were you holding your torch?" he asked.

"I had no torch," the inspector replied.

"Then how could you see, if it was dark?" Manuel demanded triumphantly.

He suggested that the police were lying; that they had known where Isabelle Cooke lay buried before leading him to the spot, and that his statement had been made under duress, with threats made against his family.

On the twelfth day came the "trial within a trial" when Manuel recalled William Watt. Now he accused Mr Watt directly of killing his own family. Mr Watt replied, "That is an atrocious lie."

Then Manuel recalled ex-Superintendent James Hendry and tried to play his master stroke. Turning to the policeman, he asked: "Did you feel confident when you arrested Watt you had arrested the man who had shot his wife?" Unfortunately for Manuel the judge would not allow the ex-detective to reply. The detective's opinions, he said, were not relevant to this case.

The following day Manuel called his own mother and father as witnesses. Then Manuel went into the witness-box himself. He gave a virtuoso performance. He denied being guilty of any of the murders, claiming that Mr Watt had admitted to him that he had shot his wife. Speaking fluently, with the odd joke here and there, he tried to persuade a hard-headed Scottish jury of his innocence. He had an answer for every allegation, claiming that the prosecution's entire case was a conspiracy against him.

Cross-examined by the prosecution, Manuel described the evidence against him as being either "ridiculous" or "just coincidence." He accused Mr Watt of being arrogant and Detective Superintendent Brown of being a "rat of man". He claimed that he simply could not have done the murders: "There was ten policemen watching my house every night."

The prosecution made its closing speech, then Manuel made his. It was an inspired and articulate performance. The judge began his summing up, first directing the jury to find Manuel not guilty of the murder of Anne Kneilands because, despite Manuel's confession, there was insufficient corroboration to establish his guilt. Referring to the prisoner's mental condition, the judge said a man "may be very bad without being mad."

The jury retired, taking two and a half hours to find Manuel guilty of all seven remaining murders. Lord Cameron then sentenced Manuel to death with the traditional formula, then placed the black cap on his head and announced the peculiarly Scottish sentence: "This pronounced for doom." Manuel's appeal was rejected and on Friday 11th July 1958, after a glass of whisky, he walked to the execution chamber at Barlinnie Prison.

Before his execution Manuel confessed to three more murders. They were of Helen Carlin, a prostitute found in September 1954; Anne Steele, fifty-four, found battered to death on 11th January 1956; and Ellen Petrie, stabbed in Glasgow in June 1956.

Peter Manuel undoubtedly obtained a morbid sexual satisfaction from the act of killing. He was a small, insignificant criminal who longed for the limelight. Andy Warhol once said that in the future everybody will be famous – for just fifteen minutes. Manuel had his fifteen minutes and more.

Lord Cameron's comment that a man may be bad without being mad was later to echo in the Old Bailey as the trial of another sex killer opened. This was the case of **Michael Douglas Dowdall**, a man who was as pathetic as he was vicious.

On Monday 15 December 1958 a prostitute was taken home in a taxi by a young man she had met while she was plying her trade. Veronica Murray, thirty-one, was subsequently found dead in her room at 58 Charteris Road, Kilburn, north-west London, on Christmas Eve. She had been dead for about a week. Her skull had been battered in, and a bloodstained dumb-bell, which was clearly the murder weapon, was lying on the floor. The corpse was naked except for a pullover drawn up over the head. Initially it appeared to be a fairly routine killing; what made this one different was the series of small circular marks found on her body. They had been made after death, possibly by someone pressing a bottle-top into the flesh with great force. Fingerprints were found in the room, but a prostitute's room can be expected to bear the impressions of many strangers. They provided few leads.

On 10th October 1959 a Mrs Hill was celebrating her birthday. She met a pleasant, good-looking youth in the West End and invited him back to her flat at Ismailia Road, Fulham. Once the door was closed the youth pressed himself up against her and tried to have sex. When she refused him he partially strangled her with a silk stocking. Mrs Hill passed out. When she recovered she found circular marks all over her body.

Mrs Hill contacted the police, who immediately made the connection between her attack and the murder one year earlier. From fingerprints found in the flat they were also to link it with a number of other crimes. One involved a 65-year-old woman who had been battered with a poker as she slept in her home near Sloane Square. She had been robbed of money and whisky. The prints also linked the mystery attacker with a series of burglaries over the previous year, including three in Chelsea, one in a Fulham pub, and another rather curious break-in at the

Westbury Hotel, Mayfair. The burglar had broken into a suite occupied by actor George Sanders, drunk some whisky and then stole a pair of shoes. The thief's own badly worn pair were recovered by the police and found to have the initials "W.G." crudely nailed into the sole.

On 19th November 1959 Scotland Yard issued a public appeal for information, publishing a photograph of the shoes, but it brought no response. A week later, however, after another housebreaking expedition in which the villain robbed four or five houses in Chelsea, leaving behind his now-familiar fingerprints on the whisky bottle and glasses, he stole an unusual cigarette lighter bearing a distinctive emblem. The owner, an Australian business-man, had a replica. Police issued a fresh appeal with a photograph of the lighter. This time a guardsman in the Welsh Guards camp at Pirbright reported to his CO that the man in the next bed to his had a lighter exactly like the one shown. His name was Michael Douglas Dowdall.

Detective Chief Inspector Bob Acott and Detective Inspector Peter Vibart had been leading the investigation. They saw Dowdall at Woking police station. He had got rid of the lighter, but showed the detectives where he had hidden it. He then made a statement concerning the murder of Veronica Murray: "Everybody has been against me. It is when I have been drinking I do these things."

Telling of how he took his victim home in a taxi, where they had sex and then went to sleep, he went on: "When she woke me up we had a row over something and she called me a filthy little Welsh bastard. She threw a vase at me... She came at me with something and hit me on the back of the head... I rushed at her and knocked her down... I remember chucking some clothes over her. I took a bottle of whisky and then I left the place." He said that only when he read of the death a day or so later, did he realize that he had killed her. Attempting to explain his criminal activities, he told the police: "My army mates think I'm queer; I've tried to show them they're wrong... My mates made me feel a nobody. So I have a drink, and then I feel better and more important."

Dowdall, aged nineteen, stood trial at the Old Bailey on 20th January 1960, before Mr Justice Donovan. The trial was to last only two days. Dowdall's defence was the new one of "diminished responsibility", and for once the psychiatrists were in agreement. Dr Brisby, Principal Medical Officer at Brixton Prison, described Dowdall as a "psychopath and a social misfit." Dr Leigh, a psychiatrist at Bethlehem Hospital, confirmed that Dowdall was a psychopath, adding: "He is a sexual pervert."

Dowdall's father had been killed in the war in 1943, his mother died in 1948, and he was brought up by an aunt in Wales. He joined the Welsh Guards as a drummer boy at the age of fifteen, and began drinking heavily soon afterwards.

The jury retired for three hours before returning to request advice on "diminished responsibility". They then took just a further eight minutes to find Dowdall guilty of manslaughter. He was sentenced to life imprisonment. He was released on licence from prison in July 1975, suffering from a fatal illness from which he died in November 1976 aged thirty-six.

Quite the worst sex killer of the fifties was **Patrick Byrne**, a man who might have gone on to become another Peter Kürten had he not been apprehended when he was. Byrne brought an atmosphere of terror to Birmingham which was surely reminiscent of the panic in London during the Ripper months of 1888. In fact, the connection with the Ripper was also more tangible. It was shortly before the murder of Stephanie Baird that a book by Donald McCormick, *The Identity of Jack the Ripper*, had been published. The killing of Miss Baird bore such a striking resemblance to those it described that the police were to try to trace every person who had borrowed the book from public libraries. Byrne is a rare creature in the annals of the sex killer – one who admitted and told in full detail his motives and methods. His statement is of prime importance to any study of the mind of the sex killer.

It began on the evening of Wednesday 23rd December 1959. Stephanie Baird was occupying Room Four at the YWCA hostel in Wheeley's Road, Edgbaston, Birmingham. She was busy packing, intending to spend Christmas with her mother, when an intruder broke into her room. The man grabbed her, felling her with such force that her skull was fractured as her head hit the floor. He was kissing her passionately even while his hands were around her throat, strangling the life out of her.

The killer had sex with the corpse, but that was not enough. He still wanted to butcher her. With a table knife he cut off her right breast. Then he attempted to cut open her stomach and mutilated her back and legs with the blunt knife. Finally he cut off her head, holding it up by the hair to look at it in the mirror. The killer then went downstairs to the laundry room. There he found twenty-year-old Mrs Margaret Brown. He struck her with a piece of rock wrapped in a brassière, but ran away when she started screaming.

Mrs Brown called the police and soon enough a team of officers were on the scene. They searched the grounds and found footprints in the earth outside an open window, then they discovered that Room Four was locked. The door was forced open. What greeted them was a sight they would never forget. The headless corpse lay on the floor, but standing on the bed, upright on its stump, was a human head, with a breast placed beside it. The only clue to the killer was a note he had left scribbled on an envelope. It read: "This is the thing I Tought would never come." The knife with which he had inflicted the torture lay close by.

So began one of the biggest police hunts in British history; 20,000 men were interviewed, and a large-scale search mounted for a bloodstained man. Every man within a three-mile radius of the hostel in the right age bracket was seen and his movements accounted for. There were many reports of a bloodstained man having been seen about that night, but nobody was ever traced.

Two Home Office pathologists called in to examine the remains of Stephanie Baird disagreed on the case. Dr Frederick Griffiths was of the opinion that the killer had used the blunt table knife, with its handle broken off, to commit all the mutilations and the decapitation. He was certain that a killer would not change knives during such a grisly ritual. Dr Francis Camps, however, was of the opinion that the killer had used a sharp knife for some of the cuts, switching to the blunt knife found at the scene for others. He also felt that the killer might have some knowledge of dissection. As a result hundreds of medical students were interviewed, as were some four thousand butchers.

Detective Chief Superintendent James Haughton, head of Birmingham CID, personally headed the hunt for the killer and appeared on TV to make an urgent appeal to the public. He was frank about the task which faced him. Every man in the area had to be traced and eliminated from the inquiry, and that meant questioning some hundred thousand people. Another difficulty was that many people had left the area to travel home for Christmas. Each would have to be traced by a laborious door-to-door inquiry.

In the end the killer was caught almost by accident. Seven weeks after the murder a routine request was sent to Warrington Police asking them to interview Patrick Byrne, a labourer who had been lodging close to the hostel in Birmingham, but had left just before Christmas to go to stay with his mother in Warrington, Lancashire. He had given notice to his landlady and his employer before the murder. A fellow-Irishman said that Byrne had been drinking with him on the evening of the murder, and as that had taken place between 6.30 p.m. and 7.15 p.m. it seemed to put Byrne in the clear. However, he had not been interviewed himself, and Haughton was insistent that every possible suspect should be seen in person. Byrne did have a criminal record. He had three convictions for housebreaking in Dublin, and convictions for drunken assault on the police in Birmingham. He also had a long record as a peeping Tom. His work-mates had nicknamed him "Acky", and on the wall of his old lodgings police found scribbled the words: Acky the Window Peeper. But Byrne was by no means a prime suspect. The request for an interview was purely routine.

Patrick Byrne called at Warrington police station on 10th February 1960 and was seen by Detective Sergeant George Welborn. The detective asked him to account for his movements on the night Stephanie Baird was murdered. Byrne answered the questions satisfactorily and readily agreed to have his fingerprints taken. Everything seemed perfectly normal. But then the policeman asked him: "Have you anything else to tell me about your stay in Birmingham?"

Either Welborn had a particularly penetrating gaze, or Byrne thought he could see into his soul, for it was then that the killer blurted out his confession: "I want to tell you about the YWCA. I have something to do with that."

That night Byrne was driven to Birmingham, where he made a full confession to Superintendent Haughton. It was sickening stuff, but the resulting document was to become invaluable for those trying to understand what goes on inside the mind of the sexual sadist.

The trial of Patrick Byrne began at Birmingham Assizes before Mr Justice Stable on Wednesday 23rd March 1960. Mr John Hobson QC, prosecuting, told the jury, "The story you will hear is one of horror and bestiality such as one would ever hope not to dream about in one's worst nightmare." He then read the long statement:

> I worked at Tarmacs in Hagley Road, facing St Chad's Hospital, until about ten of clock that Wednesday and then went to the Ivy Bush pub in Hagley Road. We had a drinking session there... I remember finishing up in Wheeley's Road, near the YWCA. I know the hostel there because I don't live far away.
> I thought I would like to have a peep through a window. I have done this a few times before... The night I killed that girl in the cubicle I went in through the front drive and into the grounds. There was only one light on in the bedrooms.... I looked through the window of the bedroom which had the light on in the block of cubicles and I saw a girl in there... She was combing her hair. I only watched for a few seconds... I decided to have a better peep from the inside. I went round the back and found a little window open a bit.

Byrne described how he got into the block, and placed a chair outside the door to Room Four so that he could watch the girl through the glass panel above it, hoping she would undress. She heard the chair squeak and opened the door, confronting him.

I didn't speak and she asked me again what I was doing. I told her I was looking for somebody. She said: "Let me get the warden." We were standing quite close together and I was just going to run but as I turned my arm touched her breast. This got me excited and I got hold of her breast. I said, "Give me a kiss," and before she could say no, I kissed her. She tried to shove me away but couldn't and for a second I got her round the waist. She only had her underskirt on and I felt very close. I was feeling her all over and kissing her but she screamed and then I put my hands around her neck.

She went over backwards inside the room with me squeezing her throat and then fell backwards. Her head bounced on the floor and I was lying on top of her kissing her and squeezing her neck at the same time. I heard a couple of small noises in her throat and kept on kissing her. I was lying on top of her alongside the bed with our heads near the dressing table. After a while I knelt up and had a strong urge to have a good look at her. I was fully sure she was dead then because I had the whole power of my back squeezing her throat. I pulled her towards me and pulled the red jumper off her and threw it to one side. I lay on top of her.... I did various things after that, I seemed to be in a hurry to do everything to her and hadn't the patience. I got up then panting and moaning... I bolted the door. I took my trousers and jacket and shirt off and I was naked apart from my shoes and socks. I rolled all over her. Her underclothes were all around her waist.

The next few sentences, in which Byrne describes his necrophiliac acts on the body of his victim, were never disclosed. The statement went on:

I got tired of that and looking up I could see the dressing table cupboard door open. There was a table knife in there... I looked at it for a couple of seconds... I got the knife in my right hand then and caught hold of her right breast and carved the knife around it. It was hard to cut round the skin but in the end I got it off. I was very surprised and disappointed it came away flat in my hand. I just looked at it and then flung it towards the bed. I scored her round the chest with the knife...

I started on the back of the neck then, catching hold of her hair and pulling her head close to my bare chest, I kept on cutting away. I remember now the knife broke off close to the handle when I was cutting her stomach and I carried on afterwards with the blade. This part seems a bit blurry, but I think I had something wrapped round part of the blade while I used it. It surprised me how easy the head came off. It's been puzzling me since – why I took the head off. It's not connected with sex in all the books I've read. I can understand the breast. I remember when the head came off I had it by the hair and I stood up...

I held it up to the mirror and looked at it through the mirror... I'd forgotten to tell you that just after I had done some of the mutilations I stood up and wrote a note with a biro on some paper on the dressing table. I can't remember the words I used but I wanted everybody to see my life in one little note.

The other times I had been definitely satisfied with peeping, but this time was different somehow.

He then tells of getting dressed and leaving the murder scene, still feeling consumed with lust. He saw another woman in the laundry room and attacked her. He described his mood in these terms: "I was pretty frantic... I was very excited, breathing heavy and thinking that I ought to terrorise all women. I wanted to get my own back on them for causing my nervous tension through sex... I felt I only wanted to kill beautiful women."

When Byrne got back to his lodgings he thought of committing suicide. He started to write a confession, describing himself as having two personalities, but then he tore it up. "I stood by the mirror in the bathroom talking to myself and searching my face for signs of a madman but I could see none."

Dr Percy Coats, senior medical officer at Birmingham Prison, said that Byrne was slightly below average intelligence, and from his own conversations with the man he had concluded he was a sexual psychopath. "I think he knew what he was doing and that what he was doing was wrong... I think his sexual emotions took complete control of him at that time." He said he believed Byrne was suffering from an abnormality of the mind and had impaired mental responsibility.

The judge asked: "Would it be fair to say that when you get such a marked degree of depravity that individual cannot be guilty of murder?" The reply was: "No, sir."

The judge continued: "Are you saying there was nothing wrong with his mind except these depraved desires to which he surrenders?"

Dr Coats replied: "'Yes."

Dr James O'Reilly, medical superintendent of All Saints Hospital, said that Byrne had a long history of gross sexual abnormality and his perversions had become increasingly bizarre. Over the last five years the prisoner had become obsessed with sadistic fantasies, including one in which he would put a woman on a circular saw and watch the blade cut through her. Even Byrne himself had been frightened by these thoughts. O'Reilly had no hesitation in declaring him to be suffering from an abnormality of the mind.

In his final speech to the jury defence counsel asked for a verdict under Section Two of the Homicide Act, saying: "In my submission there has been called before you medical evidence – most compelling evidence – which you cannot possibly shirk from accepting that this is a case of a man who comes clearly within the terms of that particular section of the Homicide Act. This means, in terms of your verdict, that he would be guilty of manslaughter, not murder."

The prosecutor reminded the jury that they were not bound to accept the medical evidence. "After all, they can only give their opinions, the ultimate decision is yours."

In his summing up the judge said that the evidence was that Byrne knew what he was doing and that what he was doing was wrong. There was no room for the application of the M'Naghten Rules, and no room for a verdict of guilty but insane.

The jury took forty-five minutes to find Byrne guilty of murder and the judge sentenced him to life imprisonment. On appeal the Lord Chief Justice decided that the judge's summing up had been wrong in law, and he quashed the conviction for murder, substituting a verdict of manslaughter. The life sentence, however, was not changed.

We end our brief survey of Britain's sex killers with an account of a murderer who, like Jack the Ripper, was never apprehended or publicly identified. He was also like his notorious predecessor in other ways: his target was prostitutes.

Between February 1964 and February 1965 six prostitutes were murdered in London, these slayings coming to be known as the Hammersmith nude murders. The killer, predictably, was labelled **Jack the Stripper**.

An attempt to make sense of the details of the case and to probe the often obscure connections between these murders makes one realise just how difficult the task was which faced the police of 1888 hunting the original and elusive Jack. Just as there remain arguments about exactly how many women Jack the Ripper killed, so in the present case it is not clear that all the murders were the work of the same man, and the generic name given to the killings – the Nude Murders – is also misleading: not all the victims were naked.

It began at 4.42 a.m. on 17th June 1959 when a police patrol car from Chiswick police station spotted the body of a woman at Duke's Meadows at the side of the Thames, close to Chiswick Bridge. The woman sat propped against a tree-trunk as if contemplating the river. She wore a blue and white striped dress which had been torn down the front – and that was all. There were no underclothes, shoes or handbag. Pathologist Dr Teare examined the body and reported that she had been manually strangled less than three hours previously. Scuff-marks on her heels and abrasions on her back suggested that she had been dragged out of a vehicle and across the ground to her final resting-place. She had engaged in sex recently, and had had a tooth removed not long before her death, the gum not yet being healed. Her stomach contents consisted of champagne.

Chief Detective Superintendent Edward Greeno was placed in charge of the case, and his first task was to establish the identity of the victim. A death mask was made, and a picture of sorts published. It was recognized by friends of the dead woman, who immediately contacted the police. The victim was Elizabeth Figg, twenty-one, originally from Cheshire. Although a prostitute, and often using the alias Ann Phillips, she had never been arrested for soliciting and had no police record. She lived in a bedsitter in Duncombe Park, Upper Holloway, at a rent of 48 shillings a week. On the day she vanished, Tuesday 16th June, she had gone to Ascot with a friend to ply her trade – hence the champagne.

Miss Figg had seen a client that evening. He had picked her up in his car. She left him later saying she had an appointment at Holland Park. The taxi-driver who took her there was traced and he said he had dropped her off at 1.10 in the morning. Thus in the space of less than an hour she had been murdered and dumped. The police surmised that it was a fairly routine murder. She had probably been murdered by her client. Who was he? It was impossible to say. The trail was cold and the case got pushed into the backlog of files awaiting attention.

Four and a half years later, on 8th November 1963 a man operating a mechanical digger at a rubbish tip at Mortlake, near the Thames, uncovered the headless body of a dark-haired woman. She was naked apart from one stocking. Her head was later found, quite close by. These remains were examined at Guy's Hospital, and from a tiny fragment of skin on one hand the pathologist was able to get a match with the fingerprints of Gwynneth Rees, twenty-two, alias Georgette Rees, Tina Dawson and Tina Smart, a prostitute with a string of eleven convictions. She too was missing some teeth: five from the upper jaw and two from the lower.

Then, on 2nd February 1964, the body of a third nude prostitute was found. It was discovered floating in the Thames at Hammersmith. Fingerprinting quickly established it to be that of Hannah Tailford, thirty, alias Ann Tailor, Theresa Bell and Hannah Lynch. Dr Teare reported that she had died from drowning – there was water in her lungs, proving that she had been alive when she entered the water. She was 5ft 2in in height, with long brown hair. The only items of clothing found were her stockings, around her ankles, and her knickers, which were stuffed into her mouth. She had been in the water for a couple of days.

Hannah Tailford was a Geordie girl, originally from Northumbria. A prostitute, she had a baby daughter and was known to be a depressive. She took barbiturates heavily and had often threatened suicide. Suicides have been known to gag themselves prior to death to prevent any involuntary cries but Dr Teare did not think that had happened in this case. He had found a large and undigested meal in the stomach of the dead woman, and in his experience people who intend to commit suicide do not first have a feast. The inquest jury recorded an open verdict.

Just over two months later, at 8.30 on the morning of 8th April 1964, another nude prostitute was found floating in the Thames. She was five feet tall with blonde hair. There was a tattoo on her right arm depicting a tombstone on which was inscribed "John in Memory". An autopsy revealed that she had been approximately four months pregnant. She was later identified as Irene Lockwood, twenty-six, alias Sandra Russell, who had lived in a flat at Denbigh Road, Notting Hill. Neighbours had heard her having a violent row with a man on the Friday night, and Tuesday morning she was dragged from the river. There was no evidence that Irene Lockwood had been murdered. She was simply a "drowner". But it was suspicious all the same.

Then sixteen days later, on 24th April, just a mile from the Thames, an assistant groundsman found a dead nude beside Beecham's Sports Ground in Acton, between Swyncombe Avenue and Boston Manor Road. The girl was lying face downward, head resting on her arms, her black hair spread out as if she was sleeping. But she was lying on rubbish and she had been choked. Commander George Hatherill was quickly on the scene. An examination of the body revealed only a tattoo on the forearm inscribed "Loving You". Fingerprints identified her as being Helene Catherine Barthelemy, 22, alias Helene Thompson and Helene Paul, originally from Scotland, last known address a flat in Talbot Road, Harlesden. She had been dead for some forty-eight hours.

Five killings in the space of five years. Both the police and the press were certain a serial killer was in their midst. Indeed, even after the murder of Hannah Tailford it was being declared that "Jack the Stripper" was on the loose. In fact, as the investigation continued, the police increasingly began to think that the first two murders were not part of the series at all. They were both separate issues. But, all the same, that still left three murders.

Helene Barthelemy provided the police with their first positive clues in the "Stripper" inquiry. Dr Teare noted that four of her teeth had been dislodged from her mouth with some force, and a broken tooth was still lodged in her throat, where there were also sperm traces. There were peculiar heat-marks on one side of the body which showed that she had been kept close to a heat-source, something like a large transformer. More importantly still, however, Dr Teare established that she had been stripped after death. Microscopic samples of metallic paint – both primer and top coat – as used in car-spraying were on her skin. The unknown killer had stored the body for forty-eight hours close to a garage of sorts. A special squad of detectives from Shepherd's Bush police station were given the task of tracing all paint-spray operations in London, of which there were hundreds, if not thousands.

It was just as the police were beginning this new line of inquiry that there came one of those incredible true-life absurdities which was to bedevil the inquiry into the case of the Hammersmith Nude Murders. Kenneth Archibald, fifty-four, the caretaker at Holland Park Tennis Club, was facing a court appearance on a theft charge. He had been questioned about the Irene Lockwood murder, since a card had been found in her flat bearing the telephone number of the tennis club and the name "Kenny". In a fit of depression he walked into Notting Hill police station on 27th April and made a false confession to the murder, saying he had pushed her into the water. His statement could not be disproved because of its very simplicity, and he duly stood trial at the Old Bailey, where he promptly retracted his confession, saying he had made it in a fit of despair. The jury took under an hour to find him not guilty.

But already another murder was on the way. On 14th July 1964, at about 2.30 a.m., a car was heard reversing from Acton Road into Berrymede Road. At 5.30 a.m. the nude body of a girl was discovered sitting propped up against a door on a garage forecourt next to a private house. The man who found it thought at first that it was a tailor's dummy. Her legs were crossed, and her trunk slumped forward as if she were contemplating her navel. She must have been posed deliberately to cause shock and outrage to whoever found her. The victim was Mary Fleming, alias Mary Turner, born in Scotland, last known address a flat in Lancaster Road, Notting Hill, where she had lived with her two children. An autopsy revealed that she had been strangled, and forensic examination showed the same tell-tale specks of car-paint on her body. Under the spectrometer the paint specks matched exactly in size, composition and colour the samples taken from the body of Helene Barthelemy. Mary Fleming had not been manually strangled, she had been asphyxiated – that is, her air supply had been cut off. Her false teeth were missing, and she had vanished three days previously. Again sperm was found in the back of the throat.

Now the killer's *modus operandi* became evident. He killed his victims during the act of fellatio by literally choking them to death with his penis, holding the victim's head firmly by the hair to prevent escape. So great was the pressure that he dislodged their teeth in the process. It was a unique method of killing. It seems that the killer then kept the bodies hidden until it was convenient to dump them, or perhaps to prevent the police from discovering that a murder had taken place until it was too late.

Margaret McGowan, alias Frances Brown, Anne Sutherland Susan Edwards, and Frances Quinn, was his next victim. The 21-year-old vanished on 23rd October 1964. Her body was kept hidden close to a spray-paint operation for almost a month, before being dumped on 25th November on waste land behind a car park in Horton Street, Kensington. She lay naked among the rubbish, her face covered with a dustbin lid. She too was small – 5ft 1in – and had a tattoo on her forearm. Originally from Glasgow, she had moved to London where she was to mix with Dr Stephen Ward, and thus became involved in the Profumo Scandal. She was a defence witness at Ward's trial; it was her brief moment in the limelight.

Dr Teare certified the cause of death as being due to pressure on the neck, or asphyxia. One tooth had been dislodged by some force, and there was sperm in the throat. Again those paint specks were present. Her clothing and jewellery were never found. Perhaps the killer kept them as a grim souvenir.

On 16th February 1965 the body of what was to prove to be the last victim was found in undergrowth on the Heron Trading Estate in Acton. She had last been seen alive on 11th January in a Shepherd's Bush hotel. The corpse was partly mummified by being stored close to a heat-source; there were the same trade-marks of missing teeth missing, sperm in the throat – and those paint specks.

By now the press had whipped up the public into a state verging on panic, and Detective Superintendent John Du Rose was placed in charge of the case. Du Rose had a reputation for never taking more than four days to solve a murder case, a talent he had already demonstrated in the case of Haigh, the acid bath murderer, and in the smashing of the Kray gang. He was expected to do the same thing now.

Du Rose's first task was to go and examine the body of the latest victim *in situ*. The woman was 5ft 2in with dark hair and a tattoo on her forearm. Her earrings had been removed, possibly taken by the killer as a trophy. She was identified as Bridget Esther O'Hara, twenty-seven, alias Bridie Moore, a native of Dublin currently living at Agate Road, Hammersmith. Du Rose had to ponder over the killer's motives for storing the body for over a month. What did he do with her? Did he play with her like a doll? Or was it to delay any murder inquiry?

A squad was formed with orders to do nothing but talk to prostitutes and discover any clients with a perverse taste for violent oral sex. Another team was still checking on all paint-spray operations. The Murder Squad had been expanded to two hundred detectives, with another four hundred officers assigned to the case on the ground. The task facing Detective Chief Superintendent Du Rose was to establish whether all the deaths, from Elizabeth Figg on, were linked. Certainly the last four were – but what about the earlier ones? They had a superficial similarity. All had taken place in a particular area of London, though over some twenty-four square miles. All had been prostitutes. But not all the bodies had been found naked, and there were other differences too. Elizabeth Figg had been manually strangled shortly before her body was discovered – but this was not the case with Gwynneth Rees or Hannah Tailford. Helene Barthelemy and Mary Fleming died from asphyxia, with no apparent marks on the neck. Margaret McGowan had been strangled, and from the marks on her neck Dr Teare was firmly convinced that this was the work of a separate killer. Bridie O'Hara had been asphyxiated without any marks.

Simple deduction leaves us with three true and certain "Stripper" murders: Barthelemy, Fleming and O'Hara. Du Rose, however, attributed at least six murders to "Jack".

Fortune was evidently keen to continue shining on John Du Rose because with this latest killing the murderer had chosen a disposal site on his own doorstep. Tests revealed that at a transformer site on the Heron Estate spray-paint was carried on the air from a nearby spray-shop. All seven thousand employees who worked in the area were questioned about their movements. Du Rose was certain that the killer worked on the Estate or had legitimate access to it. But mere questioning would not be enough. The detective had to flush out the killer, not just talk to him. He thus decided on a policy of psychological warfare. He would use the press and media in general to make the killer feel threatened. At press conferences he would announce that there was a list of twenty suspects. Later it would be halved to ten. Finally it was announced that the list had been narrowed down to three. It was all make-believe, of course, since Du Rose had no suspects at all. But it worked.

Within a month of the murder of Bridget O'Hara a security guard who patrolled the Heron Estate at night in a van committed suicide by gassing himself. He left a note saying: "I cannot stand the strain any longer." He was an unmarried man in his forties. Du Rose, in his memoirs *Murder Was My Business* (1971), states: "...the man I wanted to arrest took his own life... Because he was never arrested or stood trial he must be considered innocent and will therefore never be named."

The only proof for the security guard being the killer is that following his suicide there were no more murders. Scotland Yard announced that the killer was dead.

In his book Du Rose went on to detail the killer's method of murder: "in obtaining satisfaction he became utterly frenzied and at the moment of his orgasm, the girls died." Du Rose speculates that the first murder – he refers to Hannah Tailford – might have been an accident, a case of manslaughter, but that after the man went on killing he must have known what he was doing. Perhaps it added an extra piquant thrill: "When he continued to indulge in his particular perversion, well knowing that the girls concerned would die, he must have recognised that he was fulfilling himself as a murderer."

We shall never know just who Jack the Stripper was, and we shall never be sure of exactly how many women he killed. He remains as elusive as the killer after whom he was named.

Chapter Six
NEW LIGHT ON THE
MOORS MURDERS

G.B. Shaw wrote: "We judge an artist by his highest moments, a criminal by his lowest." It was an astute comment, recognizing as it does that the criminal and the artist are not two different creatures but that it is our judgements that make them seem so diverse. In truth, in many ways the artist and the killer are really very similar. Both want to change the world; both want fame and recognition; and both tend to live in a fantasy world where the distinctions between reality and fantasy become blurred. Creative men are notoriously self-willed, refusing to be bound by any rules – a trait that is shared by criminals. Both the killer and the poet refuse to accept the limitations of reality, of life as it is. The difference between them is that the artist sublimates his rebellion into creativity, the criminal turns it into violence. But then there is that state in between, where the desire for creativity is there but its channels are blocked. Now the psychic energy turns inward and poisons the inner life. The results can be catastrophic, even murderous.

There are killers who have retreated from reality into a world of fantasy. They kill in a curious trance-like state. For them life becomes a cinema-screen on which they are the principal actors. They become the heroes of their own imaginings, and if life is reduced to a cinema-screen, then the "bit" actors become disposable. In our own century –

the age of the cinema – we have witnessed a dramatic increase in these fantasy killings, with couples acting in combination to play out their deadly scripts. The French have a term for this: *folie à deux*, meaning a couple who support one another's fantasies and delusions. Two disturbed people come together by accident. Separately they would probably live out harmless lives. But when they come together it is like mixing glycerine and nitric acid: the result is explosive.

It has often been remarked that it was just a "million to one chance" that ever brought together such a fatal combination as Ian Brady and Myra Hindley. But in fact *folie à deux* is not that rare. The annals of murder contain many examples of deadly duos, including Bonnie and Clyde, Leopold and Loeb, Bywaters and Thompson, Snyder and Gray, Fernandez and Beck, Hulten and Jones. The Moors Murderers are just one more example of the genre.

What links these deadly couples together is that most basic of impulses, the sex drive. And sex can be a fatal will-o'-the-wisp. With some couples, after that first flush of passion has cooled and grown stale, "kinky" sex takes over in an attempt to stimulate the fading passion, but even that becomes jaded. Wilder and weirder deviations are tried, but all lead to satiation and boredom. The fact is that sex is an illusion. Every man has experienced that same baffling dilemma: you can make love to a woman a hundred times – a thousand times – but you never totally possess her. Only for that brief moment are you joined in embrace; afterwards you must always separate.

Never has the illusion of sex been more cruelly exposed than in the case of the Moors Murderers. Just as Jack the Ripper delved frenziedly with his bare hands into the entrails of women, as though seeking to discover the secret of sex, so Ian Brady and Myra Hindley practised murder as a method of divination. But in their case there was no frenzy. The witness to the murder of Edward Evans described Brady as "showing as much emotion as a butcher working in a shop... He was very calm indeed. There was no frenzy."

Brady and Hindley were heavily involved in the idea of sex. They read de Sade, studied pornographic photographs, and even took their own. They were obsessed with the illusion of sex, and tried to penetrate the veil. They ended up killing children almost as an act of magic to see if the reality of an actual corpse would bring some ultimate truth. In fact the act of murder was not so important to them. Far more important were the after-images. They derived a salacious satisfaction from the effects of their crimes, the grim souvenirs. Listening to the tape-recorded cries of the victims, looking at photographs of the graves – there was a voyeuristic madness here.

That madness is in us too, in the overwhelming public fever for sensational sex-cases, the dirty-minded gloating which crimes like the Moors Murders foster. We too chase that ephemeral illusion of sex, hoping to learn its secrets from those devotees who go further than we dare. The sad fact is that national newspapers sold an average of fifty thousand extra copies every day of the trial of Brady and Hindley. Nobody wanted to miss the revelations.

There have been at least a dozen full-length books devoted to this case and thousands of articles and reports. What justifies a fresh look at it is the new evidence which had come to light – notably the recovery of the body of Pauline Reade – and the subsequent confessions of both Brady and Hindley to other murders. This evidence throws a new light on the character of Myra Hindley and the old question of who was the dominant partner in the duo. It also helps to provide fresh insight into what it was that actually went on, and why.

I met the mother of Lesley Ann Downey during a television debate, and was humbled by the fact that even after all these years her grief is so palpable. I feel a genuine reluctance to write about the case for fear of opening old wounds; but a brief study of the case is essential to any study of sex killers. It is one of the most important English cases of the twentieth century. My personal interest in the case is the enigma of Myra Hindley. I find it interesting that most women feel that Hindley was the dominant partner, infecting Brady with the lust to kill. Men tend to blame Brady. The truth must lie somewhere in between.

Ian Brady was born illegitimate in Glasgow to tea-room waitress Maggie Stewart on 2nd January 1938. He did not live with his mother, but spent his childhood with another family, the Sloans, in the Gorbals district of the city. He grew up to be tall, with fair hair and grey eyes. At school he proved to be a better than average scholar, but was useless at sports and was teased for being a "big lassie". He retreated into a fantasy world of domination and sadism which included the cruel torturing of animals. Soon in trouble with the law – for housebreaking, for which he was put on probation – he was later convicted of nine similar offences and received two years' probation on condition that he went to live with his natural mother in Manchester. In effect, he was "deported".

In 1954, at the age of seventeen, Ian Stewart arrived in Manchester, taking the name of his stepfather, Patrick Brady. In 1956 he was convicted for theft and spent two years in Hatfield borstal. Released in 1958, he went back to live with his mother, and eventually got a job at Millward's Chemicals Ltd as a stock clerk earning £12 a week. He was a sullen, withdrawn figure, always an outsider, but now he began dressing smartly, in three-piece suits. He also started buying books on the Nazis, and building up his "special collection" of pornography. He wrote off for tapes and records of Nazi marching songs and the Hitler speeches. In his lunch-break Brady studied German grammar. The secret fantasy life of sadistic domination was developing along sinister lines: he was reading de Sade avidly. But he might have remained a law-abiding person had he not met Myra Hindley.

Myra Hindley was born on 23rd July 1942, in the Manchester suburb of Gorton, a district of back-to-back houses with outside toilets. She was the elder of two daughters, and in infancy went to live with her widowed grandmother, Mrs Ellen Maybury, at 7 Bannock Street. Like Brady, Myra was a loner, a school report describing her as "not sociable". She was a day-dreamer, good at writing essays, but she did not have the disposition one might expect of the type. She was tough, aggressive, almost masculine, and enjoyed contact sports. She was captain of the school netball team, a good swimmer and took judo lessons. The death of her boyfriend, Michael, when she was fifteen devastated her. She did not sleep for days, and finally sought solace in the Roman Catholic Church. She took her first Communion on 6th November 1958, when she was presented with a white-covered prayer-book by her aunt, Kath Maybury. That book was to play a significant role in subsequent events. In fact, seven years later it was to jail her for life.

Myra eventually found another boyfriend and was engaged to him for six months, but broke it off because she said her fiancé was "too childish". In 1961, aged nineteen, she dressed in the fashion of the times: tight pencil-skirts and sweaters. A tall girl, she missed being pretty because of a hooked nose and pointed chin. And she was still a virgin. After several jobs – and curiously enough, toying with the idea of serving with the NAAFI in Germany – she finally answered an advertisement for a typist at Millward Chemicals at £8 10s a week. Here she met and worked closely with Ian Brady. He often dictated letters to her in his nasal Glasgow accent.

From the start Myra Hindley was fascinated by the tall, slim man with the high, intelligent forehead and swept-back hair. He was withdrawn, a man of secrets, and spoke with a strange accent. To her he seemed a romantic Heathcliff figure, the ideal man. He was different. He even managed to invest the act of smoking a cigarette with a certain drama. He seemed like a man living out his own biography, as if conscious of some movie-camera focusing on his every move. She was nineteen and impressionable. He was twenty-one and rode a motor-bike.

Hindley's diary reveals her adolescent fascination with the man and her strong desire to be noticed by him. One entry reads: "The pig. He didn't look at me today." Eventually, however, as we all now know, he did.

Brady was living in Westmorland Street, Longsight, two miles away across the city from Gorton. He spent his spare time in his bedroom playing Nazi tapes and reading books on sexual perversions. Gradually he began to talk to Hindley, revealing a little of the inner man. He loaned her books on Nazi atrocities, and talked in a sophisticated manner about sexual perversions. At Christmas she asked him to go out with her. He agreed, and the evening was a success. Her diary entry read: "Eureka! Today we had our first date..." At last, Myra was no longer a virgin and a bright, happy future beckoned. Her diary entry for New Year's Day 1962 reveals her feelings: "I hope Ian and I love each other all our lives and get married and are happy ever after."

In June 1963 Brady moved in with Hindley, sharing the house with her grandmother, whose name was on the rent book. Brady introduced Hindley to German wine and Teutonic culture, persuading her to bleach her hair blonde and wear tight leather skirts and high boots. He nicknamed her "Hessie" and she called him "Neddie" because of his imitations of the Goon Show character. At this point Brady certainly dominated Hindley, teaching her his newly discovered philosophy of lust and cruelty. He bought a camera and took crude pornographic photographs of her, and of themselves in the act of intercourse and flagellations. Some of the photographs showed her with the weal-marks of a whip across her buttocks. There was a marked change in Hindley after she began cohabiting with Brady. She never again went to church, stopped baby-sitting, and became secretive and hard. Her grandmother was a frail woman who slept most of the time, and Brady and Hindley could do virtually as they liked. Soon they discovered what they liked best. It was killing.

We know now, from the new evidence, that their first victim was Pauline Reade, a sixteen-year-old girl who vanished on the evening of 12th July 1963 when she was making her way to a dance from her home (which was a short distance away from where Brady and Hindley lived). As with the other victims, the precise cause of death remains unknown, but like all their subsequent victims, Pauline found a grave on the lonely Saddleworth Moor which rises high above Manchester. It is a bleak area, with rocks standing like twisted gargoyles, buried in the soft, peaty soil. With only the earth and sky for company, it is a perfect Wagnerian setting for any Nazi superman – or woman. Brady and Hindley had started to put their sick fantasies into practice.

The date of Pauline Reade's disappearance is of some significance as it calls into question how the couple managed to transported her, or her body, to a moorland grave. Brady could not drive and Hindley did not pass her driving test until the fourth attempt, on 7th November. As the court would later hear, the use of a car was one of the common factors in all the Moors killings. It was a vital tool in their task. What happened in this first case we can only speculate.

It was on the 23rd November 1963 – the day after the assassination of President Kennedy – that the couple were to strike again. Hindley hired a car – a Ford Anglia – from Warren Autos in Manchester. That same day John Kilbride, aged twelve, disappeared from a market at Ashton-under-Lyne. When Hindley returned the car it was covered in peaty mud. John Kilbride lay on the moors in a shallow grave. There was a big police search for the missing boy while the couple sniggered quietly. In May 1964 Hindley bought her first car, a white Mini Countryman van. On 16th June 1964 twelve-year-old Keith Bennett vanished from near the home of Brady's mother. He too was later buried on the moor.

At around this time, on Brady's order, Myra Hindley joined a rifle club at Cheadle, and purchased from other club members a Webley .45 revolver for £8 and a Smith and Wesson .38 for £5. Brady, in a black shirt and with a gun in a shoulder-holster, often had "Hessie" run him up to the moors so that he could practise target-shooting. They would also use these opportunities to visit their past victims' graves, often taking Myra's dog, Puppet, with them. They evidently enjoyed doing this, and would photograph each other kneeling at the various burial sites. Later police were to use these photographs to locate some of the bodies.

On 26th December 1964 Lesley Ann Downey, aged ten years and four months, vanished on her way to a fair with a friend. Her body was to be found ten months later, in a grave on Saddleworth Moor. Her murder had been recorded on tape by Brady and Hindley, and when it was played in court at the subsequent trial it caused even hardened crime-reporters to blanch.

Brady now felt that the time had come to expand his empire of evil by recruiting able lieutenants. The person he had in mind was Hindley's young brother-in-law, David Smith. Smith was a tough, cocky character who, though he was only sixteen years old, already had a criminal record. He had married eighteen-year-old Maureen Hindley just a little while before, having made her pregnant, and he seemed the perfect choice for a disciple. Brady began to feed him on wine and de Sade, talking of "bank jobs" and other armed robberies, impressing the youth with his two guns and his air of sophistication.

Initially they had all lived together in the Gorton slums but then Brady and Hindley, together with the grandmother, were rehoused in the new overspill estate of Hattersley and given a new, three-bedroom house at 16 Wardle Brook Avenue. On 23rd July 1965 David and Maureen Smith were also moved, to a flat in Underwood Court, just a few hundred yards away. Thereafter the four became constant companions, visiting one another's homes and travelling in Myra's Mini Countryman on trips to the moors. And all the while Brady was loaning Smith books, preaching to him the mad philosophy of de Sade and talking to him of committing armed robberies. He was clearly intent on bringing the young man into his murderous fold. In the words of the prosecutor at the trial, the then Attorney-General, Sir Frederick Elwyn Jones QC, M.P.: "Brady's interest in Smith went far beyond ordinary friendship. The association was one of the steady corruption of a youth by a man... Brady was interested in murder and wanted to make Smith a student of murder."

To a certain extent Brady succeeded. David Smith began to embrace the teachings of de Sade, copying into an exercise book those quotations from the writer that interested him: "*People are like maggots, small, blind worthless fishbait... Murder is a hobby and a supreme pleasure.*" But Brady's big mistake was to imagine that anyone could be induced to put these perverse thoughts into practice. David Smith might not have been a model citizen, but he could not enter into and share Brady's sick fantasies. He was not prepared to commit murder.

On 25th September 1965 Brady had an important conversation with Smith. He told him: "I have killed before. Three or four. The bodies are buried on the moors. I have photographs to prove it." They had been drinking at the time, and Smith did not take the remarks seriously, thinking it was simply idle, drunken boasting. On 2nd October 1965 Brady insisted, "I'll do another one. I'm not due for another one for three or four months, but this one won't count." It didn't "count" in Brady's scheme of things because it was to be simply a demonstration murder designed to impress Smith and recruit him to the murder team.

At midnight on Wednesday 6th October 1965 Myra Hindley called at the Smiths' flat at about midnight, and asked her brother-in-law to walk her home. The visit was clearly a pretext to involve Smith in murder. There was no other purpose to it. When they got to 16 Wardle Brook Avenue, Myra Hindley invited Smith in, saying that Brady had some miniature wine bottles for him.

As Smith entered the house there was a cry and he rushed into the lounge. There he saw Brady standing astride Edward Evans, a seventeen-year-old youth. Evans was the "demonstration" victim.

"Help him, Dave," said Myra urgently, as Brady held an axe aloft in his hands and then brought it crashing down on Evans's head. In Smith's own words, given in evidence, "I ran in and nearly had a stroke. I just stopped dead. My first thought was that it was a life-size doll, sort of half screaming and half groaning. Ian stood over him with an axe in his right hand." Brady hit the victim at least fourteen times with the axe, then throttled him with a length of flex, all the while muttering in a dull monotone, "The fucking bastard. The fucking bastard." Then he looked up at Smith, smiled, and said: "This one was the messiest yet." He handed the axe to Smith, asking him to feel the weight of it – and thus ensuring he got his prints on the murder weapon – and Smith, dumb with terror, helped Hindley clean up the blood, and then helped Brady truss the body up in polythene sheeting. Then, in a grotesque parody of domesticity that Joe Orton would have admired, Myra Hindley made them all a pot of tea. Her eyes were glittering with excitement as she commented to Brady: "You should have seen the look on his face. The blow registered in his eyes!" She then reminisced fondly about previous murders.

David Smith left as soon as he could, promising to return the next day with a pram to wheel the body out to Myra's car – but in reality he was terrified that if he showed any sign of dissent he would be the next to die. Once back at his flat he was violently sick, and told his wife everything that had happened. At dawn the couple walked to a nearby phone-box and dialled 999, saying, "There's been a murder..."

That call was logged at 6.07 on the morning of 7th October 1965. Shortly afterwards a patrol car arrived to pick up Smith and his wife. The terrified David Smith was holding a knife and screwdriver to protect himself and virtually threw himself into the safety of the police car. Once at Hyde police station he poured out his incredible story to Detective Superintendent Talbot. At 8.40 a.m. the Superintendent, wearing a borrowed baker's roundsman's coat with a basket of loaves over his arm, knocked on the door of 16 Wardle Brook Avenue. He was unarmed, despite being warned by David Smith that Brady had two guns.

At first the Superintendent thought he must have been the victim of a practical joke. Myra Hindley seemed normal enough when she opened the door to him; a smart woman whose age he guessed at about thirty. But eventually the trussed-up body of Edward Evans was found in the locked back bedroom, and the couple were arrested.

Dave Smith's statement about Brady talking of "other murders" was now taken very seriously. Different Forces and other senior officers soon became involved in the questioning of Brady and Hindley, including Detective Chief Inspector Joe Mounsey, the new CID chief of Ashton-under-Lyne. He was interested in any connection with the missing boy, John Kilbride.

Under questioning both Brady and Hindley showed remarkable toughness. Brady admitted having killed Edward Evans, "following a row," and did everything he could to implicate David Smith in the murder. Myra Hindley was questioned by woman detective Margaret Campion, thirty-seven, and a very experienced officer. To all questions Hindley replied, "My story is the same as Ian's... ask Ian. Wherever he went, I went. Whatever he did, I did." The detective noted that Hindley did not have a hair out of place, and expressed concern only that her dog, Puppet, should be fed. Later police had to take the animal to a vet to have its teeth X-rayed to determine its age – this would have served to date the photographs found – but the dog died under anaesthetic. When told of the death of her dog Hindley screamed, "You fucking murderers!" It was almost the only emotion she was ever to display.

Detective Chief Superintendent Arthur Benfield, chief of Cheshire CID, headed the inquiry. On 13th October he told a press conference: "We have discussed the files of eight people who have disappeared without trace during the past three or four years."

Brady's story was that there had been an argument with "Eddie" leading to his death in the course of a struggle. but police found a coded list in Hindley's car. It was a carefully designed plan for the removal of all clues to the murder. Brady was later to claim that he and David Smith drew up the plan *after* the murder. GN stood for gun, and Det for detail, but PB was a puzzle. Brady said it stood for "Pennistone Burn", but there was no such place. It actually stood for "prayer book" and Chief Inspector Tyrrell was to find a ticket hidden in the spine of Myra Hindley's prayer book. It was a railway left-luggage ticket, number 74843. Two suitcases were subsequently recovered from Manchester Central Station. They contained letters, wigs, coshes, books on sexual perversions, two reels of tape, and nine photographs of Lesley Ann Downey, naked and gagged. When the tapes were played detectives listened in growing horror to the last moments of the little girl. Her death had been taped for posterity. With the discovery of this tape, the full devilishness of Brady and Hindley's crimes began to be revealed.

A vital witness in the case proved to be a twelve-year-old local girl, Patricia Hodges, who lived a couple of doors away from the pair. Brady and Hindley had befriended her, and often took her up to the moors to picnic. She was driven in a police car to Saddleworth, with instructions to tell officers when she recognized the spot where the picnics had taken place. She stopped the car at Hollin Brow Knoll, close to Wessenden Head. Police were able to match up photographs found in Brady and Hindley's house with the actual sites where they had been taken; including the picture of Myra Hindley kneeling, with a sinister smile on her lips, looking down at the earth.

An army of policemen began digging on the moor. On 16th October the body of Lesley Ann Downey was found. Five days later the body of John Kilbride was recovered,

373 yards away from the grave of Lesley Ann. The hunt continued through the next month, but by December of 1965, with the coming of winter, digging had ceased on Saddleworth Moor.

Brady and Hindley were formally charged with three murders, but still refused to talk of any other missing children and possible murders. Hindley insisted that David Smith had killed Lesley Ann Downey, and Brady said it had been Smith who had brought the child to the house to be photographed. Even now, when all was lost, they were trying to implicate Smith, displaying the manipulative traits which they were never to lose.

The "trial of the century" began at Chester Assizes – held at Chester Castle on 19 April 1966 – and was to last fourteen days. Before the trial, during the long remand in custody, Brady and Hindley had sought Home Office permission to be married: this was refused. When they appeared in the dock it was as bachelor and spinster. The court-room was packed with some 150 pressmen from all over the world, including authors and playwrights. There were few seats for the ordinary members of the public. The testimony given at the trial was to reveal much about the perverse sexual streak which bound Brady and Hindley together. For example, the pathologist's examination of Edward Evans revealed that his fly-buttons were undone, and there were traces of dog hairs around his anus. The body of John Kilbride was found with trousers and underpants down around his knees. It is likely that Hindley derived sexual pleasure from watching Brady perform homosexual acts on his victims.

The Attorney-General, Sir Elwyn Jones QC, outlined the charges and the evidence to the all-male jury. He emphasized that Myra Hindley was also firmly implicated in the murders. "She was not merely clay in the hands of a potter, but an active, and some might even think leading, participant in all that transpired." Brady looked bored, examining his well-manicured nails. The prosecution went on, "You will be wondering why this man did this to a fellow human being. You might be wondering what Evans was doing in that house at all, what Hindley was doing there, and why Smith was there. To answer these questions it is necessary to go back to the beginning and piece together the history of events." He told the court of Brady grooming David Smith to become a murder disciple, ending with the night of the murder of Edward Evans, when Hindley called for David Smith and asked him to walk her home.

Sir Elwyn Jones said, "We say this was a trick devised and executed by Hindley for one particular purpose: to get Smith back to Wardle Brook Avenue to witness the murder of Evans... The murder was prearranged by the two accused and they lured Edward Evans to the house that night for the express purpose of killing him, which they did." He referred to the fact that the victim's trousers were down, saying, "In association with his killing, as with the other two, there was present not only a sexual element, but an abnormal sexual element, a perverted sexual element."

Maureen Smith, heavily pregnant, gave evidence against her sister, telling of how she had changed since meeting Brady, and of trips to Saddleworth Moor. (Maureen would later divorce David Smith, and die young from a brain tumour.)

David Smith, now eighteen, was the next witness. He told of Brady's talk of robbing banks and of murders. "He said he had killed three or four people. I thought it was the beer talking." Smith told of the horror of having to witness the murder of Edward Evans, and being forced to help parcel up the body. "I just froze... My first thought was that Ian had hold of a life-size rag doll and was just waving it about. The arms were going all over... My stomach turned over. It was half-screaming and groaning. He was making a gurgling noise like when you brush your teeth and gargle with water..."

The prosecution asked: "Will you tell us what kind of impression Brady created upon you as you watched him?"

Smith replied: "Well, I have seen butchers working in shops showing as much emotion as he did when they were cutting up sheep's ribs. He was very calm indeed. He was not in a frenzy – no frenzy at all."

Both defence counsel – Mr Godfrey Heilpern QC, for Hindley, and Mr Emlyn Hooson QC, for Brady – cross-examined David Smith with some ferocity, trying to discredit him with his criminal record, suggesting that he was motivated by a newspaper contract to secure a conviction and insinuating that he was as closely involved with the murders as were the two accused. Mr Hooson questioned Smith about the opinions he had written in his exercise book:

Mr Hooson: " 'Every man and woman is one of two things, a masochist or a sadist' – are these your views?"

Smith: "They were my views about people."

The defence counsel pursued: "You were indoctrinated by murder, you were infected by it. Is it not the truth that you joined in?"

Smith: "No, sir."

The high-point of horror during the trial came on Tuesday 26th April, when the Attorney-General read out the transcript and then played the sixteen-minute tape recording of the last moments of Lesley Ann Downey. The victim was heard screaming and crying out. She was clearly suffering a most terrifying ordeal. That tape-recording was the most damning piece of evidence in the case.

Brady in the witness box was careful always to try to protect Hindley as much as possible and implicate David

Smith whenever he could. Asked by Hindley's counsel, "What are your feelings for Myra?" he replied, "They are as man and wife." Heilpern: "If you had different views about matters, whose views would prevail?" Brady: "Mine. She was my typist." He admitted the killing of Edward Evans, but denied any involvement in the murders of Lesley Ann Downey and John Kilbride. The photographs of Myra Hindley either kneeling over or gazing down at the graves were "pure coincidences." Brady was cross-examined for a total of nine hours by the Attorney-General, who suggested that, far from being mere coincidences, the photographs were, in fact, the killers' "trophies of murder". Questioned about his collection of pornographic books. Brady snapped back, "You'll find much worse collections in lords' manors all over the country!"

Detective Chief Inspector Tyrrell in his evidence made an interesting comment. He said that he had asked Myra Hindley about the changes in her behaviour since meeting Brady, possibly seeking to suggest that he had corrupted her. Hindley had replied, "I made all my own decisions. People go through several stages in their lives. After discussions they change their mind. Ian never made me do anything I didn't want to."

When Myra Hindley went into the witness box she was asked about her feelings for Brady. She said, "I love him. I still love him." Her voice was hoarse. Asked about her involvement in the taking of photographs of Lesley Ann Downey – she could hardly deny her voice on the tape – she replied, "I have no defence. It was indefensible. I was cruel." The Attorney-General was to call her remorse "counterfeit shame".

Brady had made a revealing slip of the tongue when describing the photographic sessions with the little girl. He had said, "Afterwards, we all got dressed and went downstairs." It was a slip that the trial judge, Mr Justice

Fenton Atkinson, was to elaborate upon in his summing up. "It possibly casts a flood of light on the nature of the activities that were going on."

The Attorney-General in his closing speech said, "As in any sphere of activity, people who commit more than one murder or other crimes tend to leave their identifiable trademarks in each case. There were eight factors in common in these cases." He listed them. The victims were all young. Had disappeared from public places. Had vanished from places in the same general area where Brady and Hindley lived. There was abnormal sexual activity with each victim. A motor vehicle had been an essential requirement in all the murders, to dispose of the bodies. The method of killing had been identical. Records, in the form of photographs and tape-recordings, had been kept of each murder. And in each case the burial place was a lonely moorland grave.

In his summing-up the judge told the jury: "If what the prosecution says is right, you are facing here two sadistic killers of the utmost depravity." At 4.46 p.m. on Friday 6th May 1966 the jury returned with their verdicts. Brady was guilty of all three murders. Hindley guilty of two murders, not guilty of murdering John Kilbride but guilty of harbouring Brady knowing that he had killed the youth. Brady was sentenced to three life terms of imprisonment, Hindley to two life sentences with an additional seven years for the harbouring charge. Brady did not appeal, but Myra Hindley did. The Court of Appeal, however, firmly rejected her appeal against conviction and sentence, describing the evidence against her as "overwhelming".

It should have been the end of the story, but it was not. It was simply the prelude to a long saga. In the decades that followed the Moors Murders were to remain lodged in the public mind as a symbol of supreme wickedness.

Had Brady and Hindley been hanged, it would indeed have been the end of the tale, but capital punishment had been abolished on 8th November 1965, just a month after the murder of Edward Evans.

Brady was now in Durham Prison, where he was to remain in solitary confinement for most of the years which lay ahead. No doubt he saw himself as some kind of Rudolf Hess figure. Just as Hess languished in Spandau Prison, refusing to be broken, so Brady would hold out, proud and aloof from the enemy which surrounded him. Hindley was in Holloway Prison, where she too spent most of the time in solitary confinement. The couple wrote to each other every week, the deadly partnership still intact. They started taking O level German together, Brady passing the examination within six months. Brady wrote frequent petitions to the Home Office, demanding to be allowed visits from Myra – the right of common-law husbands and wives. Permission was always refused, and as a consequence Brady went on hunger strike for twenty-eight days. The couple were never long out of the headlines.

After five years in prison Myra Hindley started to become impatient. The bond between her and Brady could not survive separation behind steel bars and stone walls. She longed for freedom. In December 1970 she wrote in a letter. "I feel so mashed-up mentally... The truth is that after only five years of a life sentence I am obsessed with an inordinate desire to be free." She was frequently visited by Lord Longford, the prison reform campaigner, and it was reported that she had returned to the Catholic Church. Hindley wanted freedom at any price and even now was displaying her extraordinary manipulative powers. She realised that being linked to Ian Brady reduced her chances of being released on licence, and decided to finish with him. In 1972 she wrote her last letter to him, renouncing him.

Brady was enraged by her defection, and cynically commented that her conversion to religion was a public relations exercise designed to enable her to "work her ticket". He was determined that Hindley would never escape his clutches, and at this point he began to play a cruel chess-game with her, one that seemed destined to last for the rest of their lives. Every time there was an item in the press suggesting that Hindley might be considered for release, Brady would let slip another bit of poison to damage her chances of freedom.

The years passed. Myra Hindley despaired of ever being released. She had a lesbian affair with a prison officer at Holloway. An escape was planned and keys made, but the plot was foiled. The prison officer received six years' imprisonment, and Myra Hindley, prisoner 964055, was taken to court and given an additional one year's imprisonment for her part in the plot.

Myra Hindley continued to write to influential people. In 1974 she wrote to John Trevelyan, the film-censor: "Something is slowly dying inside me, and it's the will to live..." On 8th May 1975 she wrote again: "What is life for? To die. Then why not kill myself at once? No, I'm afraid. Wait for death until it comes? I fear that even more. Then I must live. But what for? In order to die. I can't escape from that circle." After being assaulted by a fellow-prisoner and having her nose and jaw broken, Myra Hindley was given plastic surgery and had her name changed by deed-poll to Myra Spencer. When this leaked out to the press there was again speculation that the Home Office was preparing Hindley for release. Brady read the newspapers and took appropriate action. He was determined to end his days behind bars, like some Nazi martyr, and he was determined that Myra should too.

Hindley was awarded a BA Degree in Humanities from the Open University, but she could still not escape from

Brady. He was in Parkhurst Prison, making books in braille for the blind. Hindley had taken his place at Durham. In January 1978 Brady wrote an open letter saying: "I have always accepted the weight of the crimes both Myra and myself were convicted of justifies permanent imprisonment, regardless of expressed personal remorse and verifiable change." Ian Brady, prisoner number 602217, was ensuring that Myra would be damned with him forever.

Myra Hindley continued to have visits from Lord Longford and other personalities. When Lord Stonham was Under-Secretary at the Home Office he visited Hindley in prison and was so impressed by her demeanour that he said afterwards that he was worried that a person like her could be in prison. William Mars-Jones, who had been a junior counsel at the trial, retorted that he would be worried if she were not in prison. Lesley Ann Downey's mother vowed passionately that if Myra Hindley were ever released she would kill her. Patrick Kilbride, father of victim John Kilbride, made the same promise.

In 1982 Myra Hindley once again petitioned the Home Secretary, pleading for her release. She said: "I feel I have more than paid my debt to society..." Significantly, the Home Secretary did not rule it out, but he announced in the Commons that Brady and Hindley would not be considered for parole until 1985. Faced with the prospect that Hindley might be released as a "reformed character," Brady again wrote to the press. The *Sunday Times* published his letter on 16th May 1982. He declared that he had no wish ever to be considered for release: "Since the weight of our crimes justifies permanent imprisonment." Now aged forty-four, Brady wrote to the Parole Board informing them, "I will not wish to be freed in 1985 or even 2005."

Myra Hindley was moved to Cookham Wood, an open prison in Rochester, Kent, in 1983. The place was like a high-class hotel, each inmate having her own room with carpets and curtains. There was colour television, and frequent escorted walks into town. Such a move, to a minimum security jail, usually means that a prisoner is nearing the end of the sentence imposed.

It was at this time that police officers made a visit to Brady, still in Parkhurst. There was an announcement that Brady would also be moved. Gartree in Leicestershire was mentioned. There was also talk that he was providing details of other murders. Myra Hindley wrote to a friend about the rumours saying: "I couldn't make statements about something I know nothing about... My conscience is clear... Regardless of any allegations he might make."

At the age of forty-two, and after seventeen years in prison, Myra Hindley again wrote to the Home Secretary requesting once more that she be considered for release by the Parole Board. On 23rd May 1985 the then Home Secretary, Leon Brittan, announced the Parole Board's recommendations: "That neither Ian Brady nor Myra Hindley should be released. The case of Ian Brady will be reviewed in ten years' time. Myra Hindley's will be reviewed in five years' time." Lord Longford, by now Hindley's staunchest ally, denounced the decision as "brutal, revolting, astounding and disgusting." Myra Hindley attempted to commit suicide with a pair of stolen scissors. When this failed she went on hunger strike. Now, after nineteen years in prison, she was finally broken.

In cell 4 at Parkhurst Prison, Brady was now thin and gaunt, and he was hearing voices. Slowly but surely he was going insane. But not *that* insane. When he read in the newspapers that Myra Hindley had instructed her lawyers to take her case to the Court of Human Rights at Strasbourg, he let fall another drip of poisoned information. He told a reporter, "If I revealed what *really* happened, Myra would not get out in one hundred years."

In November 1985 Brady was certified insane and moved to the top-security mental hospital at Park Lane, Liverpool. Doctors had diagnosed acute paranoia and schizophrenia. In March 1987 Brady offered doctors at the hospital a bizarre deal. He would reveal the full list of victims he and Hindley had killed if the doctors would give him the means to commit suicide and let him die.

The race was on between Brady and Hindley as to who would be first to "confess". In March 1986 Brady agreed to meet Anne West, mother of Lesley Ann Downey, following an emotional letter from the bereaved woman. And Hindley was apparently moved by a letter written to her by the mother of Keith Bennett. Mrs Winifred Johnson, fifty-three, took five years to compose that letter, in which she begged Hindley to tell her what had really happened to her son.

Detective Chief Superintendent Peter Topping of Manchester CID had always been determined to solve the riddle of the missing children. He visited Hindley in Cookham Prison more than once, urging her to confess. Finally she told about the killings of Pauline Reade and Keith Bennett. Hindley was taken on a highly publicized visit to Saddleworth Moor, tramping across the peat with police officers to point out likely sites for digging. On 1st July 1987 police found the body of Pauline Read.

Brady had always refused to go back to the moor, and described Hindley's trips there as a "public relations stunt". But he too was soon back on his old killing ground. He was there to try to pin-point the grave of Keith Bennett. He failed, complaining that quarrying had altered the landscape since he had last used it as a cemetery over twenty years previously.

In August 1987 Brady told a BBC television reporter that he had given information to Manchester Police about five more killings. Police acknowledged having received this information, but could not treat the confessions as genuine until the details were substantiated. But dusty old files were reopened.

Doubtless there will be further developments in the Moors Murders case; the saga will not be over until the deaths of both participants. The latest news on the case is that early in 1995, Myra Hindley asked for and was granted permission to be hypnotised in an effort to help her remember where the grave of Keith Bennett is located. This came shortly after she had been officially informed by the Home Secretary that she is never to be released from prison, but must die within its walls. She is now back in Durham jail.

Chapter Seven
AMERICA: LAND OF THE FREE

America, land of affluence and liberty, is the ultimate dream of millions around the world. The USA is the most powerful nation in the world, and by extension the most influential. American styles are copied and reflected all over the globe. But there is also a dark side to the American Dream. It has been called "The Air Conditioned Nightmare", but the modern Sodom and Gomorrah might be a more apt description. It is the land of excess, of conspicuous consumption, and along with that has come the disposable item: the toothbrush or cigarette lighter you use once and then throw away, or in the case of the American sex killer, the human being. People are murdered by the thousand every year in the USA, bodies used to satiate a perverted lust and then thrown away like so much garbage.

Ironically the man who made modern America fully aware of the menace of the serial sex killer, **Henry Lee Lucas,** now seems never to have been the ogre we once thought. Originally he was believed to have murdered nearly four hundred people in a reign of terror that began with the rape and murder of his mother in 1960 and lasted until his arrest in June 1983. Now, however, we know that a great of deal of his confessional evidence was false. The more Lucas talked, the more cigarettes and candy the police gave him – so Lucas talked a lot. But a great deal was fantasy. His relative harmlessness, however, provides scant cause for comfort. America is still the market leader in sex killings, as even the briefest of surveys will readily demonstrate.

Just as any survey of English sex murders would start with Jack the Ripper, so the American scene begins with **Herman Webster Mudgett**, alias H.H. Holmes. He began his career studying medicine, then found that if he insured non-existent people who later "died" – he used bodies from the hospital's dissecting room to prove the death – he could make a better living by claiming on the insurance. With this initial hurdle of morality easily jumped, Mudgett then progressed to far worse crimes. In 1891 he had his "Torture Castle" built at Chicago's 63rd Street. This large, rambling structure consisted of secret rooms, concealed doors, hidden staircases, and a large chute which led to the cellar. Here Mudgett lured his female victims, whom he seduced and then drugged. Then he would dissect them. Mudgett was finally brought to justice in 1895 when he was arrested on an insurance fraud charge. His Castle was searched and some two hundred corpses recovered. Mudgett began a long and detailed confession to all the murders, but had only reached number 27 when he was executed on 7th May 1896.

Albert Fish was sixty-six when he was electrocuted at Sing Sing Prison in January 1936. He commenced his career of perversion by molesting children, then progressed to castrating several boys. Altogether he tortured and killed dozens of children. Professor R. L. Masters, in his book *Perverse Crimes in History*, describes Fish as an eater of excreta and a urine drinker; a child molester, a masochist who had driven twenty-nine needles into his body – most of them in the genital region – a vampire, cannibal and sadist. Albert Fish admitted cannibalizing at least six children.

The crime for which he was tried was the murder of ten-year-old Grace Budd. On 3rd June 1928 Fish lured Grace away from her home on the pretence of taking her to a children's party. He then strangled her and butchered her body. He took pieces of the corpse home with him and cooked them in a stew on which he feasted for nine days. He said later that this kept him in a state of continuous sexual fervour. He was caught six years later, traced through a letter he sent to the girl's parents.

When arrested he was found to have a large collection of newspaper cuttings about the case of Fritz Haarmann. At his trial the defence claimed insanity, although Fish himself stated, "I am not insane. I am just queer." Fish seems to have had a religious complex, defending the castration of boys as symbolic of Abraham's sacrifice of Isaac. He had later discovered that he was God. His killings were an act of mercy to save his victims from the horrors of life. Raised in an orphanage, where he was badly treated, he once wrote: "Misery leads to crime. I saw so many boys whipped that it ruined my mind." The psychiatrist Dr Frederick Wertham studied Fish and wrote about him in *The Show of Violence*. The doctor appeared as an expert defence witness at the trial, arguing that Fish was insane. The jury rejected this, finding the prisoner guilty. When sentenced to death in the electric chair the "Moon Maniac", as newspapers had dubbed him – most of his killings took place on or near a full moon – said he welcomed it as "the supreme thrill". He eagerly helped adjust the electrodes in the chair, and even strapped himself in. The first jolt of electricity failed to kill him, being short-circuited by the needles in his body. Witnesses reported seeing a puff of blue smoke above his head, before the second charge extinguished him.

Earle Leonard Nelson, the "Gorilla Murderer", was so named because of his large strangling hands. Born in

Philadelphia in 1897, he was brought up by an aunt who tried to beat religion into him. In his teens he was involved in a street accident which left him with brain damage. His criminal career began shortly afterwards. He started as a peeping-tom, but his crimes soon escalated. When he was twenty-one he was jailed for attempted rape. He was released in 1919, when he changed his name to Roger Wilson. For seven years nothing was heard of him. Then in 1926 he exploded into a frenzy of murders. Between February 1926 and June 1927 Earl Nelson strangled twenty-two women, all of them boarding-house landladies whom he raped after death. Moving from town to town, he was soon killing at the rate of one every three weeks. When apprehended he showed great remorse and began quoting from the Scriptures. He was hanged on 13th January 1928.

Gerald Thompson was born in Illinois in 1910. He was known as a quiet man and an industrious worker. When a workmate's daughter was raped and murdered in June 1935 Thompson gave towards a collection for her wreath. Then police discovered that dozens of girls in the area had been subjected to sex attacks. They had been induced to get into a car, where the driver held them captive and forced them to strip naked. Then he would make them pose in front of the headlights of his car while he took photographs. None of the girls had reported these attacks to the police for fear of the photographs becoming public, but following the murder they did come forward. Thompson was identified as the attacker and he was questioned about the murder of the girl, Miss Mildred Hallmark. He confessed immediately, saying that she had attacked him with her sharp nails, forcing him to kill her. "Afterwards I slept like a baby," he said, smiling. Fragments of his skin were found under the nails of his victim. He confessed to sixteen photo-rapes and said his ambition had been to commit a rape a week for a year. He also admitted to over fifty rapes since the age of sixteen. He went to the electric chair on 15th October 1935.

Donald Fearn, twenty-three, lived with his wife and young child in Pueblo, Colorado, and became obsessed with the defunct religion of the Pueblo Indians, who were known as "The Penitentes" and practised self-torture and flagellation. The quiet railway mechanic brooded over his fantasies. In April 1942 his wife went into hospital to have her second child, and Fearn took advantage of her absence to put his weird ideas into practice. His victim was Alice Porter, seventeen, a student nurse. On 22nd April he forced her into his car at gun-point, drove her to an old adobe church, and tied her naked to the altar. He spent the night slowly torturing her with various implements until she was nearly dead. Then he raped her, before smashing in her skull with a hammer. He disposed of her body down a well. He was seen when his car got stuck in mud, and was later arrested. He went to the gas chamber on 22nd October 1942.

William Heirens is the classic sex killer, often quoted in psychiatric case histories. Born in 1929 in Chicago to a puritan mother who taught him that sex was dirty, he reacted by developing such an intense aversion to women that he would vomit merely by touching a girl. At nine he was stealing women's underwear from clothes-lines, and in his teens the tall, good-looking young man began dressing in women's clothes and masturbating in front of pictures of various Nazi leaders. The power-complex allied to deviant sexuality is evident here.

At university Heirens was a good scholar but he was leading a double life. By day he was a model student but by night he was committing robberies which provided him with sexual fulfilment. He would have an orgasm simply from entering a strange woman's home. On several occasions he also assaulted the women in their homes and, in June 1945, he murdered for the first time. His victim was Mrs Josephine Alice Riss, who disturbed him when he was robbing her apartment. He stabbed her fourteen times and almost decapitated her. In December 1945 Heirens killed Frances Brown, thirty-three, in similar circumstances, first shooting her and afterwards stabbing her dead body. In lipstick on the wall in the bedroom he left police a scrawled message: "For Heaven's sake catch me before I kill again. I cannot control myself." He went on to abduct a six-year-old girl for ransom, but killed the child almost immediately and also dismembered her body. Caught six months later, Heirens confessed in the name of his alter ego, "George Murman". He was given three life terms of imprisonment with no possibility of parole.

Dr Arnold Axilrod was a respected member of Minneapolis society, having been a former mayor of the city. His dental practice brought him in a good income. It also provided him with an opportunity to rape girls. In 1955 a seventeen-year-old girl who was visiting him for a dental appointment was drugged and fell asleep in his surgery. She woke to find Dr Axilrod bent over her in a suggestive manner. She complained but was not taken seriously. A few months later a dead woman was found dumped outside the city. She had been strangled, and had had intercourse shortly before death. She was found to be three months pregnant – yet her husband could not have been the father, he had been in Korea for longer than that. Police investigated the background of the victim, Mary Moonen, twenty-one. Her dentist was Dr Axilrod... He was arrested and immediately confessed, saying: "I guess I did it." He was sentenced to five to twenty years in jail.

Melvin David Rees was a jazz musician – he played saxophone, clarinet, piano and guitar. He was also a brutal sex killer. On 26th June 1957 he held up a car containing a courting couple in Annapolis, Maryland. He shot the woman, Margaret Harold, but allowed the man, an army sergeant, to flee. He then stripped his victim and raped her. Her boyfriend summoned the police and during a search of the area they discovered a basement devoted to the worship of murder. The walls were covered with police morgue shots of murdered women and pornographic photographs.

On 11th January 1959 a car containing four members of the same family – Carroll Jackson, his wife Mildred, and their two daughters aged five and eighteen months – was stopped on a lonely road in West Virginia by another car. A tall, thin man with ape-like arms got out of the other car carrying a gun. He forced the family into the boot of his car and drove off with them. Later the Jacksons' abandoned car was found and a search for them began. It was too late – the entire family had been slaughtered. On 4th March, Carrol Jackson's body was found in a ditch. He had been shot in the head. Beneath him lay the body of his 18-month-old daughter, who had been suffocated. Three weeks later a group of boys out playing spotted a mound of freshly dug earth, and digging a little, they uncovered blonde human hair. Police were called and dug up the bodies of Mildred and Susan Jackson. Mildred had a stocking around the neck, Susan had been bludgeoned to death. Both had been raped. The grave was just a few hundred yards away from the basement which had featured in the first murder, and inside it police found a button from Mildred's dress.

Two months later the police received an anonymous letter denouncing Rees as the killer of both Margaret Harold and the Jacksons. The writer said he had confronted Rees with this, and Rees had not denied it. The police tried to trace Rees, without success. Then in early 1966 the informant went to the police in person. He said he had received a letter from Rees, who was now working as a piano salesman in Arkansas. FBI agents arrested the suspect and raided his parents' home. Inside they found a saxophone case containing a .38 revolver and a handwritten journal relating various sadistic acts. It also included an account of the murder of the Jacksons. In the journal Rees described forcing Margaret Harold to commit fellatio upon him, and commented, "Now I was the master." The entries revealed him to be a truly sadistic sex killer. The psychic Peter Hurkos had been called in after the murder of the Jackson family, and was able to give police a remarkably accurate description of the killer. He also said that the killer had committed nine murders. This was confirmed when police found connections linking Rees to the sex murders of four other teenagers: four girls who had been shot and raped. Rees was tried and executed in 1961.

Albert DeSalvo strangled thirteen women to death in the city of Boston between June 1962 and January 1964, plunging the city into a state of panic. The police were seemingly powerless to stop the killings. The Boston Strangler's trademark was the jaunty bow he tied in the ligature around the neck of his victims, like an artistic flourish. For ten months after the last killing there were no more murders, and the police and public speculated as to what had happened to the "Strangler". Then, on 27th October 1964, he struck again but this time his intended victim fought him off and was able to give police a description. The description fitted the so-called "Measuring Man" who had been arrested for indecent assault in 1960. (Albert DeSalvo had persuaded girls into letting him measure their bodies in exchange for a "free" dress.) DeSalvo was promptly arrested, and confessed to two rapes and over four hundred burglaries. He was sent to the Boston State Hospital for observation – he had threatened suicide, and there was a question about his sanity. He was not tried for the stranglings but for four cases of attempted rape where the victims had positively identified him. Sentenced to life imprisonment in 1967, he was stabbed to death by a fellow-prisoner on 26th November 1973.

Charles Howard Schmid, twenty-three, was an only child who was showered with love and money by his doting parents. As a young man he spent much of his time impressing teenagers in Tucson, Arizona, with tall stories about being a Mafia hood and running a prostitution ring. Certainly the dark-haired, handsome man was a success with the local girls and had many sexual conquests. But perhaps they came too easy...

One evening in May 1964 he was sitting with his friend John Saunders and a girl named Mary French when he suddenly announced: "I want to kill a girl tonight." He persuaded his companions to accompany him to the home of Alleen Rowe, fifteen, and then talked her into going for a drive with them. Once in a remote desert spot Schmid killed the girl with a rock, after raping her. He then kissed Mary French, telling her, "Remember I love you."

The following year – on 16th August 1965 – Schmid strangled two young girls, Gretchen Fritz, seventeen, and her thirteen-year-old sister Wendy, dumping their bodies in the desert. But he could not resist boasting to a friend, Richard Bruns, about what he had done. Bruns, who thought Schmid was lying, said to him, "If you killed them, let's go and bury them." Schmid drove him to the murder site, where they found the two bodies and buried them, Schmid telling Bruns, "Now you're in this as deep as I am." Schmid was arrested in San Diego for posing as an FBI agent and questioning girls on the beach. He was in a state of some agitation, screaming "God is going to punish me" as the police took him away. The case is remarkable in that practically every teenager in Tucson knew he had killed Alleen Rowe and the Fritz girls, but did not tell their parents – much less the police. It was Richard Bruns who finally went to the police, leading them to the bodies of the Fritz girls. Schmid, Mary French and John Saunders were arrested. Schmid received three life sentences, French only five years jail, while Saunders was given life. Another interesting facet to the case is the obvious condition of *folie à deux* that Schmid was able to induce in his followers.

Richard Speck will be remembered for his senseless killing of eight student nurses in a Chicago hostel on the night of 14th July 1966. Speck was a tall, pock-marked young man of otherwise fairly pleasant appearance, with fair hair and blue eyes. Born on 6th December 1941, one of eight children, Speck was twenty-four when he embarked on his killing spree. Semi-literate and an avid collector of comic magazines, he was drunk and probably high on drugs at the time. He entered the hostel with a gun and immediately took six nurses prisoner, tying them up and promising not to hurt them, explaining that he was only after money. When another three nurses entered the hostel he took them prisoner too, binding them with torn sheets. Then one by one he took each nurse into an adjoining room, where he killed them at roughly twenty-minute intervals. One nurse, twenty-four-year-old, Corazon Amurao, hid under a bed and thus saved her life. The last girl left was Gloria Davey, twenty-two. Speck raped her for some twenty-five minutes, asking her at one point, "Would you mind putting your legs around my back?" He sodomized her with an instrument before killing her. Miss Amurao witnessed this last killing whilst still hiding under the bed. At 5 a.m., when the killer left the scene, she raised the alarm, crying: "All my friends are dead."

Police found the hostel to be a charnel-house. Only Gloria Davey had been sexually assaulted. The other seven victims had been killed for no reason, as if Speck had been a shark in a feeding frenzy. One was killed by a single stab wound to the neck, another had stab wounds to the neck, heart and left eye. Three had been strangled and stabbed. One had been mutilated deliberately.

Speck was arrested after being admitted to hospital following a suicide attempt – he had slashed his wrists – and was positively identified by Miss Amurao. It turned out that the killer had a long record of sex offences and an insatiable sexual appetite. Speck was also suspected of several more murders: of a woman in April 1966, of three girls in July, and another mass murder in Michigan, where several victims aged from seven to sixty were butchered.

The jury took just forty-five minutes to find Speck guilty, and he was sentenced to the electric chair, but by using legal appeals he stayed alive until the death penalty was abolished. In 1972 he was resentenced to life terms totalling 400 years. Despite having maintained his innocence in 1978 be told a newspaper reporter, "Yeah, I killed them, I stabbed them and choked them." Speck died of a heart attack on 5th December 1991.

Lloyd Higdon is another example of *folie à deux* in action. On 4th July 1963 he picked up the fourteen-year-old daughter of a neighbour and raped her. In this he was aided by his wife. When the girl told her parents, police in Ypsilanti, Michigan, arrested the couple and Higdon was imprisoned. On his release he set up home with another woman, Lucille Brumitt, and again picked up a young girl, thirteen-year-old Rosanne Sandbrook, with the intention of raping her. When she resisted, however, Higdon strangled her, then dumped her body on a local garbage tip. Knowing Higdon's record, police arrested him.

They soon broke his phoney alibi, and both he and Lucille Brumitt were sentenced to life.

John Norman Collins was labelled the "Ypsilanti Ripper" by the press. This 22-year-old young man was a model student at the Eastern Michigan University in 1969. He was good-looking, but tended to be morose. The only clue to his real character came in a remark he made to a classmate: "If a man has to kill, he kills." He had reworded the Fifth Commandment. Between August 1967 and July 1969 the bodies of seven young girls were found around Ypsilanti. All had been raped and tortured before being killed with a knife. Some had been horribly mutilated, one having a branch of a tree thrust into her vagina. Psychic Peter Hurkos was called in to help, but the case was to be one of his failures. However, the body of the last victim, Karen Sue Beckemann, revealed forensic clues which helped police develop a profile of the killer. State Police Corporal David Leik realized that it fitted his nephew, Norman Collins, who was questioned but released for lack of evidence. Corporal Leik checked his basement out carefully, and found bloodstained clothing which matched the blood group of Miss Beckemann, and hair-clippings which had been transferred to the victim's body – Corporal Leik used to cut his children's hair in the basement. There were also other clues which linked the dead girl to that basement and it was concluded that she had either been killed there or her body had been stored there after death. Norman Collins was brought in again. At his trial Collins pleaded not guilty, but was convicted on the solid mass of circumstantial evidence and sentenced to life.

Juan Vallejo Corona arrived in the United States in the 1950s as an immigrant fruit-picker, but always had an eye to the main chance. Through sheer business acumen and hard work he became his own boss, becoming a contractor hiring illegal Mexican immigrants to pick fruit on various farms around Yuba City, California. He housed his workers on the Sullivan ranch. He was thirty-eight years old, and had apparently overcome a bout of schizophrenia suffered in his early years.

On 19th May 1971 a local farmer became suspicious when he discovered a large hole dug in his orchard which was then filled in again by evening. He had it dug up by the police, who found the body of a vagrant named Kenneth Whitacre. He had been stabbed, and his head battered with a machete, after homosexual intercourse. Police began a wide-scale search of the area. On 21st May a tractor driver on Sullivan's ranch discovered another grave – and then more. All the victims had been male, all had been sexually abused before being killed by knife and machete. In one of the graves was a receipt with the name Juan Corona on it. Digging continued until 4th June, when the last known victim – the twenty-fifth – was uncovered. In his pockets were bank deposit slips in the name of Corona. Corona was picked up and the names of all twenty-five victims were found, all carefully recorded in his ledger, just as the Nazis kept careful accounts of their victims. The evidence against Corona was circumstantial and the jury took forty-five hours to find him guilty of all the murders. He was sentenced to twenty-five consecutive life terms. Since his victims were all alcoholic vagrants, or illegal Mexican migrants, the case did not arouse any great public revulsion.

Sherman McCray, forty-seven, was the head of an itinerant family who wandered across the USA leaving a trail of murdered women in their wake. In June 1972 the family, consisting of Sherman, his wife Carol, son Danny, daughter Gina and her husband Carl Taylor, arrived in Santa Barbara, California, and were quickly picked up by the police following a spate of supermarket robberies. For the armed robberies Sherman McCray and Carl Taylor were both sentenced to five years to life. The other three members of the family received nine-month sentences for harbouring felons. But with the family behind bars, the police started looking into their background and uncovered evidence that they had, between August 1971 and February 1972, been responsible for the abduction, rape and murder of at least twenty young women. The McCray men had carried out these deeds but they had done so with the assistance and approval of their women-folk.

The nomad family had travelled widely, with both Sherman McCray and Carl Taylor serving time in jails for various felonies committed along the way. On 12th August 1971 Sheri Martin, seventeen, was abducted from her hometown of Salt Lake City. A week later Lenora Rose disappeared from Denver, Colorado. On 28th September Elizabeth Perryman, twenty-six, was abducted from a restaurant in Lubbock, Texas. In every case the girls had been waitresses, the tills in their workplaces had been looted, and the girls had been raped and shot. And there were more: three victims from Texas, two from Florida, and so on. Danny McCray finally broke under police questioning and confessed that he, his father, and his brother-in-law had committed the murders. It was a case where a family, like a tribe of Huns, had wandered around the USA picking up victims at random and disposing of them like trash.

Dean Allen Corll, thirty-three, was well-liked and respected in Pasadena, California, where he worked for the Houston Lighting and Power Company. But he was a homosexual with a penchant for murder. He had never really grown up, and much preferred the company of teenagers to that of adults. Some of the teenagers who went to his apartment never came out alive... Corll had two young henchmen, Wayne Henley and David Brooks, who helped him in his trade of murder. Most of the victims came from the slum area of Houston known as the Heights. The first victim was murdered in 1970, followed by two more in December of the same year: James Glass, fourteen, and Danny Yates, fifteen. Corll often murdered two at a time, including two brothers in January 1971. On 8th August 1973 Wayne Henley telephoned the police to say he had killed Corll. He told officers that Corll had tried to kill him, and he had been forced to shoot him in the back six times. Under questioning Henley admitted procuring boys for Corll, who paid 200 dollars a head, and he revealed that many of the victims lay buried in a boat-shed rented by Corll. When police dug up the floor of the shed they found the remains of seventeen corpses wrapped in plastic. At another site four more bodies were recovered, and six others were found on another dumping ground. In all twenty-three bodies were discovered, but Henley claimed that Corll's true total was thirty-one. Henley admitted that he and Brooks helped Corll strap his victims to a "torture board" where they were sodomized for days on end. Torture was also practised, with teeth-marks being found on the genitals of one of the victims. In July 1974 Henley and Brooks both received life sentences for their part in the murders.

Edmund Emil Kemper was a true freak, standing six feet nine inches tall and weighing twenty stone. He was born on 18th December 1948, and his parents split up when he was a young child. Lacking a father-figure, he modelled himself on John Wayne. His mother ridiculed his fantasies and obstructed any independent decisions he might make. He grew up nurturing dreams of torture and revenge, mainly of sadistic acts committed against female corpses. At thirteen he cut the family cat in pieces, and also the hands and feet off his sister's doll. Finally beyond his mother's control, the young Kemper went to live with his grandparents. They tried to be strict with the boy. On 24th August 1964 he shot dead his grandmother, stabbing her body repeatedly. He then did the same to his grandfather. Kemper was sent to a mental hospital for the criminally insane, where he was found to have an IQ of 136. After five years he was released as "Cured" and sent to live with his mother in Santa Cruz, California. He detested his mother...

On 7th May 1972 Kemper picked up a pair of young hitchhikers, Anita Luchese and Mary Anne Pesce. They were both girl students from Fresno State College in Berkeley. He drove them to a remote spot where he forced Miss Luchese into the car boot, then handcuffed Mary Anne Pesce, putting a plastic bag over her head. He stabbed her in the back and abdomen, before cutting her throat. He then killed the girl in the boot. He took the bodies home, decapitated them and dissected them. He played with them as if they were dolls. Later he buried the pieces in the mountains. On 14th September 1972 Kemper picked up another girl, aged fifteen, and after killing her, raped her. She too went back to his home to have her head and hands cut off, and to be dissected. On 8th January 1973 came another victim: he kept this one at home, performing sexual acts on the body. On 5th February came two more victims, both of whom he decapitated, having sex with the headless corpse of one of them. He used an axe to dissect the remains. On Easter Sunday 1973 Kemper went into his mother's bedroom and hit her on the head with a hammer. Then he used the knife he called "the General" to decapitate her. He cut out his mother's larynx and dropped it into the waste-disposal unit, telling police later that he did it because it seemed appropriate: "because she had bitched me so much." With his mother's headless body in the closet, he invited a friend of hers over for dinner and killed her too. He beheaded the woman and had sex with her remains. That night he slept in his mother's bed.

After going on the run Kemper surrendered himself to the police, saying he was afraid they might "shoot first and ask questions later". He confessed to eight murders and various acts of necrophilia and cannibalism. He was tried at Santa Cruz in April 1973 on eight counts of murder, having been adjudged legally sane. Kemper asked for the death penalty but it was refused. Instead he received eight consecutive life terms. The psychiatrist Donald Lunde said of Kemper, "In his way, he avenged the rejection of both his mother and his father."

Paul John Knowles was a petty thief who graduated to murder. From 1965, when he was aged nineteen, to 1972, he spent half of his life in prison. It was shortly after he was released from Raiford State Penitentiary on 14th May 1974 that he murdered for the first time. The tall, handsome red-haired man, now aged twenty-five, got into a fight after a messy relationship with a woman, and was locked up in Jacksonville police station for his pains. He promptly picked the lock on his cell and escaped. That same evening, 26th July 1974, Knowles broke into the home of a 65-year-old teacher and gagged her while he burgled her home. She suffocated to death. There was a large police dragnet out for Knowles, but he escaped it mainly by luck. He stole a car and picked up two sisters, aged seven and eleven, and killed them, dumping their bodies in a swamp. The next day he drove to Atlantic Beach, broke into a woman's home and strangled her with her own stocking. A couple of days later he picked up a young girl hitchhiker, strangled and raped her. On 23rd August he broke into a house occupied by Cathie Pierce and strangled her with the telephone cord while her three-year-old child looked on. On 3rd September, in Ohio, he got into conversation with an accounts executive in a bar. The man, William Bates, left with Knowles. His naked, strangled body was found later in the woods. Knowles drove away in Bates's car. Using his victims' money and credit cards, Knowles travelled across the USA, to California, Seattle, and then Utah. On 18th September, in Nevada, he broke into a camping trailer and shot dead the elderly couple to whom it belonged. He took their money and credit cards. Three days later he dragged a woman out of a car and raped and strangled her.

He was now completely out of control, killing on impulse. On 23rd September he met a woman, Ann Dawson, in Birmingham, Alabama. For the next six days they travelled around together. On 29th September, when her money ran out, he strangled her. Her body was never found. In Connecticut, on 16th October, he rang a doorbell at random. When a fifteen-year-old schoolgirl answered he forced her back into the house and spent the next hour raping her. When her mother returned home he made her cook him a meal, and then forced her to strip naked, after which he raped her several times. He finally strangled both victims. On 19th October, in Woodford, Virginia, he shot dead Doris Hovey, aged fifty-three. There was no motive; he just felt like killing. With a stolen tape recorder, Knowles began taping his confession to fourteen murders, almost as if he sensed the end was near, and he wanted his deeds preserved for posterity. On 6th November, in Macon, Georgia, Knowles picked up a man in a bar. The man was gay, and presumably the handsome Knowles made some promise of sexual activity. Once inside the man's home he stabbed him to death, then strangled his fifteen-year-old daughter, attempting to rape her after death.

In Atlanta, Georgia, Knowles met English journalist Sandy Fawkes. They spent a lot of time together in various motels and she never saw the full murderous side to his nature, although once he did pull a gun on her. She wrote a book about her experiences with Knowles, *Killing Time*. She described Knowles as being sexually incapable in bed. Also in Atlanta, Knowles tried to abduct a woman, but she escaped and got the licence number of his car. A police patrolman tried to intercept him, but Knowles warned him off with a sawn-off shotgun. Back in Florida Knowles stole another car. When stopped by a patrolman he took him prisoner and handcuffed him with his own cuffs. Knowles then drove off in the patrol car, with the officer sitting helplessly in the back. Using his siren, Knowles stopped another car being driven by a businessman – he was not satisfied with the patrol-car, complaining of its poor suspension. Knowles handcuffed the businessman, transferred the patrol car officer to the new car, and drove off with them. He drove into some woods and then shot both handcuffed prisoners in the back of the head. After crashing through a police roadblock, he ran into woods to escape, hunted by two hundred police officers with dogs and helicopters. He was captured on 17th November 1974. In four months of freedom be had murdered at least eighteen people. After appearing in court he was placed in a police vehicle to transfer him to prison. He succeeded in picking the lock on his handcuffs and attempted to grab a sheriff's gun. An FBI agent riding escort in the vehicle shot him dead.

Kenneth Bianchi was to become known as the "Hillside Strangler" and his murders display yet another *folie à deux* relationship.

Between October 1977 and February 1978 ten girls had been raped and murdered in Bellingham, California, the bodies being dumped like trash in the hills around Los Angeles. The hunt for the killer was complicated by the fact that two separate law-enforcement agencies were conducting separate inquiries. The breakthrough did not come until January 1979 when two women, Karen Mandic and Diane Wilder, vanished from the house they shared in Bellingham. Karen had told a friend that she been offered a "detective" job by a security guard named Kenneth Bianchi. The following day the bodies of the two women were found in the back of Karen's car. They had been raped prior to death. Los Angeles detectives now became very interested in Kenneth Bianchi. The 27-year-old was a police "groupie", that is, he hung around cops and studied their mannerisms. The "Hillside Strangler" was known to have used a fake police badge to lure his victims into his car. Bianchi was arrested at his home, where he lived with his girlfriend and their child. At first he denied all knowledge of the murder. Under lengthy questioning, however, he finally broke, admitting the murders of the two Bellingham girls and five of the "Hillside Strangler" killings.

When Bianchi stood trial for his crimes his defence counsel claimed that his was a dual personality, and that the killings had been committed by his alter ego "Steve". However, though Bianchi managed to convince experienced psychiatrists that he was a genuine case of dual personality, it was all a clever charade, as secret video-recordings proved. At his trial in October 1979 he was sentenced to six consecutive life terms. Like most sexual serial killers, Bianchi's background was that of a child who had been abused and rejected, and so became an emotional cripple.

John Wayne Gacy was born on 17th March 1942 in Chicago, the son of a Danish mother and a Polish father. When he was eleven he suffered a head injury which left him with a blood-clot on the brain which caused blackouts. He went to business college and became a shoe salesman, marrying a colleague. Later he ran a fried chicken business and became a member of the Junior Chamber of Commerce. He seemed the perfect citizen. However, in 1968 he was sentenced to ten years in jail for handcuffing an employee and trying to sodomize him. His marriage did not survive his imprisonment: his wife divorced him, taking with her their son and daughter. A weak character, Gacy was a liar and a boaster, although an affable man. He was a model prisoner, and was released after serving only eighteen months of his sentence. But in 1971 he was arrested again. This time he was accused of picking up a teenage boy and trying to force him to engage in sex. The boy failed to appear as a witness and the case was dropped.

In 1972 Gacy married for a second time and set up his own business as a contractor. But he had developed a violent temper and since his sexual performance was woefully inadequate, in 1976 came another divorce. One of his wife's complaints was the peculiar odour which hung round the house...

On 21st March 1978 a 27-year-old Chicagoan met a fat man – Gacy – and got into his car to smoke a joint. Gacy slapped a chloroform-soaked cloth over his mouth, and when the man woke he was in a house, being flogged with whips. He was also raped for several hours. Finally Gacy dumped the man's body by the side of a lake. In hospital it was found that he was bleeding from the rectum, and that the chloroform administered had permanently damaged his liver. He had practically to beg the police to arrest Gacy, but the case dragged on, with Gacy out on bail and the police feeling that the evidence against him was not strong enough to secure a conviction. On 11th December 1978 Robert Piest, fifteen, vanished while calling at a drug-store to apply for a summer job. The drug-store had recently been renovated, and the contractor had been Gacy. The police went to his house at 8213 West Summerdale Avenue, Des Plaines, and questioned him about the missing boy. Eventually they searched his house, lifting a trapdoor leading to the crawlspace beneath the building. There was a stench of decaying flesh and rotting corpses were in plain view.

At the police station Gacy (known as the "Fat Man") admitted killing thirty-two teenagers for sex, and said that twenty-seven of them had been buried in or around his house. The rest, including Robert Piest, had been dumped in the river. The "Fat Man" had simply run out of space. Twenty-eight bodies were finally recovered from Gacy's house. In 1980 the "Fat Man" was sentenced to death. He was executed by lethal injection on 10th May 1994.

Randall Brent Woodfield was another handsome serial killer; tall with black hair and a moustache. A natural athlete, he had been signed by the Green Bay Packers, and *Playgirl* chose a beefcake photograph of him for their centrefold. But that picture was never published. The magazine scrapped it when the truth came out that the handsome hunk was also a cold-blooded killer.

Woodfield was the leader of an organization of Christian athletes at Portland State University. Not only was he big and strong, he was also deeply sensitive, writing very moving and articulate letters to the women he dated. But he liked killing women too. His victims were to range from nine years of age to forty. He was the only son in his family, but had two sisters, and was thus brought up in a feminine atmosphere. His early years revealed him to be a disturbed child who began exposing himself at the age of thirteen. From that he graduated to rape, and finally murder. His first murder was a double event; he spotted two girls cleaning a building in Oregon one Sunday evening in 1981, and forced them at gunpoint to perform various sexual acts on him. When he was finally satisfied he shot each girl in the head. Incredibly, one of the girls survived. It was her testimony, in which she had to relive the terror of her ordeal in an open courtroom, that put Woodfield away for a sentence of life plus 155 years. Like most American sex killers, Woodfield had killed over a wide area – in his case the entire length of the Pacific Coast – and he was undeniably a monster. And yet, after being put safely behind bars, he began to receive hundreds of letters from admiring women. He replied to every one, often with tender and moving sentiments.

Christopher Bernard Wilder was a spree killer, as opposed to the classic serial killer. The FBI's Behavioral Science Unit has divided serial killers into two basic types. There are those who kill over a long time-scale, like Bundy and Bianchi; and there are those who erupt in a sudden explosion of murder. Wilder was a killer of the second type.

Born in Australia, he ended up living in Florida, where he became a genuine millionaire playboy. He had a large house, raced cars for fun, took his many girlfriends for trips on his yacht, and never forgot to send flowers. He was the old-fashioned romantic type, always standing up when a woman entered the room. But from February to April 1984 he rampaged across the USA, killing as he went.

His *modus operandi* was to go to shopping malls where amateur fashion shows were being held. He would have an expensive camera around his neck, and when he spotted a likely victim he would proffer a phoney name, show her his portfolio of photographs, and make wild promises of success. His first victim, Rosaria Gonzales, died on 26th February 1984. On 3rd March Elizabeth Kenyon died, followed by Theresa Fergusson on 18th March. On 23rd March came Terry Walden, then Suzanne Wendy Logan two days later. Sheryl Bonaventure died on 29th March, Michelle Korfmann on 1st April. Beth Dodge was his last victim. She died on 12th April.

Christopher Wilder was shot dead in a shoot-out with New Hampshire state troopers as he tried to cross the border into Canada. His death was officially listed as suicide. The psychological causes which led an attractive millionaire to become a sex killer remain unknown.

Ted Bundy was a handsome student, brimming with self-confidence and style. He could have achieved almost anything. But what he chose to do was to pursue a four-year orgy of destruction across the USA which left dozens of young women maimed or dead. Police believe Bundy killed twenty-one women, but the real figure may be as high as forty.

A narrative account of the Bundy killings is difficult to construct, since he killed in so many different locations across the USA, and intermittently over a long period of time. For our purposes, the first murder in his long series was that of Kathy Devine, fifteen, who vanished from Seattle, Washington state, on 25th November 1973. Her remains were found in a forest on December 6th. Kathy had been strangled and sodomized. Most writers on the career of Bundy do not mention this case or attribute it to him, but the *modus operandi* fits.

There are no doubts about his second victim, Sharon Clarke, whom he bludgeoned with a crowbar as she lay asleep in her basement bedroom in Seattle on the night of 4th January 1974. Bundy also thrust a speculum, or vaginal probe, deep inside her, causing internal injuries. She survived her attack, though she spent some months in a coma, but even under hypnosis she could recall no details.

Three weeks later Bundy was on the prowl again. He found an unlocked door in a student rooming house leading to a basement bedroom where Lynda Ann Healy, twenty-one, was asleep. Battering her unconscious, he carried her out to his car and drove her to Taylor Mountain, some twenty miles away. There he forced her to undress and raped her repeatedly before killing her.

Over the course of the next six months, young women began to disappear with dreadful regularity. On 12th March 1974 Donna Gail Manson, nineteen, disappeared on her way to a jazz concert in Olympia, Washington. Susan Elaine Rancourt, eighteen, another university student, disappeared on 17th April. On 6th May Roberta Kathleen Parks, twenty-two, vanished from her home in Corvallis, Oregon, and twenty-six days later, on 1st June, Brenda Carol Ball also disappeared. Eighteen-year-old Georgina Hawkins vanished on 11th June.

On 14th July, 1974, a number of young women out for the day in Lake Sammammish Park, twelve miles outside Seattle, were approached by a handsome young man who had his arm in a sling. He introduced himself as "Ted" and asked them to help him put his sailing-boat on the roof of his Volkswagen car. Twenty-three-year-old Janice Ott agreed to help. She was never seen alive again. Nor was nineteen-year-old Denise Naslund, who had also been in the park that day. On 7th September a construction worker found their bodies in a shallow grave just a few miles from Lake Sammammish. At the site police also found the remains of another identified female.

For the first time the police realised they probably had a serial killer on the loose. But they did not yet notice the striking similarities between the victims, as if the killer had picked a particular type of girl. All were white, all had long hair parted in the middle and all were slender and attractive. Each one vanished from or near colleges, all were single and had been wearing jeans or slacks when they were taken. This was the signature of Ted Bundy. Despite the fact that he was careful never to leave any clues – the police never found a single fingerprint – by his selection of victims, Bundy was signing his ghastly work.

The police now busied themselves trying to identify this "Ted" who drove a Volkswagen car. A special "Ted" hotline was set up to take information and, on at least two occasions the name Ted Bundy came up. But so did the names of countless others. In the meantime Bundy was still killing.

On 2nd August 1974 twenty-year-old Carol Valenzuela disappeared in Vancouver. Her body was to be discovered in October a few miles from Olympia, along with the remains of an unidentified female. Then, on 2nd October, sixteen-year-old Nancy Wilcox vanished. Two weeks later Melissa Smith, seventeen, disappeared from the small town of Midvale, just south of Salt Lake City. Her body was discovered nine days later in a canyon. She had been bludgeoned and sodomized, then strangled. Then on 31st October seventeen-year-old Laura Aime disappeared. Her body was found in the Wasatch Mountains nearly a month later. She too had been bludgeoned and strangled.

"Ted" made his first mistake when he attempted to abduct Carol DaRonch, nineteen, on 8th November in the town of Murray in the Salt Lake City area. Posing as a police officer and giving his name as "Officer Roseland", he persuaded her to get into his VW car. When he attempted to handcuff her, clubbing at her with an iron bar, she fought him off and fled screaming. Carole would be able to recognize him if ever he was apprehended. She had the enviable distinction of being the only living witness.

Angry and frustrated, Bundy drove seventeen miles to snatch another girl that same night. His victim was Debra Kent, seventeen, from a high school at Bountiful where a late night play was being performed. Her body was never found. The only clue was a handcuff key found in the school car-park. Ted celebrated the new year of 1975 by snatching Nancy Baird, twenty-one, from a service station in Farmington on 12th January. Her body was also never found.

With the coming of spring Bundy once again shifted his killing-ground. This time it was the turn of Colorado. While police in Seattle and Utah were still piecing together the threads, Caryn Campbell, twenty-three, disappeared on her way from the lobby to her room at the Wildwood Inn, Snowmass Village. Her nude body was found a month later, bludgeoned and raped. Julie Cunningham vanished on 15th March, then twenty-five-year-old Denise Oliverson disappeared while riding her bicycle in Grand Junction on 6th April. Melanie Cooley of Nederland, Colorado, vanished on 15th April, and her body was found two weeks later. Unlike the other victims, she was fully clothed but her jeans had been pulled down, showing that sex had been the motive for the attack. On 30th June Shelley Robertson disappeared.

Back in Utah, in the early hours of the morning on 16th August, a police patrol car stopped Bundy's car "on suspicion". He was cruising the streets of Granger, twelve miles from Salt Lake City and tried to out-run the patrol car, but lacked the speed. Asked what he was doing driving around, Bundy said he had just come from a drive-in movie where he had seen *Towering Inferno*. The cop radioed in and found that that movie was not being shown. Inside Bundy's car were found burglary tools, an ice-pick, crowbar, a ski-mask made from a pair of tights, and a set of handcuffs. The mass-killer was thus taken to Salt Lake City jail and locked up, after having his "mugshot" taken and being fingerprinted. He was held over the weekend on the minor charge of "trying to evade a police officer". On the Tuesday, when detectives at police headquarters held their regular weekly meeting, one of the items on the agenda was the case of Theodore Robert Bundy, a law student from the university, who had been speeding in Granger and found in possession of what seemed to be burglary tools and a pair of handcuffs. It was

187

routine stuff. But the handcuffs were interesting. Salt Lake City police began linking Bundy with the attempted abduction of Carol Da Ronch.

Miss Da Ronch was able to pick Bundy out of a police line-up, but the other evidence against him seemed very circumstantial. The case came to trial on 23rd February 1976 with the prosecution having little confidence of success. Nonetheless, aided by Bundy's glib and implausible responses from the witness box, the judge did find Bundy guilty and he was sentenced to a period of one to fifteen years in jail.

The police, however, were not satisfied with the result. By now they had matched his name with the suspect list for the Seattle murders. Moreover, hairs found in Bundy's car matched those of Caryn Campbell, who had been murdered in Colorado and Melissa Smith from Salt Lake City. It was all too much of a coincidence. On 11th March 1976 Bundy was interviewed in jail by detectives about the murders. He was also examined by Dr Carlisle, a court-appointed psychiatrist, who asked Bundy what he thought about death. Bundy replied: "I don't fear death, I don't believe in life after death." The interview revealed him to be a loner with feelings of inferiority. Dr Carlisle's report noted that he was "a private person... evasive... fearful of women."

On 22nd October 1976 police served an extradition warrant on Bundy in Utah State Penitentiary. He was to be taken to Aspen to stand trial for the murder of Caryn Campbell.

In Aspen Bundy sacked his lawyers and elected to defend himself. As a consequence he was granted special privileges, including the use of a typewriter, telephone and access to a law library. He grew friendly with the judge and with the jailers, as a result of which, on 6th June, he managed to escape from the court, jumping from a two-storey window and fleeing to the mountains. He was recaptured five days later.

Preparations for the murder trial continued. So too did Bundy's plans to escape. On 30th December 1977 he climbed through a hole he had made in the ceiling of his cell, crawled along the loft, and emerged in the sheriff's living-quarters. Helping himself to a change of clothes, he walked out, drove to Denver in a stolen car, and was on a plane to Chicago before he was even missed.

Bundy had made the decision to go to Florida after some deliberation. It was far enough away, he thought, and there he could change his name and begin a new life. Thus, as "Chris Hagen", Bundy began living in Tallahassee, near the campus of Florida State University. He liked being around universities; there were always plenty of vulnerable girls with long hair. It is impossible to say how genuine Bundy's dream of establishing a new "normal" life really was. He certainly intended to get a job, but somehow it never happened. Instead he found himself drifting, stealing the things he needed: television sets, cars, credit cards. And then, on 15th January 1978, Bundy's inner demon, which had seemed almost dormant, came snarling back to life. That night he attacked four girls at the Chi Omega sorority house, frenziedly bludgeoning them in their beds as they lay asleep. He left two girls dead, two more horribly mutilated.

Lisa Levy, twenty, had been raped and strangled, her right nipple almost bitten off, and she had been bitten savagely on the right buttock, the final indignity being a hairspray can jammed up her anus. Twenty-one-year-old Margaret Bowman was also dead, having been violently strangled with her own tights. She had also received a crushing blow to the right forehead, and there was massive bleeding from her head and ears, and her neck had been broken. Although she had not been sexually violated, her knickers had been torn off with such force that a burn mark was visible on her thigh. One of the survivors, Karen Chandler, twenty-one, was found rocking back and forth, moaning, blood pouring from her mouth. Her jaw, right arm and one finger were broken. Her skull was fractured, as was the orbit of her right eye and both cheekbones. Kathy Kleiner, twenty-one, had been bludgeoned in her sleep. Her jaw was broken and she had many deep gashes on her head and face. After she had been taken to hospital several of her teeth were found in her bedclothes.

Police arriving on the scene were shocked by the ferocity of the attacks; it looked like the work of an animal. But the animal wasn't satisfied. Within minutes he struck again, just a couple of blocks away in Dunwoody Street, battering Cheryl Thomas, twenty-one, in her sleep. She was found unconscious, covered in blood, her jaw broken. The only clue was a large semen stain on her bedsheet.

On the afternoon of 7th February, Bundy struck yet again. He was now a hundred miles east of Tallahassee in a stolen white Dodge van. He accosted the daughter of a Jacksonville detective outside her school. Then, on the morning of Thursday 8th February, he was in Lake City. There he abducted twelve-year-old Kimberley Diane Leach. Her body was to be found on 7th April , thirty-two miles away in a State Park. She had been sexually violated and strangled. The forensic indications were that her throat had been cut and she had been mutilated with a knife around the genital area.

Bundy was finally recaptured on 15th February 1978 in Pensecola. He persisted in denying that he had done anything wrong and remained confident and boastful. The police taped a statement by Bundy in which he refused to admit to the Chi Omega killings but hinted, "The evidence is there. Keep digging."

In his long, rambling statement, he gave clues to his condition. He said: "Years ago I saw a girl on a bicycle. I saw her and I knew I had to have her. I had to possess her." It was then, Bundy said, that what he called his "problem" began. Later in the interview he remarked: "Sometimes I feel like a vampire."

The police were now determined to build an airtight case against the killer. This time they would not let him escape. Realizing the importance of those bite-marks on Lisa Levy's buttocks, they had them photographed and took a dental impression of Bundy's teeth. That impression of the killer's teeth was one of the many bizarre pieces of evidence that would finally convict him.

Prior to his trial Bundy was once again examined by a psychiatrist. In his report the psychiatrist observed: "In a certain sense Mr Bundy is the producer of a play which attempts to show that authority can be manipulated. Mr Bundy does not have the capacity to recognize the price for this 'thriller' might be his own life."

On 29th June 1979 Bundy went on trial in Miami, a trial which was televised live across the nation. Now the evil killer was on stage; it was everything he had ever wanted. He sacked his counsel and announced that he would be defending himself. Bundy himself could face his surviving victims from the Chi Omega sorority house in court and cross-examine them, making them relive their ordeal. And this is precisely what he did. Some 40 million viewers found the trial compulsive viewing.

The case went to the jury on the afternoon of 24th July, at 2.57 p.m. At 9 p.m. the jury returned to announce their verdict of guilty. It was then that the killer's bravado disappeared. Shaking and trembling, Bundy told the judge: "I will tell the court that I am not really able to accept the verdict."

Bundy was sentenced to death in the electric chair and transported to Raiford Penitentiary, Florida, where he was placed on Death Row. He left there once, in 7th January 1980, to travel to Orlando where he was to stand trial for the murder of Kimberley Leach. There he again acted as his own counsel. There too he was sentenced to death.

On 24th January 1989 Bundy finally went to the electric chair. He was aged forty-two. He declined the traditional last meal and went to his death bearing a look of controlled anger.

What have we learned from these brief biographies of some American sex killers? The selection is by no means exhaustive, but it is representative, and what does emerge is that the sexual serial killer is extremely dangerous – the US Justice Department estimates that serial killers claim five thousand victims in America every year.

The soiled and stained characters whose stories are related here do not represent the USA of our fantasies, the paradise of a "land of the free". They are not the American Dream but the American Nightmare.

Chapter Eight
THE APPLIANCE OF SCIENCE
TESSNOW - PITCHFORK - DUFFY

The growth of the sex crime has been matched by ever more sophisticated and innovative means to combat it. Forensic science has advanced by leaps and bounds since the turn of the century and so too have many other techniques to assist detection: photo-fits, information processing and psychological profiling. Here we look at three ground-breaking cases which served to change the way that the sex criminal is sought and caught.

Ludwig Tessnow was an itinerant German carpenter who was implicated in the murder of two girls, Hannelore Heidemann and Else Langemier, who disappeared from their village of Lechtingen, outside Osnabrück. Their corpses were found on the evening of 9th September 1898 in an area of woodland. They had been raped and their bodies hacked to pieces. Tessnow was pulled in by the local police, who asked him about his movements and also asked him to explain the large red stain that they found on his work clothes. Tessnow denied ever seeing the children and said that the marks on his clothes were wood stains. With no other evidence against him, the police eventually let Tessnow go and the murder remained unsolved.

On 1st July 1901 an almost identical crime occurred on the Baltic island of Rügen. This time, however, it involved two little boys. Hermann Stubbe, eight, and his six-year-old brother, Peter, had failed to return home for supper and a search was quickly organized. The boys' mutilated bodies were found the following day. Their arms and legs had been hacked off and their organs scattered through the woods. Tessnow had again been seen in the neighbourhood – a witness had even seen him talking to the children before their disappearance – and he was arrested on suspicion of murder.

Again he declared that the stains on his clothes were from wood, though he admitted that there might be spots of cattle blood. This time, however, the police were in a position to check his claim. A German chemist named Paul Uhlenhuth had recently devised a reliable technique for identifying blood, and distinguishing human blood from that of animals. A bundle of the carpenter's clothes were sent off to him to be analysed. Uhlenhuth demonstrated that there were definite traces of human blood on Tessnow's clothing.

Confronted with this evidence Ludwig Tessnow was bound over for trial. He was found guilty of the double murder and sentenced to death. He was executed at Griefswald Prison in 1904.

Uhlenhuth's work, though now superseded by more advanced methods of analysis, crossed a major hurdle in forensic science.

The intrinsic interest of the case of **Colin Pitchfork** lies not in his murders – of two schoolgirls – but in the manner of his detection and arrest. The "Enderby Murders" became an international text-book case which made legal and medical history, and marks as great a turning-point in the fight against crime as did the discovery of fingerprinting.

In November 1983 fifteen-year-old Lynda Mann set out from her home, in Narborough near Leicester, to visit a friend in the nearby village of Enderby, taking a short-cut through a footpath known as Black Pad. She never arrived at her destination, and the following morning her body was found lying near the footpath. She had been strangled with her own scarf and raped. A lengthy police investigation led nowhere, but as is routine in these cases, the rapist's semen stains were preserved.

Three years later, in July 1986, the killer struck again. This time the victim was Dawn Ashworth, another fifteen-year-old schoolgirl who lived in Enderby. She failed to return home from visiting a friend. Her semi-naked body was discovered three days later, hidden near another lonely footpath, less than a mile from where Lynda Mann's body had been found. It bore horrific marks of violence. Dawn had been battered to death and brutally raped. There were multiple injuries to her head, face and genitals.

Police were now certain that the killer responsible for the Enderby murders was a local man. Obviously the lust-crazed killer was concentrating on his neighbours, picking off their daughters like pigeons. He could have been anybody, and when a seventeen-year-old youth was seen loitering near the murder site and looking extremely suspicious he was arrested and charged with the murder of Dawn Ashworth. The huge police murder investigation team heaved a sigh of relief, thinking their task was over.

However, the senior officer in charge of the inquiry was not satisfied, and was aware that at nearby Leicester University a unique scientific breakthrough had been made. Dr Alec Jeffreys, a biologist working there, had stumbled across a method of "genetic fingerprinting". The police decided to ask Dr Jeffreys to check their suspect's DNA code against the semen stains from the victim.

Dr Alec Jeffreys had devised the new technique in September 1984. The discovery came about almost by accident, though it could not have happened without the pioneering work that had gone before. Jeffreys had been investigating the evolution of human genetic make-up, in particular the genetic material called deoxyribonucleic acid – DNA – and found that there were variances in the DNA from each human sample. In September 1984 he discovered that by using an enzyme to fragment the DNA molecule and then separating these fragments by size using an electric field across a membrane, a unique and distinctive pattern would be formed. If the DNA was made radioactive this pattern could be detected, and would show itself almost like a barcode. The bars were the same for any bodily material from the same person. From another person, however, the bars were noticeably different. The DNA barcode was thus a unique autograph. The chances of two people having the same code were virtually nil.

The police first made use of Dr Jeffreys's technique in November 1987. In June of that year a burglar broke into a house in Avonmouth, Bristol, and raped a 45-year-old disabled woman, stealing some of her jewellery in the process. Later a man named Robert Melias was arrested for burglary, and the rape victim picked him out on an identity parade. Semen stains from the clothing of the raped woman were subjected to Dr Jeffreys's "bar-code" test, and matched exactly with the print from a blood sample taken from the suspect. On 13th November 1987 Melias was sentenced to eight years for rape and five years for robbery. The DNA fingerprint had secured its first conviction.

However, the next use police made of it had even more interesting implications. When the police suspect in the Enderby murders had his genetic fingerprint taken the bar-code obtained from his blood samples were in a completely different order to those found in the semen of the rapist. The youth could not have been the killer-rapist and he was thus released. Dr Jeffreys's test was now seen not only as a useful tool to secure a conviction it was also an invaluable means of establishing innocence. But for science the innocent young man would probably have been convicted and languished in a prison cell for years.

For the police the result was bad news. It meant that the real killer was still on the loose and the inquiry which had been brought to a halt by the arrest of a suspect had to be reopened.

The senior officer in charge of the Enderby murders inquiry now made a brave decision. Certain that the killer was a local man living in the small area around Narborough and Enderby – including the village of Little Thorpe – he decided to have the police visit all the young men in this area and request they give blood samples. Every man in the right age bracket was written to and consent obtained. It was a massive task involving more than 5000 analyses. The result, however, was disappointing. All the men had been tested, but the killer was not among them.

Then came the first break in the case. A bakery-worker having a drink in a Leicester pub boasted of having "helped out" a friend by offering the police his blood sample in place of that of his friend, who lived in the village of Little Thorpe. The conversation was reported to the police and a twenty-three-year-old man was quickly picked up and questioned. He admitted having acted as a "stand-in" for his friend and fellow bakery-worker, Colin Pitchfork, twenty-seven, who lived at Little Thorpe.

A quick search of police records revealed that Pitchfork had two convictions for indecent exposure before he married in 1981 at the age of twenty-one.

It transpired that when the police made their request for blood samples Pitchfork panicked and begged several of his workmates to impersonate him, explaining that with his record for "flashing" he would be an obvious suspect, and was afraid that the police would "fit him up". He offered one man £200 and another £500 and finally persuaded the second man to forge his signature and learn details of his family by heart. The deception was successful. The man, who lived in Leicester, offered a blood sample and identified himself as Colin Pitchfork.

Pitchfork was now arrested and a blood sample taken from him. It was rushed to Dr Jeffreys's lab, where his "barcode" proved to be identical with that of the DNA samples from the rapist-killer. Faced with this proof, Pitchfork admitted both murders.

He said on both occasions he had been out looking for a girl to whom he could expose himself, and on both occasions the realization that the girl was alone and there were no witnesses led to rape and murder. In the case of Lynda Mann he had taken his wife to night-school and committed the rape-murder before picking her up again.

On 27th January 1987 Pitchfork appeared in the dock at Leicester Crown Court, where he pleaded guilty to both murders and admitted two additional indecent assaults. Mr Brian Escott-Cox QC, prosecuting, told the court that of more than five thousand people invited to take the test, only two did not come forward. One had a genuine reason, and the other had been Pitchfork. Of the stand-in deception he said, "It worked. The other man went in and carried it off on 22nd January last year."

Sentencing Pitchfork to life for both murders, with ten years concurrently for the rapes, three years for the indecent assaults and three years for conspiracy to pervert the course of justice, Mr Justice Otton said that if it had not been for genetic fingerprinting Pitchfork might still be at large. He said of the test, "In this case it not only led to the apprehension of the correct murderer, but also ensured that suspicion was removed from an innocent man." Pitchfork's "stand-in" was given an eighteen-month suspended sentence.

The American author Joseph Wambaugh came to Britain to write a book about the Pitchfork case, amazed that no English writer had seen the potential of genetic fingerprinting. His best-selling book *The Blooding* (an obvious reference to the mass blood-testing of the males of Enderby) is a gripping account of the Pitchfork case, and both tribute and testimony to a piece of scientific history.

The first American conviction by means of the DNA fingerprint took place in November 1987, when a brutal rapist and robber in Florida was trapped by the semen he had left in one of his victims. Only one of his victims could pick him out on an identity parade, and proving the suspect's guilt was not going to be easy.

The prosecutor had read about the Pitchfork case, and knew that the Lifecodes Laboratory of New York were offering the new DNA technology under licence. The suspect's blood was of a group belonging to 30 per cent of all American males, so the DNA fingerprinting seemed the only conclusive way of proving the man's guilt. The lab tested the semen, together with a blood sample from the accused. The result was that both were identical and had come from the same man.

In September 1987 Tommie Lee Andrews, twenty-four, was found guilty and jailed for twenty-two years – the first man in the USA to be convicted by the genetic fingerprint. Tried on further rape charges with additional DNA evidence being submitted, Andrews received further jail terms totalling over a hundred years.

There can be no doubt that the development of DNA fingerprinting is one of the most significant steps in the fight against crime. But it is still not a total solution. Forensic evidence, however detailed, can only help investigators to a certain degree. Often other information is needed, other clues are required. The crime fighter has also got to know the mind of his criminal.

A recent innovation in helping to provide investigators with this additional information is the technique known as psychological profiling. This was pioneered in the United States, notably in the FBI's National Centre for the Analysis of Violent Crime, where under the leadership of John Douglas it has been developed to the state of a fine art. The technique has been used in England too, however, notably in the case of **John Duffy**, the so-called "Railway Murderer" in 1988. It was perhaps the first application of psychological profiling in Britain.

For the general public the Duffy case began with the disappearance of "Television Bride" Anne Lock, twenty-nine, a secretary at London Weekend Television who vanished on Sunday 18th May 1986 after leaving the TV studios on the South Bank to catch a train home.

She lived with her husband Laurence, twenty-six, a wealthy wholesale butcher, in a luxury home in Brookmans Park, a picturesque Hertfordshire village. On Sunday evening Anne Locke's bicycle was found at the railway station where she parked it – she would normally have cycled home – but the woman herself was nowhere to be seen.

Large numbers of police searched the surrounding area, and found her diary and address book half a mile apart, both shredded. Police frogmen searched local lakes. But they had no luck in finding the missing woman. It wasn't until some two months later, on 21st July 1986, that the body of Anne Lock was found. It was discovered lying in thick undergrowth at the side of a railway embankment by two railway workers who literally stumbled over the corpse. Forensic examination revealed the body had been lying there for about ten weeks. A police spokesman said: "The body was very carefully hidden. It's clear that somebody put it in there and packaged it in the weeds and shrubbery."

Police stated that Anne Lock had been gagged, with her hands tied behind her back. Cause of death was suffocation. An attempt had been made to set fire to the corpse, and the badly decomposed remains could only be identified from dental records.

Detective Chief Superintendent Vincent McFadden, now in charge of the case, answered criticism that the body should have been found sooner. He said: "Officers made a tremendous effort to find her body and searched over an enormous area, but the resources were limited." He then revealed that Anne Lock's murder was not the beginning of the case, but another in a series of rapes and murders by that most dangerous of criminals, the sexual serial murderer. Definite links had been established between the murder of Anne Lock and that of two girls in Surrey and East London in the previous eleven months. That feature – not revealed at the time – was a distinctive ligature used by the killer to throttle his victims. It was the killer's trademark – that and the fact that he always killed near railway lines. And there was one other distinctive clue. The killer had a minority blood group. It was this that tied him in with earlier rapes, dating back to 1982.

The killer had evidently begun as half of a rapist duo. Then, in 1984, he had struck out on his own, his first solo attack taking place in November 1984 near Barnes Common in south-west London. The next attack was in February 1985 at Hadley Wood station, two stops away from where Anne Lock met her killer. The last was in August 1985 next to the line at West Hampstead station, North London. Then the rapist turned to murder.

Alison Day, nineteen, was murdered in December 1985 after getting off a train at Hackney Wick station, East London. She was seized from behind and forced to walk into a rat-infested garage complex by the river Lea. She was raped, then killed and her body dumped into the river.

His second victim, Maartje Tamboezer, fifteen, the pretty blonde daughter of a Dutch oil executive living in Britain, was raped and battered to death in woods near the railway line at Horsley in April 1986. She was forced to dismount from her bicycle by a length of cord strung across the path, and made to push her bike 150 yards across a field to the woods where she was ambushed. She too had been bound and gagged, and a crude attempt had been made to burn her body.

All the rapes followed similar patterns, and all the rapes and murders had been linked by forensic evidence and the unique method used to kill the victim. The links between the crimes were emphasized by Detective Chief Inspector McFadden. He said, "In all three killings there has been a tying of the hands and the use of a knife and all took place on a footpath near a railway line." All details of sex attacks throughout the Home Counties were being fed into the National Crime Computer to see if there were any similar cases that fitted the same pattern.

One lucky girl had a narrow escape from the killer. She was ambushed at knife-point and sexually assaulted, but was saved by her mother, who called her name loudly. The attacker panicked and fled. From this encounter police were able to establish a description of the wanted man. Detectives said he was white, in his mid-twenties, with fair hair and an athletic build. Four police forces were now engaged in the biggest police operation in Britain since the hunt for the Yorkshire Ripper.

The police had a description of the killer, they knew his blood group, they had worked out his *modus operandi* and they had recruited the best minds – and the best computers – to find their man. And still they failed.

The killer was on the list of suspects, of course. But that list was nearly five thousand names long. Eventually it was whittled down to just 1,999 suspects – mostly made up of sex-offenders who shared the same minority blood group – but that was still an unmanageable number, especially when the real killer, though still on the list, was rated as only a "fourth-division suspect."

On 17th July 1986 Detective Constables Andrew Kelly and Peter Code of the Metropolitan Police interviewed John Duffy, a former British Rail carpenter. Duffy asked for his solicitor to be present, and this was agreed. But it was a routine affair. Duffy was only on the suspect list because he had been earlier convicted of an attack on his wife and her lover, there was nothing else to link him to the crimes. Both detectives recognized his likeness to the official identikit picture of the killer, and were not satisfied with his evasive answers. And yet he was allowed to go. He still did not seem a likely killer.

The months went by, during which time Duffy roamed about London unhindered. On 21st October he raped a fifteen-year-old Watford schoolgirl. But he was still not arrested.

It was then that a real-life "Sherlock Holmes" made his important contribution to the investigation. Scotland Yard called in a Surrey University professor to help detectives by producing a "profile" of the killer-rapist. Professor David Canter was a leading psychologist, and he sat quietly in an office going over witnesses' statements and seemingly banal and unimportant details to produce his profile. Subsequently the profile was matched on the computer with the 1,999 suspects on file. The computer threw up just one name: John Francis Duffy.

The profile later proved to be accurate on thirteen out of seventeen points, with the professor even predicting the district in which the killer lived.

John Duffy was put under surveillance. Then on 23rd November 1986 he was arrested and his trail of terror came to an end.

A search of his Kilburn home produced ample evidence of his guilt. Officers found various martial arts equipment, pornographic and violent videos and magazines, and a "rape kit" which included a bunch of more than thirty keys. Duffy claimed he could not remember what the keys were for, but the police were convinced that many of the keys had belonged to his victims, women too frightened to report that they had been raped, and that Duffy kept the keys as "trophies". Police also found a well-read copy of the *Anarchist's Cookbook* in his flat, which lists ways to incapacitate, silence, and if necessary kill.

Duffy was the most intractable prisoner detectives had ever had to interview. He fixed his questioners with a "laser-beam stare" and was never intimidated, and never spoke. He was to plead not guilty to all the murder and rape charges, simply because he would gain additional pleasure from watching his victims suffer as they testified in the witness box. They would be raped all over again, in open court.

The trial of John Francis Duffy, thirty, began at the Old Bailey on Monday 11th January 1988 before Mr Justice Farquharson.

Duffy was tried for three murders and seven rapes, all of which took place near railway lines between June 1982 and October 1986.

On 25th February 1988 the jury found Duffy guilty of two rapes, those of the fourteen-year-old and sixteen-year-old girls. The older victim, now nineteen, was in court to see him convicted. Duffy stared blankly ahead as the verdict was announced, then he walked down to the cells with his hands in his pockets.

The jury then retired again to consider the additional rape and murder charges. Earlier the judge had instructed the jury to find Duffy not guilty of the murder of Anne Lock. There was a complete lack of forensic evidence to link him to the crime. For these charges too they returned a verdict of guilty.

Duffy was finally sentenced on 26th February 1988, receiving seven life sentences for two murders and five rapes. The thirty-year-old killer stood impassive in the dock as the judge told him, "The murders of Alison Day and Maartje Tamboezer are as appalling as anything I have come across. The wickedness and beastliness of the murders committed on those two very young girls hardly bears description. Quite apart from cutting short those two young lives, you have blighted the lives of all the families of these girls. You are obviously little more than a predatory animal." The judge recommended that he should serve at least thirty years, but added, "The horrific nature of your crimes means that thirty years is not necessarily the total you will serve. It may well be more. Take him down."

Duffy displayed no emotion – certainly no remorse – throughout the six-week trial, not even when the women he had raped recounted their ordeals, at times in tears. In his crimes he had shown extreme cunning and intelligence, using his detailed knowledge of railway timetables in the South-East to stalk his victims, prowling deserted railway stations and preying on lone young women. Now he showed nothing but contempt.

Detective Superintendent John Hurst, deputy head of Surrey CID, who interviewed Duffy after his arrest, said, "In my twenty-two years' experience with crime, I have never found a man so calculating and cunning. He is a cold-blooded calculating killer with a razor-sharp mind. He is very intelligent and alert. He gave me the impression of being able to react to any type of situation in which he found himself." Although the Anne Lock case was officially unsolved, Hurst said, "Duffy did kill Anne Lock. We are certain he killed her. He knows it and we know it. We couldn't provide the forensic evidence to convict, but the similarities between this murder and the other two are just so startling. We decided to charge him with only the cases where the evidence was strongest, although we are sure he carried out many other attacks. He got his bizarre kicks from the struggles and protests of his victims. We know he pleaded not guilty just so that some of them would have to suffer in the witness-box. His final victim, the fourteen-year-old schoolgirl, told me that he locked his eyes on her as she was giving evidence. The stare broke her up and she couldn't bear to go on. Every time he looked at her she broke out in a cold sweat. She was incredibly brave to carry on." Mr Hurst added, "I spent many hours with Duffy. His laser-beam stare frightened me, and I dread to think what it did to those poor women. Not once did he confess to the rapes or killings, but he told me how he would be quite happy to spend thirty years in jail."

It is difficult to build up a picture of Duffy as a human being. He refused to see a psychiatrist and never spoke during his trial. Detective Chief Superintendent McFadden described Duffy as being one of the worst villains he had ever encountered. Even to a policeman, Duffy was exceptional. It is at once frightening and reassuring that he could be identified so easily and so precisely by a university professor.

Canter's technique and the psychological profiling methods of the FBI are now used routinely by police forces all over the world.

Chapter Nine
PETER SUTCLIFFE
THE YORKSHIRE RIPPER

If Jack the Ripper was operating today, given the advances in forensic science – fingerprinting, blood-grouping, the "genetic fingerprinting" – and other modern police methods of communication, including the use of computers and the use of psychological profiling, would he have been caught? In the light of the Yorkshire Ripper case the answer must be no. Peter Sutcliffe carried out a far worse reign of terror over a period of five and a half years – during which time he murdered thirteen women and attempted to murder seven others. The police got nowhere. He was eventually caught by pure accident. One might say that it was despite the police work rather than because of it.

Born in Bingley, Yorkshire, on 2nd June 1946, Peter William Sutcliffe was a disappointing son for his domineering father, John. His mother, Kathleen, a pretty woman and a staunch Catholic, took to him no better. The first of five children, he was weak and sickly. Bullied at school, he became secretive and solitary, often playing truant, hiding for hours in the loft.

Leaving school at fifteen, Peter became an apprentice fitter and at eighteen took up body-building in an attempt to fit in with the Yorkshire macho image of a man. In 1964 he got a labouring job at Bingley Cemetery, and there he began to display his macabre sense of humour. He desecrated corpses, played practical jokes with skulls, and stole rings from the fingers of the dead, even to the extent of snipping off the fingers if the rings proved hard to remove. Ironically, however, when he was sacked from his grave-digging job it wasn't because of his acts of desecration: it was for bad time-keeping.

In 1967, aged twenty-one, Sutcliffe met and began to court Sonia Szurma, a Czech girl who came from a rather better background than he and had realistic expectations of qualifying as a schoolteacher. The courtship was to last seven stormy years. Sonia must have had her doubts about Peter as a future husband because at one point she went out with somebody else. When Sutcliffe found out he was furious. He went with a Bradford prostitute to "settle the score", as he put it later. The prostitute cheated him out of £5, and when he tackled her in a pub about it, days later, she laughed in his face. He felt acutely humiliated. He later claimed that this incident gave rise to his hatred of whores.

In 1969 Sutcliffe carried out his first known attack – a rehearsal for murder. While out driving with his best drinking buddy, Trevor Birdsall, Sutcliffe stopped the car in Manningham and disappeared for a few minutes. He came back hurrying, and told Trevor that he had just hit a prostitute over the head with a brick-filled sock. Both were questioned by police about the assault, but since the victim declined to press charges, they were simply cautioned and let go.

On 29 September 1969 Peter Sutcliffe was arrested for hiding behind a hedge clutching a hammer. His car had been parked nearby with its engine running. He appeared in court charged with "going equipped for theft" and was fined £25. Incredibly, this early clue to the identity of the Yorkshire Ripper was never picked up. But it was just one clue among many that was overlooked.

On 10th August 1974 Peter and Sonia were finally married. Peter also got his HGV driving licence and landed a well-paid job as a long-distance lorry-driver. The pair lived with Sonia's parents till 1977, by which time they had saved up a deposit for their own house at Garden Lane, Heaton in Bradford.

The first murderous attack seems to have been in Keighley on 5th July 1975 when a young woman was assaulted by a man wielding a hammer. Six weeks later, on 15th August, another woman was struck from behind in a similar manner. She was a middle-aged office cleaner whom, earlier that evening, Sutcliffe had accused of being a prostitute. It is possible that Sutcliffe's friend, Trevor Birdsall, witnessed the attack, though he clearly did not realize the seriousness of it.

Both these victims survived. The next would not be so lucky. Wilma McCann, a twenty-eight-year-old mother of four who had taken up prostitution to help pay the rent, was found dead on a Leeds playing-field on 30th October 1975. The Ripper murders had begun.

The pathologist Professor Gee carried out the post-mortem examination on Mrs McCann. He found no traces of semen in her vagina but got a positive reaction from the back of her trousers and panties. The killer had obviously ejaculated during the act of stabbing.

Detective Superintendent Dennis Hoban, head of Leeds CID, was put in charge of the case. He had an impressive record, having solved more than fifty murders, and was a highly experienced officer who rarely made mistakes. But this time he acted rashly. He issued an internal memo to all divisions saying: "The motive appears to be a hatred of prostitutes." It was a wild assumption which didn't really have much basis in fact. As it turned out, however, this was but one of many false assumptions that the police would make before

Sutcliffe was caught.

The next to die was Emily Monica Jackson, forty-two, from Morley. Last seen alive on Tuesday 20th January 1976, she was found dead the following morning in the red-light district of Chapeltown, Leeds. She was lying face down with a coat thrown over her. Her legs had been spread apart and a piece of wood had been forced partly into her vagina. Her breasts were exposed and she had been killed with two hammer blows to the head. She had been stabbed some fifty times in the chest and stomach. Many of the wounds had been inflicted with a large Philips screwdriver, which left a distinctive star-shaped imprint. The killer had also stamped on her body, leaving the imprint of a size 7 Dunlop boot on her thigh.

Superintendent Hoban told the press, "There are links between this murder and that of Wilma McCann. Both women were prostitutes. In both cases the obvious deep-seated hatred of prostitutes manifested itself in the many stab wounds."

A coloured prostitute was the next victim. She picked up a client in Roundhay, Leeds, on 9th May 1976. The man promptly hit her over the head with a hammer. Half-conscious, she saw her attacker masturbating close by. He pushed £5 into her hand, told her not to tell the police, then drove off. Her wounds required fifty-two stitches, but the accurate description she gave of her attacker to the police was dismissed because she had been classified as educationally sub-normal.

Months passed with police working furiously on the case. The dossier of information grew daily. Hundreds of people were interviewed, but where was the Ripper? Why had the attacks stopped? The year came to an end and fear on the streets lessened. Detectives wondered why the killings had stopped. What was the perpetrator doing during the last eight months? They were to find out in horrific fashion when in February 1977 the Ripper struck again.

Irene Richardson, twenty-eight, was found dead in Soldier's Field, Roundhay, Leeds, by a jogger at 7.50 a.m. on Sunday 6th February 1977. She was lying face down, covered in blood. Her coat had been draped over her body to hide the mutilations. She had suffered three blows to the head with a ball-pein hammer, there were stab wounds to her neck and throat and three ferocious slash wounds in the stomach which had caused her intestines to spill out. Curiously, her boots had been placed neatly between her thighs. The only clue to her killer was a tyre mark nearby.

Victim Patricia "Tina" Atkinson, thirty-three, was another prostitute. She had the dubious distinction of becoming the only Ripper victim to be killed indoors. In her case, she was murdered in her own flat in Bradford. She was found dead on 24th April 1977, killed by four blows to the head and six chisel wounds in the abdomen. Her bra had been pushed up to expose her breasts and the killer had left the imprint of a size 7 Dunlop boot on her bedsheet as well as a bloody handprint on her thigh.

On 26th June 1977 sixteen-year-old Jayne Michelle MacDonald went for a night out and vanished. Her body was found at 9.45 next morning, lying in an adventure playground close to Chapeltown Road, Leeds. She lay face down with her bra pushed up exposing her breasts. She too had been hit repeatedly over the head and suffered stab wounds to the chest and back.

The police now told the press, "An innocent young woman has been slaughtered." This was a horrifying thing to say. What did they mean? Were the earlier Ripper victims somehow "guilty"?

Assistant Chief Constable George Oldfield was placed in overall command of the Ripper inquiry.

By now the Ripper's *modus operandi* was plain. He first hit his victims over the head then dragged them to the murder site. He always stabbed his victims after removing or lifting clothing, never through clothing. He liked to expose the breasts. Generally he used an engineer's ball-pein hammer and a Philips screwdriver but he also varied his instrument of killing, such as using a knife instead of a screwdriver, a rock instead of a hammer.

Since five of the victims had been attacked in Leeds and one in Bradford, the evidence pointed to a local man as being the killer. The tenth attack came on the night of Saturday 9th July 1977, in Bradford, when a 42-year-old woman was hit on the head with a hammer and stabbed four times in the chest and abdomen. This time, however, the killer was disturbed and fled before he could finish her off. She was found at 8.30 the following morning, barely alive. There was a long slash from her breasts down to her navel.

After delicate surgery, she slowly recovered and was able to tell police that her attacker had been a white man of about thirty-six, with shoulder-length hair. She said he drove a white Cortina. This description, however, was misleading. The unfortunate woman had clearly been confused by her ordeal.

The Ripper's tally was now five dead, three injured.

Intense police activity in the red-light areas of Leeds and Bradford forced Sutcliffe to cross the Pennines to seek his next victim. Jean Jordan, alias Royle, was a twenty-year-old Manchester prostitute with two children. She was killed on the night of 1st October 1977 and her body lay undetected for a week in the Southern Cross Cemetery in Moss Side. The cause of her death was established as being eleven blows to the head, eighteen diagonal stab wounds to the back and chest, with ten horizontal wounds to the abdomen, each deep enough to reach the spine.

This murder presented the police with their first major clue. The killer had paid Jean Jordan for her personal attention with a brand-new five-pound note, serial number AW 51 121565. It was one of a consecutive series issued to only one bank, and distributed as wages to only 5,943 people: Sutcliffe was one of them. He was interviewed twice about the note; once on 2nd November and again six days later. However, the coincidence of his being one of the employees paid with notes in the suspect series, and his prior arrest for being in possession of a hammer and being charged with going equipped for theft, was not recognized.

Sutcliffe could hardly believe his luck. For weeks he had been panicking about that fiver. Seven or eight days after Jordan's murder, and prior to her body being found, he had returned to where he had killed her to try and find the note. But he failed to do so. In a frenzy of frustration he stripped her corpse and slashed at it. As Sutcliffe's Stanley knife cut through her belly, the stench as her stomach blew open made him vomit. He tried to cut off her head as a means of disguising that she was a Ripper victim. To make doubly sure, he then tried to burn her on a bonfire, which is where the owner of an allotment on an adjacent site discovered her some days later.

Sutcliffe now returned to his old stalking-ground in Leeds. On Wednesday 14th December 1977 he attacked a mother of two. She survived after Sutcliffe was disturbed, but suffered a blow to the head and heard her attacker shriek, "You dirty prostitute!" She had spoken with her would-be killer and was able to give police a description. She said he had called himself "Dave", and was a white man aged between 25 and 28, and had a "Jason King" moustache. This was a crucial clue, since Sutcliffe did indeed wear the distinctive moustache and beard made popular by a character in a TV series.

The first month of the new year saw two murders within the space of ten days. Yvonne Ann Pearson, twenty-two, was murdered on the night of Saturday 21st January 1978. Her body was been hidden under an abandoned sofa on derelict land off Lumb Lane, Bradford. Stuffing from the sofa was found in her mouth. She was not discovered until 26th March and it was obvious that once again the killer had gone back to commit further attacks on the corpse, and more importantly to ensure that it would be found. Sutcliffe, evidently obsessed with his press coverage, must have been feeling neglected, because a copy of the *Daily Mirror* dated a month after her murder had been carefully placed under one of her arms. Maggots in the original wounds, but not in the fresh wounds, also pointed to the Ripper's return. She had been hit on the head with a lump hammer. Professor Gee thought it had been "something like a large stone", and at first the police did not think this was a genuine Ripper killing. She had been jumped on with such force that her ribs had cracked. Once again, however, her bra had been pushed up, exposing the breasts.

On Tuesday 31st January, ten days after the killing of Miss Pearson, the body of eighteen-year-old Helen Rytka, an Anglo-Caribbean, was found under a railway viaduct in Huddersfield. She had been hammered over the head and had several stab wounds to her abdomen. Her bra was pushed up. She was the only victim with whom the killer had sex.

The killings were now making international news, and locally the mood was close to panic. After Helen Rytka's murder, the *Yorkshire Post* offered a large reward for the apprehension of the Ripper.

On 8th March 1978 Assistant Chief Constable George Oldfield received the first of three letters posted from Sunderland which were signed "Jack the Ripper." He took them seriously. His determination was so intense it tilted the investigation in the wrong direction.

A new victim was found in the early morning of Wednesday 17th May 1978. Vera Evelyn Millward, forty, alias Brown or Barton, and the mother of seven children, was found murdered in the car park behind Manchester's Royal Infirmary. She had been hit on the head three times with a hammer and had been stabbed so viciously that her intestines spilled out. She had also been stabbed in the right eye. Her shoes had been placed neatly on her body, and a tyre print was found close by.

In June 1978 the West Yorkshire police circulated a confidential 18-page report entitled *Murders and Assaults upon Women in The North Of England* to other police forces. It detailed sixteen attacks believed to be the work of the same man, and outlined his methods. One point which was stressed was that the killer might have a fetish about footwear. On 13th August 1978 Sutcliffe was interviewed again. Police had seen his car so often in the red-light districts that he was questioned, but still not suspected. Towards the end of November that year Sutcliffe was apprehended yet again and the tyres of his car were checked to see if they matched the tracks left at the scene of Irene Richardson's murder, but by this time the incriminating tyres had long since been replaced. Sutcliffe was not detained.

Almost a year went by before the next killing; a year in which many police officers privately hoped that the Ripper had disappeared or committed suicide. At 6.30 on the morning of 5th April 1979, however, the body of yet another victim proved that the police would have no such luck. Josephine Anne Whitaker, a nineteen-year-old building-society worker, was found dead at Savile Park in Halifax. She had been hit over the head and dragged to the killing-site, where twenty-five stab wounds to her breasts, stomach and vagina had been inflicted. Machine oil was found in her wounds, together with the familiar size 7 boot prints. One of her shoes had been placed carefully between her thighs.

George Oldfield received two more letters from the "Ripper", and forensic tests on the saliva used to lick the envelopes showed that the writer had the rare blood group B, which is found in only 6 per cent of the population. A case from the files, dating back to 23rd November 1975 when a woman had been murdered and sodomized, was now pulled up. Could this have been the Ripper's work too? Many hours were spent investigating the possibility, but it was time wasted. It was just another blind alley. Later it was discovered that the "Ripper" letters had been a hoax.

The frustration within the Ripper Squad must have been pushing some members to breaking-point. Assistant Chief Constable George Oldfield's life had been taken over by the inquiry. He was giving it everything but was still getting nowhere. He has been criticized for letting the inquiry become an obsession with him, but what good detective doesn't become obsessed with the capture of a vicious killer he is hunting, knowing that until an arrest is made, he is free to murder again and again? Also, George Oldfield had taken over a badly initiated inquiry. The processing of information was being carried out by out-moded methods. Statements and card indexes were piling up at murder headquarters – computers were not made available – and there was just too much information for anyone to make sense of. But, as if this was not bad enough, the worst was yet to come.

On 17th June 1979 George Oldfield received the infamous hoax tape. He played it to the press, convinced that it was genuine. To George Oldfield, the fake tape was some kind of holy grail. He believed in it, every word.

Gone was the scepticism and detachment vital to every detective. He played the tape over and over, telling the press, "It's a personal thing between me and him."

Because the man on the tape had a distinctly Geordie accent, the police now concentrated on suspects with Geordie accents. Sutcliffe had been interviewed by the Ripper police four times: on 2nd November 1977 about the £5 note; on 8th November as a cross-check; on 13th August 1978 because his car had been spotted in the red-light areas of Bradford and Leeds; on 23rd November 1978 when his car tyres were checked. But now police dismissed him as a likely suspect because he spoke with a high-pitched Yorkshire accent.

On 29th July 1979 Detective Constable Laptew interviewed Sutcliffe at his home about his car having been seen in Lumb Lane for the thirty-sixth time in a month. Something about Sutcliffe aroused the detective's suspicions and he advised his superiors that the man should be seen urgently, as a prime suspect. Alas, his advice was not acted upon.

On 13th August 1979 George Oldfield suffered a heart attack, and Detective Superintendent Dick Holland was placed in temporary charge of the inquiry. It was he who, when asked by reporters if he was considering calling in Scotland Yard, retorted brusquely, "Why should we? They haven't caught their own Ripper yet." (A reference to the original Jack of 1888.)

On 2nd September 1979 Barbara Leach, a twenty-year-old Leeds University student, was murdered in Bradford, she was hit on the head and stabbed eight times in the abdomen. Her body was found in an alley, hidden under an old piece of carpet, on Sunday morning, by a constable. Her bra had been pushed up.

A month after Barbara Leach's murder, Detective Chief Superintendent Jim Hobson stated in a press interview,

"The Yorkshire Ripper has now made his point, after the murder of twelve women in five years, and should give himself up."

By the end of 1979 a total of 259 officers, including 120 detectives, were working full-time on the Ripper inquiry, which had cost over £5 million and had led to 169,538 people being interviewed, 161,500 vehicles checked, 51,921 lines of inquiry followed and 23,052 house-to-house searches. Another statistic was that twenty-five children had been left motherless.

Dr Stephen Shaw, a consultant psychiatrist at Stanley Royds Hospital in Wakefield, was asked to produce a psychological profile of the Ripper. He reported, "The Ripper is an over-controlled aggressive psychopath, likely to be a young man. He is waging a crusade – a holy war – against prostitutes."

Other, less scientific aides had offered their services to the police. Dozens of psychics from all over the world had come out with their personal visions of the Ripper. Most placed him in Sunderland and most were completely wrong. However, a South London woman, Mrs Nella Jones, a psychic who had been used by Scotland Yard, was interviewed by the *Yorkshire Post* in October 1979. Her description of the Ripper was never actually published but she said that he was a long-distance lorry-driver, was called Peter, drove a cab with a name beginning with "C" on its side (Clarks Transport) and lived in Bradford at number six in a street. Sutcliffe lived at 6 Garden Lane. Mrs Jones also accurately predicted the date of the Ripper's next attack: August 1980.

Before then, however, Sutcliffe would be interviewed at least three more times by the police, and on each occasion he was allowed to walk off. On 23rd October 1979, less than a month after the murder of Barbara Leach, he was again interviewed about his car. Police had long since been recording the registration numbers of cars spotted in red-light areas. Sutcliffe explained that he had to travel through these areas to get to work. He was also questioned twice in January 1980 – on the 13th and 20th – both times being asked to clarify his earlier statements about the newly printed five-pound note. By the end of that month George Oldfield had been taken off the Ripper inquiry because of his poor health.

On 18th August 1980 the body of Marguerite Walls, a forty-seven-year-old civil servant, was found buried under grass cuttings close to a house in Farsley between Leeds and Bradford. The Ripper had changed his *modus operandi*, using a ligature to strangle her. Mr Hobson declared that this was not a Ripper murder, but he was proved wrong.

The following month, on 24th September, a 34-year-old doctor from Singapore who was studying at Leeds University was attacked by the Ripper who tried to use a garotte on her. She survived, but only because Sutcliffe was frightened off by a passing patrol car. On Bonfire Night, November 5th 1980, a sixteen-year-old girl was attacked with a hammer near her home in Huddersfield. Again the Ripper was disturbed and she survived.

Not so fortunate was Jacqueline Hill, twenty, another Leeds University student who was found dead on Monday 17th November 1980. She had been hammered over the head and stabbed repeatedly with a Philips screwdriver. She had also been stabbed in the right eye.

Less than two weeks later, Trevor Birdsall, Sutcliffe's friend, sent an anonymous letter to West Yorkshire police naming Peter Sutcliffe as the Ripper. His letter was not acted upon. On 29th November Birdsall went personally to Bradford Police H.Q. and named Sutcliffe as the Ripper. He was thanked courteously for his cooperation but again no action was taken.

The situation at the beginning of 1981 was that after five and a half years the police were no nearer to catching the Ripper. Thirteen women had been killed, another seven left with severe injuries, but the investigation had brought no results. Even the basic premise seemed to be off-key. For all the talk of a crusade against prostitutes, of the twenty women attacked, half had not been prostitutes. And yet, despite Sutcliffe seeming to be immune from capture, his reign would not last much longer.

On the evening of Friday, 2nd January 1981 Sutcliffe drove to Sheffield in his brown Rover, registration FHY 400K. His usual killing-ground was swamped by police activity, so he had decided to kill in a fresh city. He picked up a prostitute and spoke to her about his wife's miscarriages and nagging. Giving his name as "Dave", he explained he wasn't able to "go with" his wife, as she wouldn't let him near her.

Two police officers on routine patrol spotted the Rover and recognized the passenger as a familiar prostitute. When they drove up expecting to make a vice arrest a quick check on the computer with the car licence centre in Swansea revealed that the car had false number-plates. Sutcliffe was taken to the police station. Initially he was charged with theft.

Once at Dewsbury, however, he was questioned about the Ripper killings. Sheffield arresting officers had found a ball-pein hammer and a Philips screwdriver at the scene of his arrest and had flashed this information ahead to Dewsbury. Detective Sergeant Des O'Boyle, attached to the Ripper Squad, questioned Sutcliffe very closely, and his persistence eventually paid off.

"I am the Yorkshire Ripper," the killer declared. Peter Sutcliffe had been in custody for 48 hours. It would now take a further sixteen hours for him to make his full, horrific confession.

Sutcliffe also confessed to three attacks the police had not linked to the Ripper: the murder of Marguerite Walls, and the two Leeds attacks on the coloured girl and the woman doctor.

Asked how he could remember his crimes in such detail, Sutcliffe said the victims "are all in my brain, reminding me of the beast I am." He admitted that he had intended killing the Sheffield prostitute but mentioned nothing of a crusade against prostitutes.

Sutcliffe's younger brother visited him in Leeds Prison, and asked him why he had committed the murders. Peter smiled as he replied, "I were just cleaning up the streets, our kid. Just cleaning up the streets."

When police searched Sutcliffe's lorry at Clarks Transport they found inside the cab a card which was hand-lettered with the legend, "*In this truck is a man whose latent genius, if unleashed, would rock the nations, whose dynamic energy would overpower those around him. Better let him sleep.*"

Sonia Sutcliffe was informed of her husband's capture marginally ahead of the press. The rest of his family heard almost by accident. News that a man had been apprehended for the Ripper murders went out over television and radio almost immediately. Senior police officers from West Yorkshire held press conferences and appeared on television with indelicate haste and clearly implied that they had caught the killer they had been hunting for so long. One can understand why they did so. Their investigation had dragged on for so long and had been subject to so much criticism that they felt compelled to break the good news quickly. But it was a dangerous thing to do. The basic principle of law is that a man is innocent until proved guilty and that his guilt must be proved beyond reasonable doubt. The Ripper Squad's ill-timed celebrations and self-congratulations could have been seen to prejudice the possibility of any fair trial. It could have been used as a powerful tool in Sutcliffe's defence from prosecution.

At the time the editors of all the national newspapers were sent letters by the Solicitor-General expressing his concern about the publicity which had been given to the Yorkshire Ripper case following the arrest of Sutcliffe. But it was hardly the fault of newspaper editors, who simply reported the news. It was the police who were guilty of premature elation.

As it turned out, however, Sutcliffe's defence counsel did not raise the issue of the possibility of having a fair trial. Instead he said that his client was prepared to plead guilty to thirteen counts of manslaughter and seven counts of attempted manslaughter – but not murder. It was plea-bargaining, which has never been a feature of English law.

The Crown was prepared to accept this deal because all the psychiatrists were united in their opinion that Sutcliffe was a schizophrenic and thus not responsible for his actions. Had this deal been accepted, it would have meant a very short trial, with none of the fruitless labours of investigating officers being made public. The trial judge, however, would not accept it.

On 29th April 1981 the trial opened in Number One Court at the Old Bailey. Relatives of some of the victims sat at the back of the court. At a table sat the detectives in the case, and on that table were the exhibits: seven ball-pein hammers, a claw hammer, three carving knives, eight screwdrivers, a kitchen knife, a cobbler's knife and a length of rope. These were instruments of death which had claimed thirteen lives, and from which the victims' relatives could hardly avert their eyes.

Sir Michael Havers and Harry Ognall QC represented the Crown, with James Chadwin QC and Sidney Levine the defence.

At 10.30 a.m. Sonia Sutcliffe arrived in court with her mother. Sutcliffe himself appeared in the dock at eleven o'clock, a slight figure with a curious high-pitched voice. He did not look like a demon. If anything his moustache and beard gave him the appearance of a benign foreign waiter. The charges took seven minutes to read out, and Sutcliffe stuttered "not guilty" to all of them.

Sir Michael told the judge that the Crown accepted Sutcliffe's pleas, saying that he had four reports from psychiatrists who had interviewed the prisoner and who were agreed that he was not responsible for his actions. "The general consensus of the doctors is that this is a case of diminished responsibility, the illness being paranoiac schizophrenia."

The judge, Mr Justice Boreham, was not happy. He responded: "I have very grave anxieties about Sutcliffe and his pleas. I would like you to explain in far greater detail than usual any decisions that you are going to make about the acceptance of these pleas."

Something extraordinary now took place. In criminal cases, if the defence wishes to plead insanity or state of mind as a defence, then the burden of proving that illness or state of mind falls on the defence. Now, however, the prosecution took up the burden for them, and argued on behalf of the prisoner!

For two hours Sir Michael spoke, trying to persuade the judge to accept the pleas. He put forward all the arguments in support of the diminished state of Sutcliffe's mind. The death of Sutcliffe' mother "greatly distressed him." (Sutcliffe had been killing for years before his mother's death.) Then the prosecution said, "He is saying that he is under the direction of God and that he has a mission... to kill all prostitutes." (Half of Sutcliffe' victims were not prostitutes.) Sir Michael also declared that Sutcliffe had heard the voice of God speaking to him from a tombstone in Bingley cemetery.

Then the trial judge listened to the evidence of the psychiatrists and their tales of Sutcliffe's "mission to kill", and he remarked: "The matter that troubles me is that all these opinions are based simply on what this defendant has told the doctors, nothing more." What the judge was saying was that if Sutcliffe had lied to the doctors, then their opinions were worthless.

The judge went on to make the point that Sutcliffe had said nothing about his mission to kill to the police, and finally said sternly, "It seems to me it would be more appropriate if this case were dealt with by a jury."

The jury should be the judges of Sutcliffe's sanity, not the doctors!

The defence, who had not expected this, applied for an adjournment, and the trial proper began on Tuesday 5th May.

Sutcliffe appeared once more in the dock. Neither by speech nor action did he give any sign of mental illness, and now Sir Michael Havers, who had already argued one way, began to argue the other.

He told the jury, "You have to decide whether this man sought to pull the wool over the doctors' eyes. You have to decide whether, as a clever, callous murderer, he deliberately set out to create a cock and bull story to avoid conviction for murder."

Sir Michael concentrated on "discrepancies" between what Sutcliffe had told the police and what he'd later told the doctors. The Attorney-General gave away his own leaning towards double standards when he said of the victims, "Some were prostitutes, some were women of easy virtue, but the last six attacks from 1979 to 1980 involved victims whose reputations were unblemished," which suggested that the court regarded the last six murders as being more grave than the previous seven.

Confirming that the letters and tape that had been sent to the police were hoaxes, the Attorney-General said, "The harsh truth is that the author of the letters and tape has nothing to do with this case. Most regrettably, it became widely accepted by a number of senior officers that this man [the hoaxer] was in fact the Ripper and that he spoke with a Wearside accent. One of the things which affected the investigating officers was that if the suspects interviewed did not speak with a Sunderland accent, they tended to be eliminated."

Peter Sutcliffe's confession, made to Dewsbury police over a period of many hours, was read out in court.

Of the first victim, Sutcliffe said: "I asked her if she fancied it. She said, 'Not on your life.' I followed her and hit her with a hammer. I intended to kill her, but I was disturbed."

Of the second victim: "I saw her in the Royal Oak. She annoyed me, probably in some minor way. I took her to be a prostitute. I hit her on the head and scratched her buttocks with a piece of hacksaw blade or maybe a knife. My intention was to kill her, but I was disturbed by a car coming down the road."

Of his first actual murder victim, Wilma McCann, Sutcliffe said: "She said, 'Come on, get it over with.' I said, 'Don't worry, I will' and I hit her with the hammer. She made a lot of noise so I took my knife out of my pocket and stabbed her about four times." (It was actually fifteen times.)

Asked by the police why he had stabbed so many of his victims in the heart, Sutcliffe said, "You can kill them quicker that way."

Of Emily Jackson he declared: "I pushed a piece of wood against her vagina to show how disgusting she was."

He also stabbed her fifty times with his screwdriver in the region of the womb.

Of his first black victim – who survived his attack – he recalled: "She went behind some trees for a pee and suggested that we start the ball rolling on the grass. I hit her once on the head with the hammer, but just couldn't bring myself to hit her again." (He had actually hit her over the head nine times.)

Of Irene Richardson: "I used the hammer and a Stanley knife on her. As she was crouching down, urinating on the grass, I hit her on the head at least two or three times. I lifted up her clothes and slashed her abdomen and throat."

Of Tina Atkinson: "I heard her using foul language. It was obvious why I picked her up. No decent woman would have been using language like that at the top of her voice. When I had killed her I picked her up under the arms and lifted her up on to the bed." He'd used the claw part of the hammer to hack at her body.

The details Sutcliffe had given in his confession were specific. After the usual stunning hammer blows to the head, he told police, he wiped his knife clean on Jayne MacDonald's back after stabbing her nineteen times. He told how he had returned to Jean Jordan's body six days after killing her in an attempt to cut her head off. Why? "To make this murder more mysterious."

He confirmed that he had used a walling hammer to smash Yvonne Pearson's skull into seventeen fragments, then took stuffing from a settee and rammed it into her mouth to stop her moaning. But it had taken more hammer blows to shut her up for good, he told police.

His account of Helen Rytka's murder was even more pathetic, since this young half-caste girl had endured such a sad life prior to meeting Sutcliffe. "She undid my trousers and seemed prepared to start sexual intercourse right away in the front seat of the car. It was very awkward for me to find a way to get her out of the car."

Why was he so anxious to get her out of the car? "Because it would have left evidence and would also have been very difficult." Sutcliffe had had enough sense to realize that leaving forensic evidence of murder in the car would be dangerous for him.

"For about five minutes I was trying to decide which method to use to kill her. She was beginning to arouse me sexually. I got out of the car with the excuse that I needed to urinate and managed to persuade her to get out of the car so that we could have sex in the back. As she was getting in I realized that this was my chance, but my hammer caught on the edge of the car door frame and only gave her a light tap. She said, 'There is no need for that, you don't even have to pay.' I expected her to immediately shout for help. She was obviously scared and said, 'What was that?' I said, 'Just a small sample of one of these' and hit her on the head, hard. She just crumbled, making a loud moaning noise. I realized that what I had done was in full view of two taxi-drivers who had appeared and were talking nearby. I dragged her by the hair to the end of the woodyard. She stopped moaning, but was not dead. Her eyes were open and she held up her hands to ward off blows. I jumped on top of her and covered her mouth with my hand. It seemed like an eternity and she was still struggling. I told her that if she kept quiet she would be all right. As she had got me aroused a moment previous, I had no alternative but to go ahead with the act of sex as the only means of keeping her quiet. It didn't take long. She kept staring at me. She didn't put much into it."

The taxi-drivers eventually drove off, and Helen Rytka took the chance to escape. She scrambled to her feet and staggered towards the car. Sutcliffe, who had dropped his hammer, had to hunt on the ground for it before going after her.

"This was when I hit her two heavy blows to the back of the head. I dragged her to the front of the car and threw her belongings over the wall. She was obviously still alive. I took a knife from the car and stabbed her several times through the heart and lungs. I think it was the kitchen knife which I believe the police later retrieved from my home."

It was in fact found in the cutlery drawer in the Sutcliffes' pristine kitchen.

The Attorney-General now turned to the death of Josephine Whitaker, describing this as "a respectable victim".

"Now we come to another sad one," Sir Michael told the court, holding up a giant Philips screwdriver, some two feet in length. "Sutcliffe told the police he used this on Josephine Whitaker and Barbara Leach. That was after he had used his hammer to shatter their skulls, leaving the tell-tale pattern of golf-ball-size indentations in the scalp. He used the round head of the ball-pein hammer. He had used that screwdriver as a substitute penis, introducing it into the vagina many times."

When asked about the murder of Barbara Leach, Sutcliffe had declared, "It was forty-six weeks after the last one. I was never urged to do it again until then."

Sir Michael held up a length of cord which Sutcliffe had used to strangle Marguerite Walls and which was found on him at the time of his arrest. When the police asked him why he had changed his method of killing Sutcliffe told them, "Because the press and the media had attached a stigma to me. I had been known for some time as the Yorkshire Ripper. I didn't like it. It didn't ring true. I had been on my way to Leeds to kill a prostitute when I saw Margo Walls. It was just unfortunate for her that she happened to be walking by. I don't like the method of strangulation. It takes them even longer to die."

He explained the murderous attack on his eighteenth victim by saying, "She was walking slowly like a prostitute and I hit her on the head with a hammer. I didn't have any tools with me to finish her off so I used the rope." But she survived.

Why did he kill sixteen-year-old Jayne MacDonald? "I attacked her because she was the first person I saw. I think something clicked because she had a straight skirt with a slit in it."

The trial continued the next day, with more details from Peter Sutcliffe's 16-hour confession. "The last I did was Jacqueline Hill at Headingley. I sat in the car... then I saw Miss Hill. I decided that she was a likely victim. I drove past her and parked up and waited for her to pass. I got out and followed. I took the hammer from my pocket and struck her on the head. I dragged her on to some waste ground. A car appeared and I threw myself on the ground, but the car passed by. She was moving about so I hit her again. I pulled most of her clothes off. I had a screwdriver with a yellow handle and I stabbed her in the lungs. Her eyes were wide open and she seemed to be looking at me with an accusing stare. This shook me up a bit so I stabbed her in the eye."

Now came the medical evidence. First came a report from Dr Hugo Milne, psychiatrist, who said:"There is no suggestion that he is a sadistic sexual deviant. I am convinced that the killings were not sexual in any way."

Trevor Birdsall gave his evidence against his former friend and spoke chillingly of that early "rehearsal", and of the night of the attack on the first victim. "On the way home we passed through Halifax. Peter stopped the car and got out. I remember seeing a woman. She was walking quickly and Peter went to the back of the car and disappeared... He was away ten to twenty minutes. When he came back he said he had been talking to a woman. The next evening I read about a brutal attack on a woman in that area. It crossed my mind that Peter might be connected with it."

Detective Inspector John Boyle went into the witness box to tell about the most important interview of his life, when he was questioning Sutcliffe at Dewsbury on the night of 4th January, almost at the end of a 48-hour period of questioning.

Boyle asked Sutcliffe why he had dumped the hammer and knife following his arrest, to which Sutcliffe replied, "I think you've been leading up to it."

"Leading up to what?" Boyle asked.

"The Yorkshire Ripper."

"What about him?"

"Well, it's me."

Prison officers testified next. One had heard Sutcliffe say to a relative, "I am going to do a long time in prison, thirty years or more, unless I can convince people in here I'm mad, and maybe then ten years in the loony bin."

Another reported a conversation he'd had with Sutcliffe in which the prisoner said, "I have been told by my psychiatrist that I will have to do no more than ten years to satisfy the public."

A third testified, "He was saying to me that the doctors considered him disturbed and he was quite amazed by it and smiling broadly and leaning back in his chair. He said to me, 'I'm as normal as anyone'."

On 11th May Sutcliffe himself went into the witness box and said:"I have killed these thirteen women. I intended to kill the other seven," before going on to tell of his religious mission from God to kill prostitutes, and of being "selected" to kill. He had taken the hoax Ripper tape as proof that God was protecting him.

Yet the fact was that Sutcliffe, who claimed to view prostitutes as "scum", had regularly paid them for sexual services. And Sutcliffe had told the police he felt an urge to kill all women.

Under cross-examination Sutcliffe was asked, "Do you think you are mad?"

"No," he replied.

"Do you think there is anything wrong with you mentally?"

"Nothing serious at all, no."

The prosecution ended by claiming that Sutcliffe had shown self-control and cunning throughout his reign of terror. He had used the "mission to kill prostitutes" story to fool the doctors.

Then it was the doctors' turn to be put on trial. They followed one another into the witness box to proclaim Sutcliffe's madness. Dr Milne was forced to admit that Sutcliffe might well have lied to him, and that the murders showed very clear sexual components.

The second doctor had seen Sutcliffe for an hour and could not be certain that he was not a liar. If he was a liar, "then my diagnosis falls".

A third doctor gave the jury a simple choice. Either he was an incompetent psychiatrist or else Sutcliffe was a very competent actor. A fourth doctor refused to agree that Sutcliffe, in inserting a two-foot-long screwdriver into a victim's vagina without tearing the tissues, was not deriving some sexual satisfaction from the act.

Attorney-General Sir Michael Havers summed up for the prosecution by urging the jury to consider whether Sutcliffe was "bad or mad".

The same point was made by the judge in his summing up.

The jury retired on 22nd May 1981.

Unable to agree a verdict after four hours, they were sent away again to reach a majority verdict. An hour later they returned, finding Peter William Sutcliffe guilty of thirteen murders and seven attempted murders. He was bad, not mad.

The verdict meant that, in the jury's opinion, Sutcliffe had indeed fooled the doctors. Insanity was not the reason for his crimes. The killer was just plain evil.

Peter Sutcliffe was later sentenced to life imprisonment with no chance of parole for thirty years.

Chapter Ten
DENNIS NILSEN
THE DEADLY SCAVENGER

Dennis Andrew Nilsen was a very rare killer. In his fifty prison notebooks, which he handed to author Brian Masters so that he could write his incisive book on the case, *Killing for Company*, Nilsen leaves you with the feeling that, in many ways, he was a thoroughly nice man. Highly intelligent and articulate, sensitive and kind, he was a person you might have valued as a friend. But he was also a twisted pervert; a killer of intense ferocity, with dirty little motives which scabbed his soul. He masturbated over his victims. Took them out from under the floorboards periodically to fondle them and "have sex with them" by placing his penis between their thighs. He sat them in the opposite armchair to watch TV with him or listen to music or simply join him in conversation. He kept one corpse in an armchair for a week because "It was so nice to have someone to come home to."

Lonely, shy, friendless, Nilsen truly killed for company. At one period he had six bodies under the floorboards of his flat and was not alone any more, but then he would burn them or cut them into pieces to flush down the lavatory. He lived a fantasy obsessed with death, but he also loved music and poetry. The closer one gets to Nilsen the greater the enigma becomes: at once potent and pathetic; innocent and demonic. He was also a man of such low self-esteem with a life he considered to be so insignificant that he was determined to create his own legend. And in this Nilsen succeeded only too well. When he stepped into the dock at the Old Bailey on 24th October 1983 he was the legendary killer of the "House of Horror"; murderer of fifteen young men and the attempted killer of seven others. Yet, since he created his own legend – this clever, manipulative psychopath – even the legend is not true.

Any attempt to view the real Dennis Nilsen objectively is a difficult task – Nilsen was very sick, his murders stomach-churning, and simply reading about them is very much like stepping into an abattoir – but the task is worth undertaking. Nilsen presents us with the classic psychiatric model of the serial sex killer, and the quest for his real identity and motives can lead to valuable insights into the drives of all sex killers.

Dennis Nilsen was born on 23rd November 1945 in the Scottish village of Fraserburgh. Son of a Norwegian father and a Scottish mother, the most important episode in his early life came at the age of seven, when he viewed the dead body of his grandfather. He could not believe that something which had once been so vital was now dead, beyond all feeling or sensation. He wrote later that the sight of the corpse had a profound effect on him, and that the experience blighted his personality permanently.

At fourteen he joined the Army Cadets and revelled in the uniform: it made him feel important. He joined the Regular Army in September 1961, aged fifteen, to train as a chef in the Catering Corps. He was taught the skills of butchery. He later served in Aden, the Persian Gulf and Germany. During this period he discovered his own homosexuality but repressed his feelings.

In 1971 he was posted to the Shetland Islands, where he developed an interest in film-making. Corporal Nilsen took many films of a private whom he instructed to lie still and "play dead". This was the first manifestation of his necrophile streak, and was an important clue to his later development. When he left the Army, in 1972, his conduct was recorded as being "exemplary".

In December 1972, aged twenty-seven, he joined the Metropolitan Police and was posted as a probationer to Willesden Green police station as Constable Q287. During the course of his duties he came across London's gay scene and visited many gay pubs. He gave expression to his homosexuality by having an affair with one man, and smuggling another back into his Police Section room for anal sex. But he was not very happy. After a year, to the surprise of his colleagues, he resigned from the Force. It lacked the camaraderie he had known in the Army.

For a time he wandered from job to job, working as a security guard until he got fed up with that. Putting on a uniform no longer conferred a sense of identity. Finally he was forced to sign on the dole, where he was persuaded to apply for a clerical post with the Department of Employment. He was appointed to the Denmark Street Job Centre in London's West End. Here he stayed for the next few years, having many homosexual affairs and contacts, picking up young men from the many gay pubs he frequented and taking them back to his home. To his colleagues at work, Nilsen was a prickly and hostile character who made it painfully clear that he wanted to be left alone. He made no friends there, and remained reclusive. But outside work he was different.

All had been well to begin with. In November 1975 he made friends with a young man named David Gallichan. Ten years Nilsen's junior, Gallichan was not a homosexual. But he and Nilsen got on well enough and very soon the two men were sharing a flat. Gallichan provided Nilsen with the sense of stability and security that was previously missing from his life. What Nilsen provided Gallichan with was harder to discern. But they lived together happily. When, in May 1977, Gallichan announced that he could not stand London any more, Nilsen was devastated. He felt rejected and betrayed. He felt no better when Gallichan's place was taken over by a young male prostitute. The relationship didn't work and the boy soon left.

Nilsen's flat at 195 Melrose Avenue, Cricklewood, now felt very empty and friendless. He began drinking himself into a stupor every night, listening to pop music over headphones with manic intensity.

By 1978 Nilsen was using make-up to give himself the appearance of a corpse – dark eyes and dead white flesh – and masturbated while looking at himself in a mirror. He had become totally obsessed with the idea of death. He spent Christmas of that year alone in his flat, with only his dog Bleep for company. He was feeling acutely lonely and depressed. At this time he picked up young men and took them home – but they always left afterwards. The next one would not be leaving.

His first victim, picked up in the Cricklewood Arms, was an unidentified Irish youth in his teens. They slept together that night – 30th December 1978 – but when Nilsen awoke in the morning he found he had strangled his sleeping companion with one of his collection of fifteen ties. He washed the body in the bath, put it back in bed and attempted to have sex with it. Later, before putting the body under the floorboards, he masturbated over it. He said later, "I took possession of a new kind of flat-mate." He added that he had been determined to have company – "even if it was only a body". That first killing shocked Nilsen: he said he shook uncontrollably for hours afterwards, wondering if he should give himself up to the police or commit suicide. The reason he gave for not doing either was that there would be nobody to take care of his dog. That first victim remained under the floorboards at Melrose Avenue for seven and a half months, until Nilsen burned the body on a bonfire in the garden 11th August 1979.

There had been an earlier clue to Nilsen's homicidal nature. In 1976 he had attacked a young man he had brought back to his flat, again attempting to strangle him with a tie. The young man fought him off and fled, reporting the incident to the police. Nilsen found himself being questioned at the police station at which he had once served. But as there was no obvious injury to the young man – who didn't want to press charges anyway– and since Nilsen had said he was drunk and could remember nothing, the matter was dropped.

On 31st October 1979 Nilsen picked up a young Chinese student in a pub near Trafalgar Square. He took him back to Melrose Avenue, and after a few drinks attempted to strangle him. The intended victim, Andrew Ho, fought him off, knocking him unconscious with a brass candlestick. Mr Ho reported the incident to the police because he feared he might have killed Nilsen. Again Nilsen pleaded drunkenness, and again the matter was dropped.

The second victim was a young Canadian tourist, Kenneth Ockenden, aged twenty-three. He was not a homosexual, but was delighted when a polite Englishman took an interest in him. Nilsen met him on 3rd December 1979, in the Princess Louise pub in High Holborn. He took the young man on a guided tour of London, then escorted him back to Melrose Avenue for a meal and some drinks. After a bout of heavy drinking Nilsen persuaded Ockenden to listen to pop music on the headphones. Then he strangled him with the headphone cord. Nilsen said later, "I kept him with me for the rest of the night. There was no sex, just caressing etc." He sat the body in an armchair and made the face up with cosmetics. He watched TV with the corpse and held conversations with it. Eventually Nilsen put it under the floorboards, but took him back out at least four times in the next fortnight. He had sex with the corpse via the thighs. He washed the corpse, as he was to do with most of his victims. This ritual washing of the corpse was a demonstration of his total power over the victim, a ritual of symbolic importance.

Nilsen said he felt remorse after the death of Kenneth Ockenden, especially when he saw TV news reports about the young man's disappearance. He was bewildered and frightened by his own actions and again wanted to give himself up to the police. But again he never did.

After two murders Nilsen said he came to feel "less emotional" about it all, and accepted the fact that he was a compulsive killer. So unconcerned did he become about the act of murder that he kept small items belonging to his victims around his flat. He wore a watch belonging to one victim, and a pair of spectacles belonging to another. He told police: "I did not feel that it was theft as the owners hadn't really gone away." Indeed they hadn't, they were still under the floorboards.

In May 1980 Nilsen picked up his next victim, Martyn Duffy, sixteen, a Liverpool youth who had a record for petty theft and drug-addiction. Once at Melrose Avenue Nilsen strangled him unconscious and then drowned him in the bath. Afterwards he washed the corpse and placed it on the bed, masturbating over it. Duffy too would later be put under the floorboards. To cover the smell of putrefaction Nilsen was using air-fresheners and disinfectant. When the "smell problem", as Nilsen termed it, became too strong to ignore, Nilsen took the bodies up and dissected them on the kitchen floor. The heads went into plastic bags, the bulky parts into two suitcases which he stored in the garden shed. Duffy's arms and hands were buried in a hole in the garden, and the internal organs of both men were just dumped in the street. A man found a plastic bag full of entrails and reported it to the police: they dismissed it as being simply refuse.

Billy Sutherland, twenty-seven, was a hard-case from Edinburgh. He was picked up in a pub near in Piccadilly Circus, and, having nowhere to sleep, agreed to accompany Nilsen back to Melrose Avenue. There Nilsen strangled him. He left him sitting dead in an armchair for two days before putting him under the floorboards. Nilsen liked to keep his victims as long as he could, bathing them and changing their underwear so he could fondle them.

The next four victims were never identified, but all were young men. Number 5 Nilsen called the "Mex" because of his Latin appearance. Number 6 was Irish, picked up in the Cricklewood Arms. The seventh was a pathetic creature, a young man of emaciated looks who Nilsen said reminded him of a Belsen victim. Nilsen took him home and fed him, then when he fell asleep in the chair strangled him with a tie. He was later to describe how the young man's legs had cycled frantically in the air as he fought for life. Nilsen said that this murder "was as easy as taking candy from a baby." That body too went under the floorboards.

By now, of course, all these corpses were becoming something of a nuisance. They were all over the place. Nilsen would take them out periodically to cuddle, caress or just talk to, but he wouldn't necessarily put them back in the same place. Occasionally he forgot where he had put them. In September 1980 he went to get a shirt from the wardrobe and a body fell out on top of him. Even for Nilsen this was a bit of shock, and with a sigh of exasperation, he decided something had to be done.

He took all the bodies out and dissected them. He said later, "The flesh looked just like any other meat one could see in a butcher's shop, and having been trained in butchery I was not subject to any traumatic shocks." It was then that he had his second bonfire in the garden, putting car tyres on the blaze to disguise the smell of burning flesh. Children gathered round to watch as the fire burned all through the day. The following morning Nilsen used a roller to crush the remaining evidence, the skulls and bones, into fragments. With a sense of relief – the bodies finally out of the way – Nilsen went out that night to a pub and picked up a young man, taking him back to the flat for sex. He did not kill this one: he left next morning. But on 10th November 1980 he picked up Douglas Stewart, twenty-six, a fellow-Scot. Stewart agreed to go back to Melrose Avenue for a drink and fell asleep in the chair. He woke to find his ankles tied and Nilsen trying to strangle him with a ligature. He managed to fight Nilsen off and grabbed a carving knife to make good his escape. Stewart reported the attack to the police, but the two officers who responded to his call concluded that it had been a homosexual lovers' quarrel and took it no further.

Five more people died in 1981. Nilsen's murderous lust had not died with that fire. He had been turned down for promotion, and had also been mugged in the street and robbed. With his self-esteem at rock bottom he needed to kill again. He killed for fear of something worse. Murder was a safety-valve, it served as a catharsis and stopped him from going insane. That year, 1981, had been a bad one all round for Nilsen. On 8th June his flat had been vandalized and he had called in the police. Detectives stood in his flat, unaware of the bodies under their feet. The next victim, the eighth, was a tall young hippy with long fair hair. Nilsen picked him up in the

West End, and his strangled body went under the floorboards. Victim number nine was another Scot, picked up in a Soho pub early in 1981. His strangled body went under the floorboards. Victim number ten was Irish. Nilsen could not remember strangling him, but woke up one morning to find him dead on the floor. Victim eleven was an aggressive Cockney skinhead with a dotted line tattooed around his neck with the inscription: "Cut along dotted line." Nilsen had picked him up in Leicester Square, took him back to the flat and plied him with drink. When he passed out Nilsen strangled him. Of this victim Nilsen wrote:"I went to bed thinking: end of a day. End of the drinking. End of a person." He too went into the crowded space beneath the floorboards.

The next victim literally fell into Nilsen's lap. Malcolm Barlow, twenty-four, was an orphan from Rotherham. Of low intelligence, he suffered from epilepsy. On 17th September 1981 he had a fit in Melrose Avenue, and Nilsen found the vagrant slumped against a wall, sitting on the pavement. He telephoned for an ambulance. The following day Barlow had himself released from hospital and went in search of the Good Samaritan. He found Nilsen's flat and waited for him to arrive home from work, then invited himself in for a drink. Nilsen was seriously concerned about him, warning him not to mix alcohol with the tablets he was taking because of the possibility of an adverse effect. But Barlow insisted on a drink. Later, Nilsen admitted that he strangled him because he was a "nuisance" and for no other reason. He was hidden under the sink, later to be placed intact on the going-away bonfire.

Nilsen had been offered another flat at 23 Cranley Gardens, London N10, and was promised £1,000 by his landlord if he would agree to move. Nilsen arranged to move into the new flat in October, but first he had to get rid of the embarrassing four bodies under the floorboards. He dissected them, cutting along the dotted line on the skinhead's neck, and then had another huge bonfire, burning the bodies and throwing the entrails over the garden hedge for vermin to dispose of, before moving out on 5th October 1981.

Cranley Gardens is a long and pleasant road in the Muswell Hill suburb of north London, lined with large semi-detached houses. It was into one of these – number 23 – that Nilsen moved. Managed by a local estate agent for an Asian owner, the house had been converted into six flats, and Nilsen moved into the very top flat in the attic, an apartment consisting of two rooms and a kitchen and bathroom. Here he lived with his dog, Bleep.

By now Nilsen had been promoted to executive officer and was working at the Job Centre in Kentish Town, where he was known to his colleagues as "Des". He had also become branch officer for the civil service union, CPSA, and seemed to delight in tweaking the nose of authority, battling against the system. The tall, thin, stooping figure of Des Nilsen, wearing the spectacles of victim Martyn Duffy, was a man of mystery to the people who shared the house. He hardly ever spoke, and made friends with none of them. He lived alone in his dingy flat, making no attempt to clean it or keep it tidy.

Between January 1978 and September 1981 Nilsen had killed twelve men at Melrose Avenue. At Cranley Gardens he was to begin killing again. In 1982 he killed twice, but before these successes he attempted to kill Paul Nobbs, nineteen, a student he met in a West End pub on 23rd November 1981. He took him back to Cranley Gardens and cooked him a meal, after which they went to bed together for sex-play. Paul Nobbs woke at six in the morning to find that he had a raging headache, and when he looked in the bathroom mirror he was astonished to see that his eyes were bloodshot and his throat badly bruised. Nilsen told him that he had probably caught his neck in the zip of the sleeping bag. The fact was that he had attempted to strangle the youth during the night, but for some reason desisted from killing him. When Paul Nobbs left that morning a solicitous Nilsen advised him to see a doctor and gave him his telephone number, expressing the hope that they would meet again.

The first victim to be murdered at Cranley Gardens was known to Nilsen only as "John the Guardsman". He was later to be identified as John Howlett, twenty-three, from High Wycombe. He was a drifter who lied that he had been in the Guards. They had first met casually in December 1981, but met again by chance in March 1982 in a pub. Nilsen invited him back to the flat for a drink, but was annoyed when his visitor made himself too much at home. Nilsen remarked acidly: "I didn't know you were moving in." When Howlett fell into a drunken stupor Nilsen put a ligature around his neck, saying viciously, "I think it's time you went!" He throttled him unconscious and then placed him in the bath to drown.

Nilsen dissected Howlett quickly: a friend was due to visit the next day. He boiled the head in a large pot on the stove then flushed the internal organs and some flesh down the toilet. The rest he packed into a tea-chest which stood in the corner of the flat. He later told police, "I put all the large bones out with the rubbish for the dustmen."

In April 1982 Nilsen met Carl Stottor in the Black Cap pub in Camden Town. Stottor, twenty-one, was a six-foot-tall male dancer known professionally as "Blondie". Nilsen took him back to Cranley Gardens and they went to bed together. In the middle of the night Stottor awoke to a living nightmare. He was being strangled, and was too weak to resist. He felt himself being lifted and carried, then plunged into a bath of water. Several times his head was pushed under the water, while he tried to beg for mercy. He then lapsed into unconsciousness. "Blondie" awoke to find himself back in bed with the dog licking his face. In actual fact Nilsen thought he had succeeded in killing the dancer, and was surprised when he revived. But once he realized he was alive Nilsen made every attempt to bring Stottor round, turning on all the bars of the electric fire to warm him. He persuaded Stottor that he must have got his neck stuck in the zipper of the sleeping bag and almost choked himself. Much was to be made at the subsequent trial of this strange episode. Why had Nilsen spared Stottor? How had he been able to snap out of his killing state? It seemed to suggest that there were two Nilsens, a Jekyll and Hyde in real life.

The next murder was that of twenty-eight-year-old Graham Allan, from Glasgow. The exact date of his death is unknown, but it was some time in mid-1982. Allan, a drug-addict, was strangled and then dissected in the bath. He was later identified from an X-ray plate of his skull, which bore a distinctive fracture.

On New Year's Day 1983 Nilsen attempted to strangle Toshimitu Ozawa, a young Japanese student. Ozawa managed to fight Nilsen off and fled the house in terror. Because there was no obvious physical injury, police dismissed the matter.

Nilsen was later to tell police that he never went out looking for a victim to kill. He simply went out looking for company, and never knew when the urge to kill might come on him. Sometimes he could not remember having killed. On 27th January 1983 he woke to find a dead man in the armchair with a tie around his neck. A piece of string had been attached to the tie to make it long enough to function as a noose – this suggested premeditation, since the ligature must have been constructed in advance. But Nilsen claimed it was all a mystery.

This time the victim was Stephen Sinclair, twenty, a punk and drug-addict. He had a borstal and prison record and suffered from hepatitis. Something of a social misfit, Sinclair had been a foster-child. Nilsen had picked him up in the Charing Cross Road on the evening of 26th January. Back at the flat Nilsen strangled him, then lay naked beside the body with an erection. Nilsen later told police of how he had attempted to dispose of Sinclair. "I put the head in a pot, popped the lid on and lit the stove. When the head was coming to the boil I turned the pot down to simmer, then I took the dog out for a walk... Later I watched TV as the head was simmering." Most of Sinclair's dissected corpse was found in two black bags in the wardrobe. Nilsen tried to flush pieces of flesh down the toilet, but the toilets became blocked.

In February 1983 the residents of the other flats reported the blocked toilets to the landlord, who arranged for a plumber to call on Saturday 5th February. He arrived, but decided that the job was too big for him and advised the estate agent to call in DynoRod.

On Monday 7th February Nilsen went to work as usual. The DynoRod engineer arrived at 6.15 p.m. on Tuesday. The engineer, Michael Cattrann, lifted a large manhole cover and climbed down into the sewer. There was a revolting smell, and he noticed what looked like lumps of flesh blocking the outlet pipes. It was getting dark, and since he had not been long with the company and did not want to make a fool of himself, he packed up for the night, saying he would return the following day. However, he reported his grim find to his boss by telephone.

That night Dennis Nilsen went down into the sewer and removed most of the flesh into plastic carrier bags, throwing them over the back garden hedge. But his neighbours had seen him at his midnight task.

Nilsen knew that the next day would be crucial: his luck was running out. Again he thought of suicide, but again the thought of his dog Bleep deterred him. He went to work as usual, and before leaving at the end of the day he left a note in an envelope in his desk. The note said that if he were to be arrested there would be no truth in reports that he had committed suicide in his cell.

While Nilsen was at work the plumber and his boss returned to the manhole at Cranley Gardens with police officers. Portions of flesh were recovered from blocked pipes and were taken to a pathologist who declared them to be human tissue. When Nilsen returned home on the evening of 9th February he found three burly policemen waiting for him. They were Detective Chief Inspector Peter Jay, Detective Inspector Stephen McCusker and Detective Constable Jeffrey Butler. They had checked Nilsen's background, and knew that he had been a policeman and might therefore prove tricky.

Inspector Jay said to the 37-year-old Nilsen: "I've come about your drains."

Nilsen replied: "Why should the police be interested in drains?"

Jay went on: "The reason I'm interested in your drains is that they are blocked with human remains."

Nilsen said: "Good God! That's terrible. Where did it come from?"

The policeman would have none of this. "Don't mess about," he said. "Where's the rest of the body?"

Nilsen confessed immediately, all resistance gone. "In plastic bags in the wardrobe," he said.

He took the officers up to his flat and showed them. Nilsen was immediately charged on suspicion of murder.

In the police car taking them to Hornsey Police Station, DI McCusker asked Nilsen idly: "Are we talking about one body or two?"

Nilsen replied: "Fifteen or sixteen since 1978. I'll tell you everything. It's a relief to be able to get it off my mind."

Once at the police station an incredulous Detective Chief Inspector asked Nilsen: "Let's get this straight. Are you telling us that since 1978 you have killed sixteen people?"

"Yes," Nilsen replied. "Three at Cranley Gardens and about thirteen at my previous address, 195 Melrose Avenue in Cricklewood."

The human remains recovered from Nilsen's wardrobe were examined at Hornsey Mortuary by pathologist Professor Bowden. He found several plastic carrier bags inside the two large black plastic bin-liners. In one bag was the left side of a man's chest including the arm, in another a torso, in a third a heart, lungs, spleen, liver, gall bladder, kidneys and intestines. Dissection had been skilful, the pathologist noted. Slowly he was able to reassemble the body of Stephen Sinclair.

The questioning of Nilsen began on 11th February 1983 at Hornsey Police Station, led by Peter Jay. It was to last thirty hours spread over a week, and the story which emerged chilled the listening detectives. With dispassionate calm, like the civil servant he was, Nilsen dictated a precise and detailed account of his many murders. He said that of the three people murdered at Cranley Gardens he knew only Stephen Sinclair by name. He said he was relieved he had been caught now, because "If I had been arrested at sixty-five years of age there might have been thousands of bodies behind me."

While telling detectives about how he had cut up bodies and flushed them down the toilet, he asked for an ashtray to stub out his cigarette. When a young constable told him to flush it down the toilet Nilsen replied drily, "The last time I flushed something down the toilet I got into trouble." He cooperated fully in the interrogation, as if anxious to have all his deeds recorded. While in custody he wrote a document entitled *Unscrambling Behaviour* in which he attempted to explain his motives. He displayed no signs of remorse at any time and admitted, "I can't weep for my victims."

The detectives tried to establish if the murders had been premeditated, if Nilsen had lured young men to his flat with the express intention of killing them. "No," said Nilsen, "it just happened." He said that far more people had visited his flat and left alive than had been killed. Asked how he could have cut up bodies and dabbled in flesh without feeling sick, Nilsen replied simply: "The victim is the dirty platter after the feast and the washing-up is a clinically ordinary task." He also told detectives about the seven attempted murders.

The detectives noted that there had been a gap of a year between the first and second killings, and then ten victims had been strangled within eighteen months, in 1980-81. Was there any reason for this? Could Nilsen supply any motive for the murders? Nilsen said he could not. He wasn't a sex-maniac or a robber or a sadist. "What I am is totally irresponsible," he said.

When his solicitor had finished reading his terrible confession he raised his eyes to Nilsen and asked, "Why?" Nilsen shrugged. "I was hoping you would tell me that," he said.

Nilsen was remanded to Brixton Prison, from where he sent a letter to the detectives handling his case, complimenting them on the professional way in which they had handled the inquiry. He was very conscious of the media interest in him, conscious that he had at last become a *somebody*. Once in prison Nilsen was made a Category A prisoner and was surprised at the hostility shown against him by fellow-prisoners. But he made a bad prisoner. He tried to fight the system, protesting and going on hunger strikes. He once tried assaulting the prison staff: he got a black eye and lost a tooth as a result. Convinced that he was being treated unfairly, he complained bitterly to the prison governor, and ended by sacking his legal counsel.

At this time he also fell in love with a fellow-prisoner, David Martin, a transvestite who eventually committed suicide in prison. Nilsen had begun writing his own account of his crimes in his many notebooks in an attempt at self-analysis. Like Kürten, he wrote he would welcome being executed and complained that he had been "used" by a power to which he had surrendered control. He seemed convinced he was a victim of demonic possession, a fact that explains the cryptic words written after he was convicted. "They think they have the real me safely locked away here, but the real me is hundreds of miles away . . ."

The trial of Nilsen began at the Old Bailey on Monday 24th October 1983, with Mr Justice Croom-Johnson presiding. Mr Alan Green prosecuted, with Mr Ivan Lawrence for the defence. Nilsen was charged with six murders and two attempted murders. He pleaded not guilty to murder but guilty to manslaughter on the grounds of diminished responsibility.

The prosecutor told the jury of eight men and four women the facts relating to the arrest of Nilsen. He said that seven victims had now been identified, although only six were on the indictment. The prosecution set out to show the pattern of the murders. Each victim was a man. Each had been picked up in a pub. All were strangers to Nilsen. All, with the exception of Ockenden, had no permanent address. All had been strangled. Some were homosexuals or male prostitutes. Nilsen had had sexual connections with six of the bodies.

Nilsen's confession was read out to a shocked court. When the police had asked him about the ties which he used to strangle his victims Nilsen said he had started out with fifteen and only had one left at the time of his arrest. Asked how many bodies were under the floorboards at any one time, he had replied flippantly: "I'm not sure. I did not do a stock check." He had told police he had taken on a "quasi-God role" in killing.

The first prosecution witness was Douglas Stewart, twenty-nine. He was a married man, and stated that he was not a homosexual. He told of Nilsen's abortive attempt to strangle him. On Tuesday 25th October two witnesses told of having been attacked by Nilsen. Paul Nobbs told of sex-play in bed with Nilsen, then waking up to find himself half-strangled. "There were no whites to my eyes; they were all bloodshot. I had a sore throat and I felt very sick." He said Nilsen had told him:"God, you look bloody awful."

Carl Stottor told of being picked up in a pub by Nilsen. Stottor had been feeling very depressed at the time, and told Nilsen he wished he were dead. Nilsen told him not to be silly – he should not throw his life away. They went to bed, and then "I woke up feeling something around my neck. My head was hurting and I couldn't breathe properly... He was saying in a sort of whispering shouting voice: 'Stay still! Stay still!' Then I passed out... I vaguely remember hearing water running... I was being carried. I knew I was in the water and he was trying to drown me. He kept pushing me into the water. The third time I came up I said: 'No more, please, no more' and he pushed me under again... I passed out." Stottor said he woke up to find himself on the couch, the dog licking his face. Nilsen was solicitous and helped him to the tube station.

The defence counsel asked him: "Was the defendant both calm and concerned before and after the 'incident' as though he was unaware that he had done anything to harm you?"

When the witness replied yes Mr Lawrence ruminated aloud, "How odd that was..." and then sat down.

Defence counsel established that the police only knew about the various attempted murders because Nilsen had volunteered the information. Now they showed how Nilsen had spared Stottor's life when he had him at his mercy. It was an attempt to establish the prisoner's claim to "diminished responsibility".

The document *Unscrambling Behaviour*, written by Nilsen at Hornsey Police Station, was read out in part:

> I guess I may be a creative psychopath who, when in a loss of rationality situation, lapses temporarily into a destructive psychopath... At the subconscious root lies a sense of total social isolation and a desperate search for sexual identity... God only knows what thoughts go through my mind when it's captive within a destructive binge. Maybe the cunning, stalking killer instinct is the only single concentration released from a mind which in that state knows no morality... There is no disputing that I am a violent killer under certain circumstances... It amazes me that I have no tears for the victims. I have no tears for myself. . .

His personal letter to Chief Inspector Jay had read: "My remorse is of a deep and personal kind which will eat away at me for the rest of my life... I have slain my own dragon as surely as the Press and the letter of the law will slay me."

Mr Jay agreed with defence counsel that Nilsen had been totally cooperative, and had given his confession in a matter-of-fact manner – a confession which Mr Jay said he found "horrific". Under cross-examination DI

Chambers agreed that the police had managed to trace fourteen men who had visited Nilsen's flat and come to no harm.

On Wednesday Mr Lawrence rose to open the defence case. He told the jury that he did not have to prove that Nilsen was insane – just that at the time of the murders he had been suffering from an abnormality of the mind. He called the first witness for the defence, psychiatrist Dr James MacKeith, who said that Nilsen suffered from a "severe personality disorder" and at the time of killing was in a state known as "disassociation", as if watching someone else do the deed.

Under cross-examination the doctor admitted that all a psychiatrist could know of a person's mental condition was what that person told him. There was the usual clash between the prosecution and psychiatrist which is endemic in these cases. The prosecution asserted that Nilsen was cunning, resourceful and had presence of mind. Mr Green said the fact that Nilsen had spared some of his victims proved that he could desist from killing when he wanted to; he had the power of *choice*. There was a shouting match between Mr Green and the witness, which ended with the doctor withdrawing his diagnosis that Nilsen had been suffering from diminished responsibility.

Dr Patrick Gallwey fared no better. He said Nilsen suffered from a "false self syndrome", a theory developed by R.D. Laing from ideas postulated by Jean-Paul Sartre. It was simply another formulation of the "Jekyll and Hyde" story. According to the doctor, this type of personality is fine when things are going well, but quickly falls apart under stress. The doctor went so far as to say:"I don't see how he can have had malice aforethought when he had no feelings." This brought a stern rebuke from the judge, who said he was trespassing on the law and should confine himself to medical matters.

The prosecution had stressed Nilsen's ability to make choices. He *chose* to invite men to his flat. He *chose* to kill Barlow because he was a nuisance. Re-examination of Dr Gallwey by Mr Lawrence clarified the issue. The doctor said that Nilsen killed to save himself from going insane. The acts of murder pointed the prisoner's destruction outward instead of inward. Without the acts of murder Nilsen's mind would have collapsed into psychosis. The doctor said that while Nilsen had known intellectually what he was doing, he had not known emotionally, and without emotion a man behaves like an automaton, a robot.

The prosecution psychiatrist was Dr Paul Bowden. He had seen Nilsen on sixteen occasions over an eight-month period and had determined that Nilsen was not sick. His report had stated "I am unable to show that Dennis Nilsen had any abnormality of mind."

Mr Lawrence asked Dr Bowden: "Were not his murders evidence of abnormal behaviour?"

The doctor replied, "Of course strangling people is not normal behaviour."

Mr Lawrence was able to trip him up on a number of points, establishing that the law and psychiatry do not mix. One deals in intangibles, the other in tangible evidence.

In his closing speech the prosecutor said: "You are dealing with a defendant who liked killing people and derived satisfaction from the act itself. The defence says this man was simply out of his mind. The defence says he couldn't really help it. The Crown says, oh yes he could."

For the defence Mr Lawrence opened by saying: "Does not common speech oblige one to say of the perpetrator of these killings, he must be out of his mind?"

The judge spent four hours summing up the case to the jury, and his bias against Nilsen and psychiatry was evident. He said: "There are evil people who do evil things.

Committing murder is one of them... A mind can be evil without being abnormal."

The jury retired on the morning of Thursday 3rd November. At 4.30 p.m. the judge asked the jury if they could agree a verdict. The response was no, and the jury were sequestered in a hotel overnight. They resumed their deliberations at 10 a.m. the next day. At 11.25 a.m. the judge told them he was prepared to accept a majority verdict, and at 4.25 p.m. the jury returned. On every count the decision was a 10-2 majority verdict of guilty, except for the attempted murder of Paul Nobbs when all twelve jurors agreed on guilty. The judge sentenced Nilsen to life imprisonment, with a recommendation that he should serve a minimum of twenty-five years.

Here then are the bare facts of the Dennis Nilsen case. What remains are the disturbing reflections about motive.

It so happens that years ago a Dr Brittan built up a portrait of the serial killer based on his experience of observing murderers for twenty years. That "IdentiKit of a Killer" bears a striking resemblance to Nilsen.

The doctor reported that this kind of killer is usually introspective and withdrawn. He engages in solitary pursuits. He is retiring, shy and uncommunicative. He rarely shows temper, and does not retaliate to violence. He feels different from other people, isolated. He is at his most dangerous when he suffers a loss of self-esteem, such as demotion at work or a failed relationship. He is arrogant, vain and narcissistic...

Generally under thirty-five years of age... usually of high intelligence. Leads a complicated fantasy life... shows little or no remorse and is without pity for his victims. He plans his murders well and cunningly... is a plausible liar.

The desire to have power over others is an essential part of his abnormality.... Although these are essentially sexually motivated crimes, sexual intercourse or even orgasm does not always occur but sometimes the murderer masturbates beside his victim.

Dr Brittan could almost have been describing Dennis Nilsen himself.

Chapter Eleven
ROBERT BLACK
MURDERER OF CHILDHOOD

For eight years the police knew that a monster was on the loose: a predator picking off children, as a fox preys on chickens. Where he might strike next could never be forecast, for his victims would be plucked from areas hundreds of miles apart. Only one thing was certain: no little girl was safe while he remained at large.

It was on the afternoon of 30th July 1982 that Susan Maxwell, a pretty eleven-year-old, failed to return to her parents' farm at Cornhill-on-Tweed, Northumberland near the Scottish Borders. She'd been playing tennis, and was on her way home when she disappeared.

Two weeks later senior police officers called at the farm to see Mrs Maxwell. The stunned mother listened in disbelief as a detective told her as gently as he could: "Your child is dead." The badly decomposed body of her daughter had been found more than 260 miles away in Staffordshire. She had been murdered, and the motive for the killing had been sexual.

The next victim was fair-haired Caroline Hogg, who was just five years old. She was last seen alive at a funfair near her home in Edinburgh's Portobello district on the evening of 8th July 1983. Witnesses were found who had seen the little girl being led away from the fair by a furtive-looking man who was holding her by the hand. Ten days later her decomposed remains were found in a ditch near a lay-by close to Twycross in Leicestershire, not far from the M1.

The following March a reconstruction of Caroline's abduction was televised in the hope that it would jog someone's memory and lead to the capture of the killer. In the television appeal Caroline's father expressed his fear of another killing. "You think it can never happen to you," he said, "but it has been proved time and time again that it can, and it could once more if this man is not caught."

His grim prophecy came true on 26th March, 1986. Sarah Jayne Harper, a bright ten-year-old who was a member of her local Salvation Army choir, was sent by her mother to a corner shop, less than 100 yards from her terraced home in Brunswick Place, Morley, West Yorkshire. It was about 7.50 in the evening when Sarah went on the errand. She arrived at the shop and bought a loaf of bread – the shopkeeper remembered serving her – but then she vanished.

At a press conference on 3rd April the girl's mother tearfully told journalists that she feared the worst. In a faltering voice and staring straight into the TV camera, she said:"I just want her back even if she's dead. If someone would just pick up the phone and tell us where the body is..." She revealed that the worst torment of all was the waiting. As she left the press conference she collapsed.

The body of Sarah Jayne Harper was found three and a half weeks later, on 19th April, in the swollen waters of the river Trent at Nottingham, over 70 miles away. She had been badly battered and sexually abused.

Forensic evidence and other clues, including the fact that all three victims' socks were missing, indicated that the murders – of Susan Maxwell, Caroline Hogg, and now Sarah Harper – were the work of one killer. The police had no leads to speak of and were quick to realise that they would not make much more progress unless they consolidated their efforts. It was obviously inefficient to have three separate police forces pursuing three separate inquires. But which force should have overall command? The decision was made to place the investigation in the hands of the Deputy Chief Constable of the Lothian and Borders Police, Hector Clark. He had led the initial inquiry into the murder of Susan Maxwell, the first victim in the series.

Forensically there was very little to go on. Advanced decomposition had hampered examination of Susan and Caroline's bodies, but in the case of Sarah the pathologist was able to gather some important clues. He reported that she had been raped vaginally and anally, and the killer had used an instrument of some kind, some dildo-type device.

There was also a mass of other information. Already 30,000 statements had been taken from witnesses of one sort or another and more than 75,000 people had been interviewed. The murder team also had to take on board other cases of missing children which might be linked to the three child-murders. Similar cases included the baffling disappearance of Genette Tate, thirteen, who had vanished while delivering newspapers in the village of Aylesbeare, near Exeter, in August 1978. She had apparently been knocked off her bicycle by a vehicle. The bike was found – but she was not.

A summit meeting at Scotland Yard was attended by officers from sixteen forces, discussing a total of nineteen unsolved child-murders. Mindful of the Yorkshire Ripper inquiry, in which the sheer volume of paperwork clogged up the investigation, the officers decided early on to use the latest technology. Priority was to be given to getting every scrap of relevant information on to a computer.

In March 1987 it was announced that a Government computer dubbed HOLMES was being used to collate and cross-check all data coming into the Murder Incident Room. HOLMES, which is an approximate acronym for Home Office Major Enquiry System, was being used to link investigators from six forces. More than 40,000 names were being held in its database, and among the facilities it offered was free text reference and retrieval. For example, if one single piece of information was being sought – such as the number of times witnesses had mentioned a leather jacket – then all the databases could be merged to seek out all references to a leather jacket. Clark said that the half-million pound machine, based at the Child Murder Bureau in Bradford, would be used "to determine whether or not the girls were killed by one man."

In only one case – that of Caroline Hogg – did the police have a satisfactory description of the suspect to work from. The man, who had been seen walking hand-in-hand with the child from the Edinburgh funfair, had been described as being between 25 and 45, about 5 feet 10 inches tall, of shabby appearance and wearing spectacles.

"My own view", Clark told reporters, "is that the person we are looking for is probably a man between twenty-five and forty-five who travels a lot in Britain and possibly abroad, and has previous convictions of a similar nature involving female children."

It was also revealed that details of all three murders had been sent to the FBIs Behavioral Science Unit in Virginia, USA, where specialist investigators would draw up a psychological profile of the wanted man.

Despite all this activity, however, no arrests were made. The inquiry seemed to be going on forever, and the police seemed to be nowhere nearer to finding the culprit. But then came the breakthrough.

On July 14th, 1990, a man living in the Scottish Borders village of Stowe, on the A7 trunk road linking Scotland with England, was mowing his lawn when he saw a neighbour's child being dragged into a Transit van. He raised the alarm, and police road-blocks were quickly set up. By a supreme irony of fate the girl's own father was manning the road-block which stopped the wanted van. In the rear he found his daughter bound and gagged, hooded and trussed in a sleeping-bag. Even in that short space of time she had already been sexually assaulted.

The van-driver was Robert Black, forty-three. He came from London, and regularly travelled to the North to deliver advertising posters for the firm for which he worked. All his trips to Scotland took place on Friday nights. The capture of Black excited the police hunting the killer of Caroline Hogg, Susan Maxwell and Sarah Harper. He fitted the profile of their unknown killer almost perfectly. He had previous convictions for the sexual molestation of young girls, and when his home in Stamford Hill, north London, was searched police discovered a cache of child pornography. This included 110 magazines and 58 videos or films of young children being sexually abused. Moreover, a check on Black's work-sheets revealed that he had been in the area of all three killings at the relevant time. He had, for example, been delivering posters to a firm in Morley on the very day Sarah Harper was abducted.

Ideally Black should now have been charged with all three murders, but there was insufficient evidence at the time and it is unlikely that the cases could be proved. Black exercised his right to silence and never made any confession. But he pleaded guilty to the abduction of the little girl – he could hardly do otherwise, having been caught red-handed – and at his trial in Scotland on 10th August 1990 he was jailed for life for this offence.

Pressure now grew to bring Black to trial in England for the three schoolgirl murders. What the press and public failed to appreciate, however, was that the Crown Prosecution Service had to be confident that there was more than a 50 per cent chance of a conviction before a case was brought to court ... and there was not a shred of forensic evidence linking Black to any of the murders.

But the police did have something else: an attack on a fifteen-year-old girl in Radford, Nottinghamshire, in 1988. A man had tried to drag her into his van, and only the intervention of a passing boy had foiled the attempt. The girl could describe her attacker and was prepared to testify. Moreover, because of the similarities between this attempted abduction and the case in Stowe it would seem permissable to also refer in evidence to the Stowe kidnap, for which Black had already been found guilty. It would be a powerful weapon for the prosecution.

In August 1991 Black was formally charged with this attempted kidnapping and the three child-murders, but it was not until 13th April, 1994, that he stood in the dock at Newcastle upon Tyne Crown Court, pleading not guilty to all counts.

In his opening statement for the Crown, Mr John Milford QC told the jury that the pattern of the killings indicated that all three girls had been murdered by the same man. All were bare-legged and wearing white ankle socks when they disappeared. All had been sexually abused and each body was dumped without any effort at concealment. Mr Milford said: "The points of similarity are so enormous and so peculiar that it is submitted to you that you can safely conclude that they were all the work of one man." Mr Milford went on to say that this man was Robert Black. He was always there at the scene of the crime. In the case of Sarah Harper, Black was delivering posters to a warehouse 150 yards away from where she disappeared. He was in Portobello, Edinburgh, delivering posters, on the day Caroline Hogg vanished, and was almost certainly on the A697 on the Scottish border when Susan Maxwell was taken. Each victim was abducted near main roads which Black would have used in the course of his job. "The Crown allege," Milford continued, "that Robert Black kidnapped each of these victims, that he did so for his own sexual gratification, that he transported them far from the point of abduction and then murdered them."

The prosecutor said that Susan Maxwell disappeared after playing tennis with a friend not far from her home at Crammond Hill Farm. It was around 4 p.m. when she set off on the short walk home from the tennis club. She was wearing a yellow T-shirt, shorts and ankle socks, and she was carrying a tennis racket and an empty flask which had contained orange juice. The route took her across the border into England "where she disappeared as if into thin air." Thirteen days later her decomposing body was found 264 miles away in a copse next to a lay-by on the A518 in Staffordshire. Her knickers had been removed and were folded beneath her head. It was only by a cruel twist of fate that Black made the fateful journey to Scotland that day, the prosecutor said. A workmate was supposed to have done the Scottish run but was unable to do so for personal reasons. Black volunteered for the job. He liked the long-distance runs. He slept in his van and saved on subsistence expenses.

Black was drawn to the spot where Susan vanished by the sight of semi-clad children who were bathing in the river Tweed Mr Milford said:"A bathing place like this would be attractive to a man with an unhealthy interest in children in various stages of undress. It is common sense that watching them would excite and arouse. It may take someone with that unhealthy interest to turn fantasy into reality and lead to the commission of a serious criminal offence... We say the child was snatched, and snatched very quickly, from the roadside."

There were two sightings of a van near the river and a third further along the road. This suggested that Susan was first "stalked", and then at a safe distance trussed and gagged. Almost a year after Susan vanished Caroline Hogg disappeared while playing near her home in Beach Lane, Portobello, near Edinburgh. She was seen in the company of a man matching Black's description. Two witnesses said she went with him to a nearby fun-fair where he paid for her to ride on a roundabout. Her decomposing body was found opposite a lay-by on the A444 near Twycross, Leicestershire, 308 miles from her home, but only 24 miles from where Susan Maxwell's body was discovered.

On the dark, wet March night when Sarah Harper disappeared witnesses reported seeing a stocky, balding man in the area. They also saw a white Transit van in the vicinity, similar to the one Black drove. Mr Milford said: "It is no distance at all that the child had to walk, but again, as she walked down that street, just like those two other little girls, she disappeared into thin air." Later that evening a balding man and a white Transit van were sighted near the river Trent not far from junction 24 of the M1, the exit for the village of Donisthorpe, where Black went to visit friends. The police believed that Sarah was thrown into the river that same night, close to that junction.

Mr Milford claimed that Black had dumped the child in the river alive, after having caused her grievous internal injuries during his sexual assault. Her body, bound with rope, had been trapped in the Trent for days before being dislodged as the river swelled after heavy rain. It was eventually found at a weir. Sarah had been thrown in the river within a couple of hours of having been abducted, at about the same time that a witness saw a white Transit van parked at a gateway leading to the Trent.

"The gateway gave access to a path leading to the river used by fishermen," Mr Milford said. "But this was the close season for coarse fishing and it was 9 p.m."

Sarah's body bore bruising to the face, forehead, neck, arm and thigh, and it was thought she was probably unconscious when she was put into the river. A post-mortem examination showed the cause of death to be drowning and she had been dead within five hours of being abducted. Marks on her face showed she had been gagged, the gag being held in place with sticky tape of the type Black had later used in kidnapping the little girl in Stowe.

Turning to the attempted kidnapping of the teenager in Nottinghamshire, Mr Milford described how, as the girl was walking home after parting from her boyfriend, she noticed a blue Transit van parked with its bonnet raised. The driver attempted to engage the girl in conversation by asking if she could fix engines. Then suddenly, "she was grabbed in a bear hug", and a determined effort was made to put her by force into the van. But the would-be victim, only 4ft 10in, and looking much younger than her age – "she had the appearance of a child, fitting in with the appearance of the other children murdered by this man" – put up a spirited resistance.

A boy with whom she had been earlier spotted her plight and rushed to her aid. "The abductor realised that he was not going to get away with it and sped off," Mr Milford said. He pointed out that Black had been driving a blue Transit van that day in that area, and the girl's description of her attacker fitted his appearance at that time.

She told police that the man was aged 40 to 50, was 5ft 6in to 5ft 8in in height, wore spectacles, was heavily built – she described him as being pot-bellied – and had facial stubble and a moustache. She also noted that he smelled. Mr Milford said that members of the family with whom Black lodged knew him as Smelly Bob.

Mr Milford then turned to the background of the defendant. Scottish by birth, Black had moved to London in 1969, and lodged in Stamford Hill, north London, with a Scottish family. One of the sons of that family had once gone into Black's room and had found a blue suitcase full of pornographic photographs. He had been fifteen at the time and had gone into Black's bedroom with a friend. The son was now called to give evidence.

The prosecutor asked him what sort of people were depicted in the photographs. The witness said: "The majority of the photographs were of children." He added that he had also found a girl's swimming costume in the suitcase. He had felt disgusted and had panicked. "I just wanted to get out of the room. I put the suitcase back where I found it."

Sergeant William Ormiston of Lothian and Borders Police, who had driven Black to Galashiels police station after his arrest for the abduction and rape of the little girl in Stowe, was also called to give evidence. He said that Black had started talking about what had happened, saying: "What a day it's been. It should have happened on Friday the thirteenth ... I snatched her because of a rush of blood. I have always liked young girls since I was a young kid."

The officer said he asked Black if anyone else was involved in the abduction, and Black replied: "It's not the sort of thing you do with witnesses around, is it? I just seen her and got her into the van. I tied her up because I wanted to keep her until I delivered a parcel to Galashiels."

Ormiston said he asked Black if he had assaulted the girl. Black replied: "It just happened so quick. I only touched her a little ... I wanted to keep her until I went to somewhere like Blackpool so I could spend some time with her." He claimed he had intended to let the girl go afterwards ...

Black's defence counsel, Mr Ronald Thwaites, tried to dismiss the evidence against his client as being purely circumstantial. He claimed that everything put before the court, including the pornographic pictures from Black's collection, was merely propaganda designed to colour the minds of jurors and to paint a picture of a monster who must be guilty.

"However wicked and foul Black is – and I am not here to persuade you to like him or find any merit in him at all – it is not unreasonable to suppose that there might be some evidence to adorn the prosecution's case other than theory," Mr Thwaites declared. "This case has been developed before you using one incident of abduction in Stowe, which he admitted, as a substitute for evidence in all these other cases. There is no direct evidence against Black. If the prosecution had not been able to refer to Black's previous conviction for the child-abduction, then they would not have been able to bring him before this court on a single one of these charges. There is no forensic evidence linking Black to any of these crimes and you cannot convict him of them unless you are prepared to convict him on thin air."

Mr Thwaites said that Black would not give evidence on his own behalf, saying: "No man can be expected to remember the ordinary daily routines of his life going back many years, and in England there is not yet a presumption of guilt attached to a man who remained silent."

The defence counsel then read out his client's criminal record. It was chilling stuff. At sixteen Robert Black had been "admonished" by Greenock juvenile court for sexually assaulting a seven-year-old girl. Four years later he had been sentenced to borstal training for three similar offences against a six-year-old. Then in 1990 he was jailed for life for the abduction of the little girl in Stowe.

"The judge saw fit to give him a life sentence," Mr Thwaites said. "No one can be surprised by that and everyone must applaud it. Our children must be protected from human predators who prowl the streets, patrol the parks, scan the beaches looking for children temporarily detached from their parents to pounce on.

"Black's unhealthy lifelong interest in children is further confirmed by the haul of pornography found in his home. It is revolting and sickening to look at. But although Black was a wicked and foul pervert presently serving a life sentence, and although he was a child-molester and had a sensual obsession with young girls, that does not mean that this wretched man is a murderer. There is no automatic progression from pervert to killer. Unfortunately, there is no shortage of perverts, and child-molesters like Black are far from unique. The question for you to determine in this case is whether it has been proved he graduated from molester to murderer."

On the 19th day of the trial Mr Milford rose to make his closing speech for the prosecution. He said that Black's capture in 1990 had halted the activities of a cruel child-murderer and ended "a series of offences which are unlikely ever to be forgotten and which represent man at his most vile."

Because nobody ever voiced any suspicion about Black, "he was able to move anonymously around the country in his plain, unmarked van, a man without a wife or family, who could keep his own odd hours, who could come and go as he pleased." And Black's activities as a killer would have continued, said Mr Milford, but for his chance arrest.

Meticulous research into his daily runs and petrol receipts which had established his whereabouts at the dates of the crime were crucial evidence in the case, he said. Had it shown that Black was elsewhere in the country when the girls were abducted, then he would have been eliminated. The defence had argued that it was only coincidence that Black had been in the murder areas at the time of the offences. If that were so, Mr Milford commented, it would be "the coincidence to end all coincidences". It would mean, he said, that someone else had been Black's shadow, moving around the country like him, someone who shared his depraved sexual tastes and abducted young girls.

Although Black had told a policeman that he had taken the child at Stowe because of a rush of blood, his actions had been premeditated, Mr Milford suggested. He had with him in his van a roll of sticking plaster to gag his victim, black cord to tie her up, a cushion-cover to put over her head, and a set of "revolting probes."

"What Black actually did to that child, kidnapping, indecently assaulting, gagging and blindfolding her, demonstrates in this man a quite appalling capacity for cruelty... Wherever Black was going to take her, it was a long way from her home. Whatever indignities lay in store for her, what would her ultimate fate have been in the hands of one so calculated, so determined, so callous, so cruel?"

Mr Milford asked the jury to consider whether once she had served her purpose – almost too horrible to contemplate – Black would have let her go. It was more likely, he suggested, that "what we would have found in the heat of the summer would have been yet another decomposing little body."

The jury retired on 16th May to consider their verdict. After more than thirteen hours' deliberation spread over three days, the jury filed back into court. They had found Black guilty of all charges against him.

The judge told the prisoner: "You have said nothing in this court. Neither you nor the public will expect me to say more than a few words in sentencing you. You are an extremely dangerous man. You are already detained for life in Scotland. I sentence you on each of these counts to life imprisonment. In respect of each of these I expect you will be detained for the whole of your life, but on the murder counts I propose to make a public recommendation that the minimum term you are detained is thirty-five years. Take him down."

Black had remained impassive during the trial. Now he spoke for the first time, just four words. As he was led from the dock he looked at the row of senior detectives whose work had secured his conviction, and sneered: "Tremendous. Well done, boys."

For those officers it was the end of a marathon inquiry which had cost £12 million. Outside the court Hector Clark said: "I am totally satisfied with the verdicts for the three murders and the abduction of the girl. Had he been acquitted on any one of the charges, I would have been concerned." He added bleakly, "Black is a man of the most evil kind, but no longer important to me. I care not about him."

Critics of the investigation claimed that there had been an intolerable delay in linking the three murders to one culprit. Hector Clark admitted that it had not been until eight months after Sarah Harper's murder that the police had linked her death to those of Susan Maxwell and Caroline Hogg. He said frankly: "It was a mistake but the man who never made a mistake never made anything."

However, he reacted sharply to criticism that given Black's background of sex convictions he should have been spotted years earlier. He pointed out that Black's convictions were 20 years old and of a relatively minor nature. Had the police checked every man in Britain with minor sex convictions it would have involved over 50,000 men being questioned, which would have been logistically impossible. Black had never been considered because his name had never been forwarded to the inquiry.

However, when further details of Black's past were revealed there were more than a few raised eyebrows. For those who study serial killers, his history had a depressingly familiar ring. He was illegitimate, his factory-worker mother dumping him at birth on the Social Services. He was then fostered out with a strict elderly couple, never knowing his real mother or father. When his foster-mother died in 1958 he was moved to a mixed children's home, where he indecently assaulted a young girl. No action was taken, but he was moved to an all-boys school in Edinburgh – just two miles from Portobello. There he himself was sexually abused by a member of the staff for several years.

Psychiatrist Mervyn Glasser said: "If a man has been homosexually abused as a boy and then starts to abuse little girls, he is taking on the role of the abuser and the girl is representative of his weak victim self."

Certainly a close examination of Black's previous minor convictions raises some alarming questions. The list records that in 1963 he appeared in court charged with indecently assaulting a seven-year-old and was merely admonished. What this doesn't reveal is that Black took his victim into an air-raid shelter, half-strangled her when she cried out, and masturbated over her body, leaving her for dead. A psychiatric report given to the court suggested that it was an aberration on Black's part, unlikely to be repeated. But it was. Later he was sent to borstal for indecently assaulting his landlord's six-year-old daughter. And then he moved to London, where his first job was at

Hornsey Swimming Baths... and he was sacked for indecently assaulting a young girl swimmer.

His workmates remember him as a loner who hid his secret life well. His only outside social activity appeared to be pub darts, at which he was quite good. But he was less proficient as a driver, having to buy his own van and become self-employed when his firm refused to insure him any more.

A psychiatrist who interviewed Black in prison tape-recorded a conversation in which he confessed to indecently assaulting at least 40 young girls.

This was the perverted logic of his thinking: he loved young girls, he told the psychiatrist, and didn't want them to suffer pain from his probes. So he killed them. Dead, they couldn't feel any pain...

And now the police revealed him to be a prime suspect in at least twelve other schoolgirl murders, including three in France, where he is known to have been when three young girls disappeared south-east of Paris: their bodies were dumped after being sexually assaulted. Two child-murders in Ireland may also be his work. He was certainly in that country at the time.

The most disturbing case now linked to him is that of Lesley Molseed, the eleven-year-old girl whose body was found on the moors above Halifax, West Yorkshire, in 1975. Stefan Kiszko wrongly served 16 years in jail for her sex-killing before being cleared. Freed in 1991, he died just over a year later, aged 42. The torment he had endured in prison as an innocent man had broken him for ever.

Chapter Twelve
THE STOCKWELL STRANGLER

It began in the spring of 1986 and was to last four terrifying months. Old people began dying...Nothing strange in that; in most cases death was expected. But these elderly men and women had not died natural deaths. They had been murdered and sexually assaulted. The killer had tucked up his victims so neatly after he had satisfied his perverse desires, pulling the sheet modestly up to their necks, that at first it was assumed they had died in their sleep. The victims all lived alone or in old people's homes, and ranged in age from sixty-seven to ninety-four. It needed hardly any pressure to strangle such frail people, and in most cases the slight bruising to the neck was almost invisible. Four of the victims lived in the Stockwell district of south London – hence the killer's nickname.

In each case someone had entered their bedrooms through windows, leaving no sign of forced entry, and had killed using a one-handed grip, placing his other hand over their mouths. He left no signs of disturbance at his death-sites. He was like a wraith, drifting through the night to steal lives.

The first victim was Miss Eileen Emms, seventy-eight, who was found dead in her basement flat in West Hill Road, Wandsworth, on 10th April by her home-help. A doctor certified that death was due to natural causes, and Miss

Emms was due to be cremated before it was realized that she had been murdered.

It was the second victim who alerted the police to the fact that something was wrong. Sixty-seven-year-old Mrs Janet Cockett, of Warwick House on the Overton Road estate, Stockwell, was found dead in bed on 9th June. Her nightdress had been torn off, but lay neatly folded on a chair. Palm-prints of a stranger were found in the flat, and another factor which was to become common to most of the murders was that photographs of relatives were turned to the wall. The killer did not like to be observed...

If the police had begun to suspect that they might have a madman on the loose, an attempted killing on 27th June confirmed their fears beyond any doubt. Retired engineer Mr Fred Prentice, seventy-three, was attacked in his bed at an old people's home in Clapham, south London. An intruder got into his room and jumped on his bed, pinning him down.

The man began pinching his neck, and mumbled: "Kill!" Mr Prentice would never forget his face – he had glaring eyes and an evil grin. It was as if he was playing a cruel game with the old man, one which gave him a secret amusement. Finally Mr Prentice managed to free his mouth long enough to shout, and also pressed the alarm buzzer by his bed. The would-be killer banged his head into the wall and then fled.

The following night – 28th June – as if being thwarted had left him frustrated, the killer committed a double-murder. He broke into Somerville Hastings House, an old people's home in Stockwell Park Road. The victims were found in adjoining rooms. Valentine Gleim, eighty-four, was a former lieutenant-colonel in the British Army. Zbigniew Strabrawa, ninety-four, had been a judge in his native Poland, and had worked for British Intelligence during the war. Both men died in quick succession.

Another feature was noted by police to add to the killer's distinctive pattern – the victims were sodomized.

Now the police launched a hunt in earnest, with special night surveillance mounted on old people's homes. Forensic experts worked non-stop, gathering what information they could. Mr Prentice had given the police a sketchy description of the man they were seeking. He was aged twenty-eight to thirty, 5ft 8in tall, with short dark hair and a tanned or reddened face. The skill with which the unknown killer had gained access to flats and bedrooms led police to suspect that he was a professional burglar who might well have passed through their hands in the past. If so, his details would be in the Criminal Records Office at Scotland Yard.

Meanwhile the killings continued. The fifth victim was Mr William Carmen, eighty-two. He was found dead in bed by his daughter at his flat on the Marquess Estate, Islington. He had been sodomized, and photographs in his flat had been turned to the wall. He had been killed between 6th and 9th July.

By now the murder team hunting the killer – the "Stockwell Strangler" as the press had dubbed him – consisted of over a hundred detectives working from four murder incident rooms. Detective Chief Superintendent Ken Thompson, who coordinated the hunt, told a press conference held on 22nd July that police were studying "the probability" that one mass-killer was preying on elderly people. He warned elderly people, especially those living in South London, to be especially vigilant. Extra police patrols had been ordered in the danger areas. Pressed to state if the killings had all been done by one man, Mr Thompson said, "Certainly, if all the offences are by the same person, he must be caught before he strikes again. This man is extremely dangerous." Mr Thompson also revealed that Scotland Yard had called in a psychologist to study the murders and produce a profile of the likely killer. All the data on the murders was being fed into the super-computer HOLMES.

Because so many of the murders had taken place in old people's homes, police naturally had to investigate the possibility that a council employee might be responsible – someone who knew where the victims lived, knew they lived alone, and had means of access. However, Camden Council refused to give the police details of present or former employees, and twenty-four members of the Trade Union NUPE – half the staff at one home – refused to have their fingerprints taken. The police angrily accused the council of hindering their hunt for the killer; the council strongly denied any obstruction. Murders or no, civil rights had to be protected.

The sixth victim had provided the police with very useful clues. Mr William Downes, seventy-four, a virtual recluse, was found on 9th July by his son at his bedsit in Stockwell. The son had arrived to prepare breakfast for his father. He found him dead, lying naked in bed with the sheets pulled up to his chin. He had facial injuries, and had been sexually assaulted. On the garden gate and a wall, police found impressions of a palm-print. They were getting close; they could sense it, as hunters do.

The seventh and final victim was disabled Mrs Florence Tisdall, eighty. She was found murdered at her home in Fulham on 23rd July. She had spent the day watching the wedding of the Duke and Duchess of York on television before meeting her death at the hands of a sex-fiend. Mrs Tisdall too had been sexually abused. Police also found valuable clues at this murder scene. Within three days of this killing police arrested the murderer.

They had known his identity before the last killing – they had matched those palm-prints. After two days of painstaking checks through more than four million records, police had come up with a name, and were confident they had made a major breakthrough. They spent all weekend combing his usual haunts for him, but he was not to be found. So police waited at his local DHSS office in Southwark for him to arrive on 28th July to sign for his dole money.

The short, thin figure of Kenneth Erskine duly arrived and the police arrested him, driving him to Clapham police station. Erskine sat giggling in the back of the car. The evidence to connect him with all the killings consisted of a pattern, and those palm-prints at the homes of two of the victims. Mr Prentice subsequently picked out Erskine from an identity parade.

The police found it difficult, if not impossible, to question the killer about his bizarre sexual appetite. They had his record – pages of it – revealing him to be an incompetent burglar who had served time for his offences. But they had no idea where he had been living for the past few months and they had great difficulty in getting any answers to their questions. Erskine would grin and giggle when details of the murders were put to him, and he unnerved his questioners by engaging in continual masturbation during interviews. Detective Superintendent Bryan Jackson, who led the team of questioners, found his most experienced men baffled by their prisoner.

The police took the unusual decision to publish a photograph of Erskine in the national press before his trial, in the hope that it might bring forward witnesses who could fill in the missing pieces of the jigsaw. The photograph duly appeared in all the dailies on 12th August, with an appeal for anyone who knew the man in the picture to contact the police, who wanted to trace property stolen from the home of the victims, and to check Erskine's lodgings for possible forensic evidence. Police still did not know where Erskine had lived.

The appeal worked. A young businesswoman came forward who had come face to face with Erskine on Putney Bridge shortly after the murder of Mrs Tisdall. The woman was struck by his horrific grin, and had no trouble picking him out from an identity parade.

Erskine appeared at the magistrates' court in Battersea to be charged with the murders of Mrs Cockett and William Downes. He stood barefoot in the dock, grinning, and was formally remanded in custody. Police knew at this stage that he had killed seven people, but they suspected there might be many more victims whose deaths had been attributed to natural causes. During his four-month killing spree there were at least four other cases of old people who died in similar circumstances to his victims. They included Wilfred Parkes, eighty-one, who died at his Stockwell council flat, and Trevor Thomas, seventy-five, found dead in the bath at his Clapham home.

The police were also delving into Erskine's past for clues. They discovered that while in jail in 1982 for burglary he spent his time painting a gallery of old people lying in bed with gags stuffed in their mouths, knives sticking in them, or burned to death. Other drawings showed headless figures with blood spurting from their necks. He pinned these drawings up above his bed, and alarmed doctors at the prison, who pleaded with the authorities not to release him. But he had to be released once his sentence was completed. To be detained one day longer would have infringed his civil liberties. Fellow-prisoners were traced who spoke of Erskine boasting to them of killing old people. Yet he had been released upon society like a bomb waiting to explode.

From Erskine himself police could gather little. He was a giggling, deranged drifter who had a mental age of ten. He had moved around London from squat to squat, supplementing his dole money with the proceeds from burglaries. He may have been mentally retarded, but he had the cunning of a fox. He had two bank accounts into which he paid hundreds of pounds gained from crime.

Psychiatrists called in to examine him were as baffled as the police. Dr Gisli Gudjohnsson of London University said later, "He was giggling, smiling and looking out of the window when serious matters were being discussed. He had serious difficulty distinguishing reality from fantasy."

All that was known of Erskine's background was that his mother and Antiguan father had decided early on that they did not want him living with them at their Shepherd's Bush home and as a child he had attended schools for maladjusted children in and around London. When he was sixteen they disowned him completely, and ever since the retarded and difficult youth had lived rough.

On 13th August 1987 Erskine was charged with an additional three murders and one attempted murder. Erskine always appeared in court without shoes – and sometimes without socks – grinning inanely from the dock as the charges were put.

The trial of Kenneth Erskine began at the Old Bailey on Tuesday, 12th January 1988. The thin, short figure of Erskine, wearing a blue denim jacket, just stood there grinning, unaware of his surroundings or of what was being said about him by prosecuting counsel. He pleaded not guilty to the seven counts of murder, speaking in a barely audible whisper.

Mr James Crespi QC, prosecuting, told the jury that the "appallingly wanton" murders of seven pensioners in London between April and July 1986 were marked by such striking similarities that they could only have been the work of the same man. "They were committed by a killer who likes killing, and that man was Kenneth Erskine." Telling of the deaths of the seven victims, Mr Crespi said that five of them had been sodomized immediately before or after their deaths. All died from manual strangulation. Mr Crespi said that after Erskine had murdered and finished "playing with" his victims, he placed their naked bodies in their beds and tucked the sheets tidily up to their necks.

Mr Crespi said the murder toll could have been eight had not the killer panicked and fled while attacking Mr Frederick Prentice. Mr Prentice was ambushed by an intruder in the early hours of 27th June. "Mr Prentice told him to get out of the room and the man put his fingers to his lips as a gesture to be quiet. He then jumped on Mr Prentice, putting one knee on each of his hands to immobilize him, and his hands around his neck with his thumbs over his windpipe, pressing with a pumping action. He appeared to be playing with his victim and uttered only one word throughout:'Kill!'"

Mr Crespi told how Mr Prentice had picked Erskine out from an identity parade, and thumb and palm-prints found at the homes of Mrs Cockett and Mr Downes, and shoe-prints at the homes of Prentice, Gleim and Stabrawa, linked Erskine to the murders. Mr Crespi admitted that there was only indirect evidence linking Erskine to three of the murders and the attempted murder, but said a pattern was visible through all the counts. The common features were that all the victims were elderly people living alone; they were attacked by an intruder who left no signs of forced entry, and almost all were attacked late at night or in the early hours of the morning. In each case the intruder made his entry through a window. All the victims were killed by one-handed strangulation while the other hand was held over the mouth. All the victims were found in bed, and five of them had been sodomized.

Mr Crespi went on:"In all these cases the killing was wanton. It was not done for the kind of reason which would encourage a burglar under normal circumstances to kill. In our submission, putting all these things together, there is not only a pattern but a striking pattern."

On the second day of the trial, after forensic evidence, the only surviving victim of the Stockwell Strangler went into the witness box to relive the night of the murderous attack on him. Mr Prentice described to the jury how he had been woken by an intruder and looked up to see a pair of "black glaring eyes" staring at him. "I could only see his head and his glaring eyes, and he grinned. He had a terrible grin on his face." By the electric light from the corridor outside, Mr Prentice could see something of his attacker. "I saw the figure and I shouted at him to get out... he jumped on top of me... he had his legs on top of me. I couldn't move my hands and arms because they were pinned. I could feel him pinching my neck and I was screaming. I thought I was finished. I could feel his hands around my neck. He would stop for three or four seconds and then start again. It went on three times and the last time he chucked my head against the wall and ran off."

Six weeks later Mr Prentice, a severely disabled man who could only walk with crutches, picked Erskine out from a police identity parade. "I know the man I saw that morning," Mr Prentice said, "and I never want to see him again. He ruined my life. I have still got pain." Replying to Mr Roy Amlot, defending, Mr Prentice said the light from the corridor was sufficient for him to see his attacker. "I'm sure it was the man," he said. "I recognized him by his hair, the top of his face and his glaring eyes." He denied having seen any press pictures of Erskine before attending the identity parade.

Miss Denise Keena, twenty-five, the young woman who had seen Erskine leaning over the rail of Putney Bridge, apparently being sick, told the jury about the encounter. It came on the evening of 23rd July, the day when Mrs Florence Tisdall was found murdered at her home in Ranelagh Gardens, Fulham, a short walk from Putney Bridge.

When she was about eight feet away from Erskine, Miss Keena testified, he looked over his shoulder at her and she saw his expression. "It was a sort of terrible grin," she said. "He looked almost as if he was out of control. It was a horrible, awful, disgusting expression. All the muscles in his face were taut and all the tendons strained across the bone structure. He had wide and staring eyes. His mouth was open."

Miss Keena told the jury that she had to look away, because Erskine's expression shocked and scared her. She said that when she looked back at him "he was walking as if in a daze or a trance." She later picked Erskine out of an identity parade.

The following day Detective Chief Superintendent Bryan Jackson went into the witness box to tell about the arrest, interrogation and background of Erskine. He described him as being a loner, without family or friends, who lived off the proceeds of burglary. He had no visitors during his eighteen months in custody, apart from legal representatives and doctors. Erskine had made no admissions to the offence. He just said: "I don't remember killing anyone. I may have done it without knowing it."

The trial lasted an astonishing fifteen days, and for that time Erskine repeatedly grinned in the dock. On Friday 29th January 1988, after the final speeches by defence and prosecution counsel and the judge's summing-up, the jury retired, returning with guilty verdicts on all the counts. Erskine appeared to be tearful as the judge addressed him.

Mr Justice Rose told him: "I doubt whether the time will ever come when you can be safely at large. I have no doubt that the horrific nature and number of your crimes requires that I should recommend, taking your age into account, a prison sentence of forty years." It was the longest sentence ever passed in a British murder trial. Erskine was given seven life sentences.

Chapter Thirteen
HEIDNIK

The pornography of an age reflects its fears and fantasies, and modern pornography seems to be a perversion of the will-to-power. It may be argued that it is not too different from the writings of de Sade or Nietzsche – but they were unique in their age, and their evil philosophy is now commonplace. John Fowles's powerful novel *The Collector* is not pornography but literature. However, even literature can inspire devotees to act out the fictional fantasy. The novel is a study of a clinically obsessive man who wins the football pools and puts his fantasy into action. He buys a house in an isolated spot, has the basement turned into a prison cell and then "collects" a girl and keeps her prisoner in his private dungeon.

The pleasure he derives from his captive is compared to that felt by a fanatical butterfly collector with a rare specimen, but what is captured so strongly in the book is the sheer power-kick of having a woman completely submissive to the man's will – rather like a sultan with his harem. The book, which was a best-seller and turned into a film, seemed to capture something of the spirit of its age; a feeling that women should exist only to serve the whims of men, and in a sense the novel was a prophecy which was to be fulfilled in the USA in 1987 in a case which the press called Philadelphia's "House of Horror".

Just before midnight on 24th March 1987 a black prostitute, Josefina Rivera, banged frantically on the door of her boyfriend's apartment in Philadelphia. He had not seen her for four months, ever since she had gone out on a November evening to "turn a trick". He was shocked to see how appallingly she had changed; she looked thin and haggard and had deep scars and sores around her ankles.

The boyfriend, Vincent Nelson, said later, "She came in rambling on, you know, talking real fast about this guy having three girls chained up in the basement of his house and she was held hostage for four months. She said he was beating them, raping them, had them eating dead people... a dog was in the yard chewing their bones. I just thought she was crazy..."

However, he and the girl went to the phone box and rang the emergency number for the police. Two officers arrived in a squad car and listened to her extraordinary tale. They were initially sceptical, thinking she was perhaps on drugs, but the scars around her ankles convinced them it was a story worth checking out. She said she had been kidnapped on 26th November 1986 by a bearded white man driving a Cadillac Coupé de Ville, whom she described as well-dressed and wearing a Rolex watch. The house in which she claimed to have been held was just three blocks away. She said she had been tortured and sexually abused and had seen other women in the house being treated in a similar fashion. She had also witnessed the murder of a fellow-captive.

Police kept the house under observation while a warrant was obtained and a search-team of officers was assembled. The two-storey brick house was in a white working-class neighbourhood and had bars over its windows. On the outside was a placard reading United Church of the Ministers of God, and the house was guarded by two fierce dogs, a German Shepherd and a Doberman. The address: 3520 North Marshall Street.

Police forced entry into the house at 4.30 a.m. on 25th March, and were confronted by a bearded white man who raised his arms when he saw drawn guns. He said his name was Gary Michael Heidnik, forty-three.

He was taken into custody and removed to the Sex Crimes Unit at headquarters. He seemed to think the police had called about his late alimony payments...

In his basement police found two naked black women chained to a sewer pipe by their ankles. At first they were terrified, but when they realised it was the police they cried out in joy, "Hosanna – we are free!" and kissed the officers' hands in gratitude.

Sergeant Frank McCloskey asked them: "Is anyone here but you?" The two women, one eighteen and the other twenty-four, pointed to a board on the floor.

"She's there. She's in the hole."

Pushing the board aside, the officer discovered a pit in which crouched another naked black woman. She too was shackled, and her hands were cuffed behind her back. She was so weak she had to be lifted out of the hole – and immediately started screaming.

"It's all right," the other two women assured her. "It's the police. We're free."

Still in shock, the woman who had been in the hole began raving: "He took my thirty dollars; get my money back!"

Police had to use bolt cutters to remove the shackles, and the women were rushed to hospital. All were extremely thin and weak, and covered with bruises. The police now searched the house, finding a stack of pornographic magazines, all of which featured black women. On the stove was a blackened cooking pot, its interior covered in a thick crust.

An officer opened the fridge and was confronted by a human forearm. That did it. He ran outside and vomited.

Officers sent for forensic experts from the medical examiner's office to assist them. Detective Lamont Anderson, at the scene, told reporters that "other body parts" had been found in the house and it was believed that at least two women had been killed in the basement.

The following day, all the newspapers led with lurid headlines which tried to include the elements of murder, rape, bondage, torture and cannibalism. It was known from early on that Heidnik was a "Bishop" in his own invented church and had extensive dealings with the stock exchange. He was worth in excess of half a million dollars, and had a Rolls-Royce in the garage of his run-down home. Newspapers called him the "Rolls-Royce Reverend" and stated that he was into "stocks and bondage".

Other headlines declared: MAN HELD IN TORTURE KILLINGS; MADMAN'S SEX ORGY WITH CHAINED WOMEN; and WOMEN CHAINED IN HORROR DUNGEON.

While police continued to take cardboard boxes filled with human remains from the house, the four surviving captives were questioned in hospital and the grotesque and sickening details of their ordeal emerged. Three of them had been imprisoned for three months, tortured and raped daily by the white man, who kept them alive on a diet of dog food, bread and water. They were kept shackled in the basement, being released from their manacles only for further sex and torture sessions upstairs. Police later learnt that at times the starving captives had been fed on human flesh which had been put through a food-processor and blended with the dog food. A dog had been seen chewing on a human leg...

One of the freed victims guided police to where another woman's body lay buried. Survivor Lisa Thomas, nineteen, said she'd seen a woman she knew only as "Sandy" fall while handcuffed to a chain from the ceiling and strike her head on a concrete floor. Sandy was later identified as Sandra Lindsay, twenty-four.

Miss Rivera, the woman who'd raised the alarm, told police that the white man had been boasting that he had fed the boiled remains of "Sandy" to herself and the other captives. Police also heard that Debbie Dudley, twenty-three, had been murdered by being placed in a pit filled with water and electrocuted by wires attached to her chains.

That pit had also served another purpose; it was the "hole" in which the captives were kept when being punished, as well as to prevent escape whenever the "master" left the house. A wooden board would be placed over it, held down by a sack of sand.

Josefina Rivera had been the first captive, picked up on 26th November 1986, for sex. Heidnik had driven her to his house where, after sex, he'd begun to throttle her into submission. He handcuffed her and took her down into the basement, shackling her by the ankles. She had to watch him dig a pit in the concrete floor, and feared it was going to be her grave. But he had assured her that the hole was only for punishment if she misbehaved, confiding that he was only attracted to black women. His ambition was to have ten women captive in the cellar and to have children by them all. "We'll all be one big happy family," he promised.

Hetold her that he had served four years in prison after being found guilty of the rape of a mentally retarded black woman by whom he wanted to have a child. It had been unfair, he said, because sex had been voluntary. He also told her that the daughter he'd had by another black woman had been put in a home.

"Society owes me a wife and family," he told Josefina, before forcing her to perform oral sex on him.

Later that day Josefina had managed to force open a boarded-over window and scream for help. Nobody came, but Heidnik heard her and came down and beat her, then threw her into the pit. He left her alone, with a radio playing rock music at full volume to drown out any more cries for help.

On 29th November, three days later, Heidnik brought his second captive down into the basement. She was Sandra Lindsay. She had known Heidnik for years and had once been pregnant by him. He had been furious when he discovered she'd had an abortion. Heidnik forced Sandra to write a letter to her mother saying she was all right, and later posted it from a box in New York.

The basement was cold, lit only by a bare bulb. The floor was covered in litter. The routine each day was the same: beatings and forced sex, a prison diet of oatmeal and bread. Later Heidnik began giving them dog food from tins, which he spread on sandwiches.

One by one other captives were brought down to the basement.

On 22nd December Lisa Thomas was accosted by a white man sitting in a Lincoln. She accepted his invitation to dinner and afterwards agreed to go home with him to watch video-tapes.

"I fell asleep and the next thing I know he was choking me and had handcuffed me," she said. "He took me down to the basement and put chains on my legs. He beat me with a wooden stick. There were two other women down there. They were chained too."

Later, Heidnik brought a further two unfortunate women down to the basement. The first, Deborah Dudley, arrived on New Year's Day 1987. Heidnik came to regret taking her because she was a strong character and argued back, inciting the others to revolt. She had to be beaten frequently. Then, on 18th January, Jacquelyn Askins, eighteen, was captured. Her ankles were so thin that she could not be shackled. Heidnik used handcuffs instead.

By now Heidnik was treating Josefina Rivera as a "trusty", allowing her out of the cellar to have meals with him and keep discipline among the other captives. She reported any talk of escape attempts. On 23rd March Heidnik took Josefina out driving and together they picked up Agnes Adams, twenty-four, another prostitute. She was necessary because by that time two of the other captives had died.

On 7th February Sandra Lindsay died. She had been suspended by her hands from the ceiling for a week as a punishment for attempting to escape from the hole, and died from sheer exhaustion.

On 18th March, Heidnik filled the pit with water and made everyone except Josefina climb in. He gave them electric shocks from a bare wire. It touched Deborah Dudley's chains and she was killed instantly.

Heidnik disposed of Sandra by putting her body through a meat-grinder, and boiled her head in a pan on the stove. Neighbours complained about the stench of the cooking meat, but Heidnik simply told the investigating policeman that he had burnt his dinner. The officer did not bother to look inside the saucepan on the stove...

Next came another refinement in cruelty. To make the girls deaf so that they would not hear any rescue attempt Heidnik jabbed a screwdriver into their ears, twisting it around to rupture their ear-drums. Josefina was not subjected to this. She had by now gained Heidnik's trust by snitching on her fellow-captives and beating them on Heidnik's orders. She was often taken out to fast-food restaurants for meals, or for a ride in his Cadillac or Rolls-Royce.

She was with him when he buried Deborah Dudley in a New Jersey park on 22nd March, and when he stopped on the way back to buy a newspaper. "I want to check my stocks," he told her.

On 24th March, 1987, Rivera had become so trusted that she persuaded Heidnik to let her see her family to put their minds at rest. She promised to return... Heidnik dropped her off at the same corner that he had picked her up from four months previously. Once out of his sight Rivera hurried immediately to Vincent Nelson's apartment and blurted out her astonishing story.

When arrested on 25th March, Heidnik was found to have almost $2,000 on him, and numerous credit cards. There were documents for four cars, and a statement from the stockbrokers Merrill Lynch, showing his account standing at $377,382.52.

Within hours of his arrest, Heidnik was attacked by disgusted fellow-prisoners who broke his nose. In isolation for his own protection, Heidnik attempted to hang himself in the shower on 2nd April. He was rescued unconscious, but alive.

Police continued to search Heidnik's house, dredging the sewers and tearing apart the walls in their search for further bodies. They had already recovered parts of the dismembered body of a girl wrapped in plastic from the freezer and were seeking a third body.

Meanwhile other detectives began investigating Heidnik's background. He was a wealthy, self-styled "Bishop", who insisted that police address him as "Reverend". He had a record of violence, having been charged the previous year with "spouse rape" by his Oriental wife, who had since left him. Police established that his *modus operandi* was to seduce women with a mixture of religion and kindness – then terrorise them with sadism.

Born in November, 1943, in Cleveland, Heidnik is the archetypal serial killer; the product of a broken home, his parents had separated when he was two years old. His mother committed suicide in 1970 when she learned she had cancer, and Heidnik had not seen his father in twenty years.

Heidnik had a loveless childhood, which he spent in solitary fantasizing. He was also a bed-wetter, a fact which enraged his heavy-drinking father, who beat him often for it. At school Heidnik was an object of ridicule because of the shape of his head: classmates called him "football head". His head was slightly deformed following injuries after a fall from a tree. (A high proportion of serial killers have a history of head injuries.)

Following his son's arrest his father told the press:"I hope to hell they hang him, and you can quote me on that. I'll even pull the rope."

Gary Heidnik's younger brother, forty-one-year-old Terry, gave an interesting insight into the Jekyll and Hyde character who was now being labelled the "Beast of Philadelphia". He explained that he and Gary had been raised in a family atmosphere of violence and racism. It was an unhappy childhood.

When Heidnik left school he joined the army where he became a loan-shark and started making money. His childhood fantasies had always centred around money and on dreams of becoming a millionaire.

On 25th August 1962 he complained to an army doctor about headaches, dizzy spells and various other ailments that he was suffering. The doctor diagnosed him to be either schizoid or schizophrenic. On 23rd January, 1963, he was given an honourable discharge and awarded a 100 per cent mental disability pension for life because his condition was considered to be service-related. He had served just fourteen months of his enlistment.

For over twenty years Heidnik lived on his pension, some $2,000 a month, plus social security payments.

Having failed in an army career, Heidnik settled in Philadelphia. At first he tried to gain credits at the University of Pennsylvania in a number of subjects. He had an IQ of 130, 30 above average. His attempts in the 1960s to live first with his mother, then his father, were failures, so he drifted from job to job, the last one as a male nurse. He never lasted long.

In the years that followed he was admitted to mental hospitals at least twenty-one times, and attempted suicide on thirteen occasions. In the spring of 1971 he founded his own church, registering it as a charity with himself as Bishop for life. He seems to have held genuine services with his flock, but his church's money-raising ventures included bingo and loan-sharking.

In 1975 Bishop Heidnik opened an account with Merrill Lynch in the name of his church, and began playing the stock-market – with remarkable success. By 1976 he was a wealthy man. In that same year came his first arrest, for carrying a firearm on a public street. He had let an apartment to a man, but when his tenant climbed in through a window one night Heidnik fired at him with a revolver. The charge of assault with a deadly weapon was dropped, however.

In March 1978 Heidnik became a father. A mentally retarded black woman bore his child, a baby girl. Heidnik also attempted to father a child with this woman's sister, who was in a psychiatric institution. On 9th May 1978 he helped her escape and hid her at his home, in the basement. He considered he was doing her a favour. When the police found the girl it was obvious that the she had been grossly sexually abused. She had a venereal infection of the throat, so oral sex was not hard to prove. Heidnik was charged with unlawful imprisonment and deviant sex. In November 1978 he was sentenced to from three to seven years in the state penitentiary. He served four years, being released on parole on 12th April, 1983, aged thirty-nine.

Heidnik bought the house at 3520 North Marshall Street soon after, and became noted for his extraordinary sexual behaviour. Every night he seemed to have three-in-a-bed sex, always with black women, some drawn from his congregation.

Deciding he wanted an Oriental wife, he got one through a matrimonial agency, and Filipino girl Betty Disto flew from Manila to Philadelphia to join him. They were married within three days. A week later she came home from shopping to find him in bed with three women. Heidnik tried to assure her that this was a normal custom for American males, but after being subjected to forced sodomy she left him in January, 1986. The court ordered him to pay her $135 a week.

It was in November of that same year that Heidnik began stocking his harem, first kidnapping Josefina Rivera...

Gary Heidnik's trial began on 20th June, 1988, in Philadelphia City Hall, room 653, before a woman judge, Lynn M. Abraham. It was obvious from the outset that the defence tactic would be to claim insanity; however, Assistant District Attorney Charles Gallagher made it plain that he would seek the death penalty. Defence counsel was Charles Peruto, a flamboyant lawyer with a good record of acquittals, but in this case he knew he would be fighting a losing battle. It took a long time to choose a jury. The defence, for some reason, sought an all-white jury. The prosecutor told this jury that Heidnik had murdered, raped, kidnapped and assaulted six young women aged between 18 and 25.

"Gary Heidnik took these women home with him," Gallagher said. "He plied them with food and in some cases sex. He assaulted them. He choked them. He handcuffed them and took them to his basement where he put shackles on their ankles. He starved them. He tortured them. He repeatedly had sex with them."

He added that Heidnik had killed two of them, one of whom he dismembered, cooked and fed to the others: "The evidence will show that, from the eve of Thanksgiving, 1986, up to 25th March 1987, the defendant committed repeated and sadistic malicious acts. He did them in a methodical and systematic way. He knew exactly what he was doing, and he knew it was wrong. He took advantage of underprivileged people."

When defence counsel rose the judge reminded him that he need not make an opening statement; that his client was innocent until proved guilty.

Peruto retorted:"My client is not innocent. He is very, very guilty." He said his client had indeed done all the things he had been accused of, but added that while the prosecutor had promised to construct a trail of evidence leading right to Heidnik's door, he didn't want to stop there. He wanted to take the jury through that door and show the man inside.

"There's no mystery here," he went on. "This is not a whodunnit. If all we had to decide here was who did it and what was done, it would be easy. You're not here to determine if Gary Heidnik is going to walk out of here a free man. He's never going to see the light of day. He will be put behind bars or in some mental institution. Any person who puts dog food and human remains in a food processor, calls it a gourmet meal and feeds it to others is out to lunch!"

Peruto said the defence would be one of insanity, telling the jury that he would be calling expert witnesses to testify to that fact.

"Understand two things," he intoned to the jury. "One: Gary Heidnik didn't want anybody to die. Two: because of his mental illness, he couldn't tell right from wrong."

Witnesses were called one by one. Josefina Rivera was asked what the women had done to pass the time in the basement.

"Nothing too much... outside of just having sex and staying in the hole. Three times we were down in the hole and we ran out of air. We couldn't breathe. We started screaming and hollering and Gary came down and beat us... We didn't take any baths or wash our hair... Music was going twenty-four hours a day."

In telling of the death of Sandra Lindsay, Josefina said: "He carried her body upstairs and we heard an electric saw. Then we smelt a terrible odour. He smelled of it and so did the food he brought us." She said that Heidnik had stopped beating her in January because he was beginning to feel he could trust her. But he was having problems with Debbie Dudley. "He always had trouble with Debbie, Debbie always fought back."

Not long after Lindsay died, Heidnik took Debbie upstairs. "In about five minutes she came back. She was very quiet." Josefina said she asked her what had happened, and Debbie told her, "He showed me Sandra's head cooking in a pot. Her ribs were cooking in a roasting pan in the stove and her legs and arms were in the freezer. He told me if I didn't start listening to him, that would happen to me." Six weeks later, Debbie Dudley was dead.

The black woman's shocking testimony continued, clear in the silence of the court. "Everybody went on punishment in early March. We were eating dog food mixed with body parts."

She was asked if she knew where Heidnik had got his ideas from, and replied brightly, "Yes, he got them from watching movies and TV. He got the idea of feeding us parts of Sandy's body from *Eating Raoul*, and his ideas on punishment from *Mutiny on the Bounty*. He also saw *The*

World of Susie Wong and said he liked the way Oriental women were. That's why he picked a Filipino wife."

Lisa Thomas was the next witness. The day after he'd first shackled her, Heidnik seemed to have shown a touch of compassion and fitted a longer chain between her ankles.

"Why did he do that?" Gallagher asked.

"So I could open my legs wider to have sex," she replied.

"Did he beat you too?"

"Yes, almost from the first moment. He hit me five times with a thick brown stick... He told me to beat Sandy regularly; he'd get his kicks from seeing us beat each other. Then he'd get on top of me and make me suck his penis."

Jacquelyn Askins was the youngest of the witnesses, still only nineteen when she took the stand. She looked frightened to death as she described the sex-parties Heidnik forced her to join in from her basement cell. "I'd suck his penis and another girl would suck his balls. Then he'd have sex with one girl and I'd lie next to him so I could catch his juice." She told of the frequent beatings she endured, and of having to eat dog-food sandwiches.

The remaining witnesses were policemen and doctors. Detectives told of what they found in Heidnik's house.

Dr Robert Catherman, who'd performed the autopsy on Dudley, confirmed that she had died of electrocution. "It was an almost classic example of electrothermal injury," he said.

Dr Paul Hoyer had examined the body parts removed from Heidnik's freezer. He testified that he had found a bone covered in dog hairs in the yard. It was from an upper left arm and matched the other frozen limbs in the freezer. They included several ribs, a number of tooth fragments and one whole tooth. Positive identification of the remains came from a wrist found in the freezer. Lindsay had injured her wrist a year earlier and her X-ray was on file. "The overall size and shape matched, plus the pattern matched. There is a pattern in bone and each pattern is unique. By comparing this we were able to say that this was Sandra Lindsay."

The prosecution rested its case.

A psychiatrist called by the defence, Dr Clancy McKenzie, argued that there existed within Heidnik's head an adult mind and a mind only 17 months old. It was the infantile part of the mind that kidnapped and raped women. Heidnik was a schizophrenic, he declared firmly.

The judge was openly sceptical of this explanation and ruled that the defence could not call in evidence Heidnik's twenty-year history of mental illness, or even produce the records from various doctors in evidence. It was a blow which sunk the defence.

A broker from Merrill Lynch said that "Bishop" Heidnik had opened an account with a cheque for $1,500. Over the next seven years, Heidnik had bought shares over the telephone and his original stake increased to over half a million dollars.

District Attorney Gallagher asked the witness, "What kind of investor was he?"

"A very astute investor," was the broker's reply.

In his closing speech for the defence, Peruto told the jury, "What was Gary Heidnik's purpose? His purpose was to raise ten kids, not to kill anybody. Third-degree murder in reckless disregard for human life. This is a classic case of third degree."

He said of Heidnik's captives that one was retarded and three were prostitutes.

"As sick as it is, these were his chosen people. These were the girls he wanted to reproduce with. Is that sane? It's a case of Dr Jekyll and Mr Heidnik. Isn't it more likely that he's more insane than not? What kind of mentality does it take to have human flesh in front of you; a human being, and to cut through that body? To cut through flesh? To cut through bone and to take some of those body parts and wrap them up and put them in the freezer? And then to cook some and feed it to the others? Who was he trying to impress with that delusion?"

Peruto demanded a verdict of not guilty by reason of insanity.

District Attorney Gallagher countered by saying that Heidnik had planned each of the abductions, killed in a cold, premeditated fashion and disposed of Sandra Lindsay's body by dismembering it and cooking those parts that could have led to her identification – the head and hands. "Just because someone does bizarre acts, the law doesn't recognise them as insane... What he did was premeditated, deliberate murder," he declared.

On 1st July, 1988, the jury found Heidnik guilty in the first degree on all counts in the indictment. Under Pennsylvania law, the jury that returns a guilty verdict for first-degree murder must also decide the penalty, and they have two choices: life in prison, or death in the electric chair. The jury returned the following day with a decision of death.

Peruto was angry, insisting that the jury had acted emotionally, not intellectually. Then he asked Judge Abraham to issue an order to prison officials to make sure Heidnik was kept in isolation. "If he is put in the general population, the jury's wishes will be carried out immediately," he warned.

Judge Abraham said, "If your client is going to commit suicide, he's going to do it. Prison officials don't want that, but neither do they want prisoners killing other prisoners. I don't have the authority to order him held in isolation, but I will suggest they carefully watch him for suicide and carefully house him."

She then immediately sentenced Heidnik to death for the murder of Sandra Lindsay, setting a date three months ahead for sentencing on the Dudley killing. A reporter telephoned Heidnik's father with the news and asked for his reaction. The father replied, "I'm not interested. I don't care. It don't bother me a bit."

Chapter Fourteen
JEFFREY DAHMER:
THE MILWAUKEE CANNIBAL

On the evening of 22nd July, 1991, Jeffrey Dahmer, a white man aged thirty-one, met a black man called Tracy Edwards, a thirty-two-year-old father of six. They met in a shopping mall, and Dahmer invited the man back to his apartment for a beer. Edwards wrinkled his nose at the foul smell which permeated the apartment – which Dahmer explained was due to faulty plumbing – but stayed seven hours. "He seemed like a regular guy," Edwards said later.

In the early morning of the following day Edwards ran out of the apartment building with handcuffs dangling from his wrists, and flagged down a passing police patrol car. Edwards told the police officers how he had been lured to the home of Jeffrey Dahmer at 213 Oxford Apartments, in the predominantly black area of Milkwaukee.

Edwards never did reveal what he and Dahmer talked about or did for seven hours, but he said that at one point he willingly snapped the handcuffs on to one of his wrists. Then he got scared; he saw that Dahmer had a knife.

As a result of Edwards's statement the police raided Dahmer's apartment. They found a chilling scene inside. Swarms of flies hovered over the remains of at least eleven corpses. A soup pan on the stove contained human brains which had been simmered in tomato sauce. In the refrigerator were three human heads wrapped in cling-film, and a selection of hands and feet in another pan had apparently been boiled. A number of glass jars in the kitchen contained the genitalia of at least three men, all preserved in a saline solution.

Police officers had to wear rubber protective suits and special breathing apparatus to remove the evidence from that flat. They were all warned what they might find. Even so, all the officers who entered that chamber of horrors had to undergo specialist counselling to help them recover from the shock.

Officers noticed that there was very little actual food in the apartment, just one or two packets of savoury snacks. It is claimed that Dahmer lived on the flesh of his victims and little else. Newspapers reported that, following his arrest, Dahmer described eating the flesh of his victims, relating in gory detail how he had sliced off one victim's biceps and fried it in vegetable oil.

Over the years Dahmer had killed and sodomized at least eleven men in his apartment, dismembering their bodies with the aid of a chainsaw. All of them were black. Dahmer was that rare serial killer: a man who crossed the racial line to kill. Usually, whites kill whites, and blacks kill blacks. But not Dahmer.

In other ways, however, he was very typical. Like so many serial killers, he liked to keep mementoes of his crimes. Police found scores of Polaroid photographs of the nude victims, Dahmer's little souvenirs of his exploits. The photographs were found stuffed down besides bags of dismembered limbs.

Dahmer – who worked in a chocolate factory – said that his desire to kill stemmed from the time when he was gang-raped by a group of blacks while he was in prison. This claim was never proved, but Dahmer had certainly spent time behind bars. In 1989 he was jailed for eight years for child-molesting (though he served only ten months of that sentence before being released in March 1990). He was also a homosexual.

The police came in for criticism when it was revealed that one of Dahmer's earlier victims, Konerak Sinthasomphone, had tried to escape from his clutches. He had run out of the building naked and screaming, bleeding from the rectum and begging police officers to rescue him. They had laughed the incident off as a "homosexual lover's tiff", and had returned the victim to Dahmer. Sinthasomphone was a boy aged just fourteen years.

Police transcripts of the radio call made by the patrol car on that evening of 27th May 1991 revealed that the officers joked with their dispatcher about the plight of the boy, reporting: "Intoxicated Asian, naked male. Was returned to sober boyfriend." The boy's parents had in fact reported their son missing several hours previously. The police said they would keep an eye open for him.

The adult Dahmer was able to fool the police and his neighbours, but as a child he had never fooled his class-mates. They knew him to be a highly disturbed loner. One said: "By junior high school, everyone gave him a wide berth. He always tried to be the class clown, but his sense of humour was cruel and dark. He would run through shopping malls acting like he was mentally retarded, just to get people's attention. He didn't win a lot of friends that way."

After dropping out of high school, Dahmer joined the army and served a two-year stint in Germany at the US Air Force Base at Baumholder, twenty-five miles south-west of Mainz. During this period – between 1979 and 1981 – the remains of five mutilated murder victims were found close to the base. The murders had baffled the German police. Now they were anxious to question Dahmer...

Following his release from prison on parole in the spring of 1990, Dahmer was given a job at the Ambrosia chocolate factory in Milwaukee. He spent his spare time cruising the seedy gay bars in the neighbourhood, and would often stay in them all day. He was eventually sacked from Ambrosia for absenteeism in the summer of 1991.

Might it be significant that, at about this time he went to see a film playing at the local cinema: *The Silence of the Lambs*? It is a tempting connection to make, but in fact reports indicate that Dahmer had begun killing and eating human beings long before that film was made or the novel written. It appears that he committed his first murder shortly after he left school, when he picked up a hitch-hiker, nineteen-year-old Steven Hicks, and battered him with a bar-bell, then strangled him to finish him off. After his arrest Dahmer provided the police with a map of the burial site. Human bones were subsequently recovered.

Nevertheless, Jonathan Demme's horrific film did seem to have some effect on him. Most of Dahmer's victims were butchered, cooked and eaten in the six-week period between his seeing *The Silence of the Lambs* and being arrested.

When the police did bring Dahmer in, they found him to be polite and cooperative. He readily told them what he had done, how he had lured his victims back to his apartment with promises of sex or free beer. Once he got them inside he found some way of drugging them before killing them. Some fought back with phenomenal strength, but Dahmer always prevailed.

The FBI Behavioral Science Unit in Virginia were naturally appalled by the revelations of Dahmer's crimes. But they were not surprised by the horrific details surrounding the case or the background of the killer that subsequently emerged. Jeffrey Dahmer, they said, fitted the serial killer profile perfectly. According to their psychologists, a serial killer is likely to be a loner, possibly the victim of school bullies, and someone who consistently underachieves his outward promise. Generally they have been pressurized into setting their goals too high, and resort to lying – even to themselves – to cover their inadequacies and inabilities.

The typical serial killer is white, unable to hold down a job for long, with abnormal sexual needs. That was Dahmer. Such a man would feel a compulsion to treasure trophies of his killings. That was Dahmer too. Cruelty to animals in childhood is a key element in the profile of a serial killer. As a child Dahmer had killed and mutilated a dog, nailing its carcass to a tree.

The most chilling aspect about the serial killer, however, is not these various obscene characteristics and traits. It is their apparent normality. Jeffrey Dahmer, described by his neighbours as a pleasant, polite man, was a reasonably good-looking thirty-one-year-old, clean-cut but unremarkable. He came from a respectable middle-class family who concerned themselves with his education. As one neighbour said when he discovered what the police had learned about Dahmer: "Who the hell would have thought we were living with that monster in our building? He's so damn ordinary!"

Prosecutor Michael McCann told reporters about the scene inside Dahmer's apartment and about one of his victims in particular. Oliver Lacy was twenty-three. Dahmer "dismembered him and placed the man's head in the bottom of the refrigerator – and kept the man's heart in the freezer to eat later."

McCann claimed that Dahmer was responsible for "at least seventeen killings."

Through his lawyer, Dahmer issued a terse statement. It read simply: "Tell the world I am sorry for what I have done."

The trial of Dahmer began on 27th January 1992. After the charges had been read out Dahmer's lawyer, Gerald Boyle, the court-appointed defence counsel, told Judge Gram that although Dahmer admitted killing fifteen young men and boys, he had been insane at the time. "The decision to plead guilty is Dahmer's defence," Boyle said. "This case is all about his mental condition."

The defence presented its case first. Dr Frederick Berlin, a psychiatrist specialising in sexual disorders, said that Dahmer's obsession with having sex with corpses took over his mind and drove him out of control. The doctor said that in his opinion Dahmer did not have the capacity to control or adapt his behaviour to the requirements of the law. "He lacked the capacity to appreciate the wrongfulness of his actions."

The court heard how Dahmer had attempted to perform crude lobotomies on some of his drugged victims, drilling holes in their skulls and then pouring in acid in the hope of deadening a portion of their brains. "Dahmer had hoped to control and keep them around longer by turning them into zombie-like creatures," the doctor said. The defence counsel asked Dr Berlin: "In your medical judgement, does Jeffrey Dahmer suffer from a mental disease?"

"Had a policeman been standing beside him, he would not have killed," replied the doctor. "But left to his own resources, he lacks control due to his mental disease. His disorder is necrophilia, a type of sexual deviation."

Gerald Boyle declared that his client had been a "steam-rolling killing machine" who had been out of control at the time of the killings and that he was plainly mad.

Prosecuting district attorney Michael McCann insisted the opposite. He said that Dahmer was sane and rational, and called Dr Frederick Allan Fosdal to the stand to substantiate the claim. Dr Fosdal testified: "A mental status examination showed Dahmer to be in control, in my professional opinion. He does have a psychiatric disorder, and had this disorder before, during and after his fifteen slayings. This disorder is of a sexual nature, principally necrophilia, but this disorder does not in itself make him lack substantial capacity to conform his behaviour to the requirements of law."

The defence called Dahmer's last intended victim, the young black man Tracy Edwards. He told the jury: "He seemed friendly and normal at first, but then turned crazy. Like I told the police the first time, 'This freak, this guy, is trying to hurt me'."

Gerald Boyle asked him: "What impression was made on your mind by the conduct of Jeffrey Dahmer, by the acts of Jeffrey Dahmer, by the manner, experiences and the circumstances of Jeffrey Dahmer that you observed?"

Edwards replied: "It's like I told the police: this guy is crazy."

Dahmer sat in court wearing a bright orange prison suit. He did not wear his steel-rimmed spectacles because he did not want to look at the witnesses, and he did not even glance at the young man who had escaped his clutches and brought about his downfall.

Tracy Edwards told the court about his ordeal at the hands of Dahmer. He had gone to Dahmer's apartment for a drink, but suspected that his rum and coke had been drugged since he started to feel dizzy. Then Dahmer shoved a twelve-inch butcher's knife into his armpit, the blade directed at his heart. "If you don't do what I say, I'm going to kill you," Dahmer said. "I've done this before. Don't make a move..." Dahmer then handcuffed Edward's left wrist and led him into the bedroom.

Edwards was waiting for the right moment to escape, and was attempting to placate his tormentor. Inside the bedroom he saw that the walls were covered with prints and photographs of nude men in almost every homosexual sex-act imaginable. As he was led to the single bed Edwards noticed to his horror a large bloodstain on the top coverlet, and a human hand protruding from under the bed.

"You'll never leave here," Dahmer told him. "It won't be long. I'll show you things you won't believe." After telling Edwards he planned to eat him, Dahmer put a video cassette of the film *The Exorcist* on TV and said: "That was the best movie ever made." He then went over to a filing cabinet and took out a human skull, saying to Edwards: "This is how I get people to stay with me – you will stay with me too." He also showed Edwards photographs of corpses in various stages of dismemberment.

Dahmer forced Edwards to lie on the floor, then put his head to his chest and said: "I can hear your heart beating. Soon it will be mine. I'm going to cut your heart out."

Edwards kept chattering to keep Dahmer's mind off killing, and persuaded Dahmer to take him back into the living room for more drinks. He nearly fainted when he saw the severed human head in the fridge from which Dahmer took the cans of beer, but he managed to keep hold of his senses. As they sat on the settee Dahmer began rocking backwards and forwards, sending himself into a drink-induced trance.

"It's time. It's time," he kept chanting. Edwards knew that if he did not escape now, he never would. Standing up, he punched Dahmer with all his force, then kicked him in the chest before fleeing the apartment and flagging down two police officers.

Gerald Boyle, Dahmer's counsel, used blackboard diagrams to chart Dahmer's increasing madness for the jury. "He begins by living for the weekends, and ends by

eating his victims and spending most of his time in bed...
As a total human being, that is what I see in Jeffrey Dahmer.
A person who is into cannibalism, a druggie obsessed with
sexual fantasies and perversions, rocking and chanting...
this is Jeffrey Dahmer... He started to experiment more
and more, because his sickness is growing greater and
greater. He began taking pictures of his victims' corpses.
He didn't even know that he was mentally ill – he just
thought he was bad."

Mr Boyle pointed out that Dahmer had never tried to
blame anyone else for his acts, but took the total blame.
"All I wanted was my own selfish gratification..." Boyle
pointed a finger at his own head and said bluntly: "He was
nuts." He went on: "This was a crazy man would couldn't
stop until he was stopped... I submit to you that Jeffrey
Dahmer is so out of control that he cannot be punished
by ordering imprisonment. He is *out of control*."

The prosecutor argued that Dahmer had a disordered
mind, not a diseased one, and was responsible for his
actions. He likened him to an alcoholic: out of control,
but with the ability to stop drinking. The testimony of the
detective who arrested Dahmer supported this view: "I
began questioning him about the way in which he selected
and approached his victims. He stated that before going
out for the evening he generally knew whether or not he
planned to commit a homicide... He would study the gays
in the bar and select one which he found attractive."

Saying that Dahmer's killing had been cold-blooded
and planned, the prosecutor asked the jury to identify with
the victims, not the defendant. He held up photographs
of the victims, fanning them out for the jury to see each
face.

On Saturday, 15th February 1992, the jury returned
after deliberating for six hours with a 10-2 majority
verdict. Squeals of delight greeted the fifteen verdicts –

one on each count. Fifteen times Judge Gram asked the jury: "Did Jeffrey Dahmer have a mental disease?" Fifteen times the jury said no.

It was incredible that the spectators cheered not because Dahmer had been found guilty, but because he had been found *sane*. In an unusual move, the judge allowed the relatives of the victims to address the court to tell of their feelings. Most wept, some raged, one girl yelled at Dahmer: "I hate you, mother-fucker!"

Sentencing was set for the Monday, 17th February, when Dahmer was allowed to address the court. He put on his spectacles for the first time and rose to his feet, the TV cameras zooming in on his face. He said:

> Your honour, you know it is all over now. It has never been a case of trying to get free. I never wanted freedom. Frankly, I wanted death for myself. This has been a case to tell the world that I did what I did not for reasons of hate. I hate no one. I knew I was sick or evil or both. Now I believe I was sick. The doctors told me about my sickness and now I have some peace. I realize how much harm I have caused. I did my best to make amends after my arrest, but no matter what I did I could not undo the terrible harm I have caused. My attempts to help identify the remains was the best I could do, and that was hardly anything.
>
> I feel so bad for what I did to those poor families, and I understand their rightful hate. I also know I will be in prison for the rest of my life, and I know I will have to turn to God to get me through each day. I should have stayed with God. I tried and failed and created a holocaust. Thank God there will be no more harm that I

can do. I believe that only the Lord Jesus Christ can save me from my sins.

I decided to go through with this trial for a number of reasons. One of these was to let the world know that these were not crimes of hate. I wanted the people of Milwaukee, which I deeply hurt, to know the truth of what I did. I did not want the world to think that these were hate-crimes. I did not want any unanswered questions. Now all the questions have been answered...

Dahmer continued:

I wanted to find out just what it was that caused me to be so bad and evil, but most of all Mr Boyle and myself decided that maybe there was a way to tell the world that they could get some help before they end up being hurt, or hurting someone. I think the trial did that. And I take the blame for what I did. In closing, I just want to say that I hope God has forgiven me for what I have done.

Thank you, your honour, now I am prepared for your sentence, which I know will be the maximum. I ask for no consideration.

Judge Gram then sentenced the prisoner to fifteen consecutive life terms – totalling 1,070 years – thereby making parole impossible. Jeffrey Dahmer was led away to start serving his sentence in an isolation cell at the Columbia Correctional Institute in Wisconsin.

At the same time plans were already under way to bring charges against him in Ohio, where he killed his first victim, the hitch-hiker. Dahmer had identified this victim from the police photograph as Steven Hicks, nineteen, whom he murdered on 18th June 1978.

Dahmer could yet have got his wish for death, since Ohio has the death penalty on its statue book and an electric chair waiting. But as it turned out the question proved to be academic. Dahmer was murdered in prison by fellow-inmate Christopher Scarver, a black man, on 28th November 1994.

Chapter Fifteen
THE MONSTER OF FLORENCE

Oscar Luigi Scalfaro, the Minister of Justice, had no doubts. "The perpetrator of these crimes cannot possibly be Italian," he said. Serial sex killing was unknown in Italy at the time. It was regarded as being a specifically Anglo-American curse. At a push, it could also be German. But it just couldn't be Italian. The police were instructed to investigate all the tourists in the area: German, English and American.

It was the summer of 1981 and *il Mostro di Firenze*, the Monster of Florence, had struck twice. The killings had been widely spaced in time, but the gruesome remains told the police that they were the work of the same man.

The Monster had first struck seven years before, on the night of 17th September 1974. He had come across eighteen-year-old Stefania Pettini, eighteen, and boyfriend Pasquale Gentilcore, nineteen, making love in their car in a park on the outskirts of Florence. The boy was shot through the driver's window in the left shoulder and the heart. The girl was shot four times, then her body was mutilated. An autopsy revealed ninety-seven curious small black marks on her chest and pubic area. The pathologist concluded that they had probably been made with a scalpel. It was also discovered that a vine-stalk had been inserted into her vagina. The psychiatrist solemnly assured the police that this represented a "sacrifice to the earth" ritual. It was an insight that was of help to neither the victims nor the investigators.

In the months and then years that followed, no other similar killings were reported. It was assumed that the tragedy was just a bizarre one-off. Nobody was arrested, or even apprehended for the murders, but there was no great public outcry. But then, on 6th June 1981, the killer struck again.

Carmela Di Nuccio, 21, and Giovanni Foggi, 30, were shot dead in their car. Once again the man had been shot through the driver's window, before the gun had been turned into the car's interior to blast the girl with five shots.

Afterwards the killer had dragged the girl some fifteen yards across the ground, where he carried out a gruesome operation. With a razor-sharp scalpel he removed the girl's entire pubic triangle with three neat cuts.

In both this killing and the similar double killing seven years earlier, the killer had used the same gun, a .22 Beretta, and the bullets had come from the same batch. They were Winchester .22s, manufactured in Australia between 1962 and 1965. Each of the bullets bore the identifying letter H. This was the most important clue the police had to go on. Find the man who owned the tell-tale weapon, and you found the killer – or so the theory went.

In fact, as it turned out, almost the opposite happened. The police didn't find the killer, but they did find two more victims.

On the evening of 21st August 1968 Antonio Lo Bianco, 29, and Barbara Locci, 32, had also been shot to death while making love in a car. This killing had been particularly horrific because Barbara's six-year-old son Natalino had been asleep on the back seat. He woke screaming when the shots blasted, and ran for help.

The police carried out a routine inquiry. Barbara was known to have had many lovers: what was more likely than that her humiliated husband, Stefano Mele from Sardinia, had committed the deed? He was quickly arrested, tried and convicted. Mele was released in 1981, having served twelve years' imprisonment for a crime he clearly had not committed. The bullets that had killed his wife and her lover were Winchester .22s, "H" series.

Before the Italian police had time to dwell on this evident miscarriage of justice, however, there was yet another double killing. In October 1981 another couple, Susanna Cambi, 24, and Stefano Baldi, 26, were shot dead with the Monster's bullets and methods. And in June 1982 he struck again. This time his victims were Antonella Migliorini, 20, and Paolo Mainardi, aged twenty-two.

On 9th September the Monster made an error. He came across a homosexual couple - two German lads - necking in their camper van in the village of Vicchio, near Florence. Since one had long fair hair and was slim he evidently assumed they were male and female. He killed them both, but did not mutilate their bodies. Horst Meyer and Uwe Rusch had only arrived in Italy a few days before, as tourists.

Following this pair of murders, the eleventh and twelfth in the series, the police set up a special full-time anti-Monster squad. The killer replied by murdering another two couples. On the night of 29th July 1984 Pia Rontini, 18, and Claudio Stefannaci, 21, were shot dead in their car. Once again the woman's body was dragged away from the vehicle, before the tell-tale mutilations were carried out on it. The pubic area was removed, and her left breast was also cut off.

The final pair of victims were both French tourists. Nadine Mauriot, 36, and Jean-Michel Kraveichvili, 25, were killed at Scopeti as they slept in their tent in an olive grove on the night of 8th September 1985. The murder was followed by the now all-too familiar ritual of the women's genital region being removed. In this case also the female victim's left breast was cut off. The only difference between this pair of killings and the others was that the Frenchman had not been killed instantly, despite having been shot three times. He managed to crawl away from the car while the Monster was busy with his ritual mutilations. But he wouldn't live to tell the tale. The killer pursued him and finished him off with a knife.

By now couples were afraid to go out courting, and if they did they went in packs, parking nose to bumper. Among them were policemen in discreet cars, keeping watch for the Monster, who by now had assumed mythic proportions. A reward of $150,000 was now on offer for the capture of the killer, as Florentine authorities feared the impact the murders might have on their lucrative tourist industry.

The police had some clues to work on. The killer always followed the same method, used the same gun and left the ejected cartridge shells at the scenes of his kills. A footprint, size 44, was found close to the scene of the last murders. If it belonged to the murderer, then it meant that the Monster was likely to be around six feet tall. Another clue was the fact that nearly all the killings – apart from the first two – had been committed during a weekend, five of them on a Saturday or Sunday, one on a Thursday. That would indicate that the monster had a full-time job which kept him busy during the week. Incidentally, it was also discovered that six out of the eight double killings had taken place on nights when the moon was full.

It was the instruments of killing, of course, that provided the biggest clue, and thinking that perhaps the Monster kept his weapons in a safe-deposit box, taking them out only when it was time to kill, the police obliged the banks to open hundreds of boxes in a search for the gun or scalpel, without success.

What sort of man was the killer? Perhaps a deranged surgeon? Gynaecologists were questioned by the score, as was anyone found in the woods as a likely peeping tom - or *guardone,* as the Italians call voyeurs. Perhaps there were even two Monsters, working together...

The police had scores of suspects – in fact, too many. They had 100,000 names on their computer database, and these were being added to by the day. In 1985 an anonymous letter arrived at the Monster Squad office denouncing a certain Pietro Pacciani, but it was never followed up. But then, the police were receiving hundreds of such anonymous letters every week.

And some were not so anonymous. Rumours spread that the owner of a café near Pistoia was the Monster. These rumours reached the ears of the café owner himself, Giuseppe Filippi. After being frequently pointed out in the street, he became afraid for his life. Soon he refused to leave his home. And then in a fit of depression he went upstairs to his bedroom, telling his wife he was going to rest. It was the evening of 3rd July 1982. He lay down on his bed and cut his own throat. In his own way Signor Filippi became another victim of the Monster.

Lacking any firm leads, the police arrested six suspects, each one amid a fanfare of publicity. Each in turn, however, was eventually released, their innocence proved.

In the meantime, as the police fretted with impotence, the killer sent them three bullets in an envelope, along with a cryptic note. It was clearly not a hoax – they were genuine "Monster" bullets – but it provided no clues. Worse was the clue he sent the woman magistrate involved in the case. Silvia della Monica received a piece of human skin which analysis showed was cut from the breast of one of the last victims. She was taken off the case and placed under full protection.

A year after the last double murder the police began despairing of ever catching their man. It was at this point that the Justice Ministry asked a leading Italian detective to take over the entire investigation. Ruggiero Perugini was then working with the FBI's Centre for the Analysis of Violent Crime at Quantico, Virginia. He was familiar with psychological profiling and the use of the latest computer techniques to identify criminals.

A strictly rational and methodical detective of the new breed, trained in the analysis of crime through statistical methods, he first commissioned a psychological profile of the Monster from a professor at the Department of Criminology in Modena, Professor Francesco de Fazio. The eventual profile ran to over a thousand pages.

Since the conventional wisdom among the FBI's Behavioral Science Unit's experts was that such killers tend to be driven by a compulsion to confess, Perugini now made a national television appeal directly to the Monster. It made for riveting viewing.

Staring straight at the camera, Perugini said: "I don't know why, but I have the impression you are watching me now. Listen to me. People call you a monster, a maniac, a beast, but I believe I have come to know and understand you better. I know that you are only the slave of a wretched obsession which has dominated you for a long time. You are not the madman people have described. Your fantasies and dreams have taken you over and control your behaviour. I also know that from time to time you try to resist them. We want you to know that we are here to help you. You know how, when and where to find me. I shall be waiting."

If Perugini expected the Monster to appear at his office the next day and confess, he was disappointed. The appeal went unanswered, save for another taunting letter, this time to Perugini himself. The detective therefore now resolved to follow another method.

Perugini had all the anonymous letters received over the years analysed and fed into the computer database. The letter which the police had received in 1985, incriminating an elderly farmer, Pietro Pacciani, was among them.

The Anti-Monster Squad had already investigated the gruff-speaking, ill-educated farmer, who had a wife and two grown-up daughters, but they had dismissed him from their inquiries on account of his age and his ignorance. At this stage they hadn't bothered to check his record, which would have revealed a history of sex-related crimes...

Perugini identified Pacciani solely by computer. To begin with his was just one of the 100,000 other names of suspects. But, checking with alibis and known absences, the computer had already whittled those names down to some hundreds, then to three hundred. After adding previous convictions for sex offences, the computer reduced the number down to ten, then finally to one: Pietro Pacciani. He lived in the area of the killings, had known all the murder scenes, had been seen in those places at various times, and had two convictions for sex offences. Pacciani was promptly arrested.

Why should anyone believe the police had the right man now? The police case was simple. Pacciani was in jail before the series of killings began, and was in jail again when they suddenly stopped. It seemed an open-and-shut case, and one can imagine the detectives shrugging their shoulders as if to say: "Isn't it obvious enough? The murders stop when he's in jail, and start again once he's out..." The one obvious problem, however, was that he didn't match the profile of the killer at all. Pacciani was a small, rotund and almost illiterate peasant – exactly the opposite of the clever murderer the police had been led to expect. Born on 7th January 1925, he came from a long line of peasants who had worked the earth for centuries, more used to a hoe than a scalpel. He spoke with a thick Tuscan accent, full of oaths. He could only write in capital letters, and even his spelling was poor. He couldn't have written those letters to the police, so who had done? A friend? Still, perhaps all was not as it appeared.

His background was of some interest. During the war Pacciani had fought with the Partisans, becoming a crack shot in the process. Then in 1951, when he was aged twenty-six and engaged to be married to sixteen-year-old Miranda Bugli, he saw his fiancée going into the woods with Severino Bonini, a man in his forties. Pacciani followed the couple, and when he saw Severino attempting to seduce his future wife, exposing her left breast in the process, he became so enraged that he stabbed the man nineteen times, then forced Miranda to make love with him close to the corpse. For this murder Pacciani had served thirteen years of a 22-year sentence.

Released in 1964, he went to live with his mother, taking jobs as a manual labourer and a cobbler – which made him adept with a knife. Shortly afterwards he married Angiolina Manni, a woman, it was said, he had bought from gypsy peddlers. It was the only way people could understand why she tolerated a marriage that was so full of violence and in which she was treated worse than a dog. In court Pacciani referred to her as "a half-witted chump."

As his two daughters reached puberty Pacciani forced his wife out of the marital bed and put the girls in her place. He forced them to perform sexual acts with him and beat them if they refused. Angiolina refused to testify against her husband in court, but both daughters testified in some detail, with the public prosecutor, Paolo Canessa, eliciting specific descriptions of the sexual acts, to the delight of the Italian viewing public.

For the sexual abuse of his daughters, Pacciani was sentenced to prison for the second time. That term lasted from 1987 until December 1991.

Pacciani was now arrested and formally charged with being the "Monster".

The police were anxious to build up a watertight case against him, but it proved to be hard work. Certainly the periods of his freedom and incarceration dovetailed with the dates of the murders and clearly Pacciani could be a violent and bestial man. But, if Perugini was to secure a conviction, he would have to find more concrete evidence of the suspect's guilt.

The farmer's house was searched on five different occasions: the first time in June 1990, when he was still in prison; again in December 1991; then over a twelve-day period from 27th April to 8th May 1992, and twice more in June 1992.

It was during the twelve-day search that a cartridge was found on his land. It matched all the 67 bullets fired in the 16 murders, and bore the identifying letter H. But its discovery was controversial to say the least. Pacciani's lawyer was present when the bullet was found and had this to say: "I had lunch with Perugini and we got back to the farm about four in the afternoon. The place was still swarming with police. As we walked down a path which was lined with concrete posts, Perugini suddenly said that he saw something glistening, reached into a hole in the post and retrieved the cartridge." The lawyer said the cartridge was lying on its side and had certainly not been dropped by anyone. It had been neatly placed later. Pacciani was later to say that it was "that shit-head Perugini who put it there."

That single bullet was the only forensic evidence found during that 12-day search. But following another anonymous letter, the police went back on 2nd June and searched the farm again. This time they took away a note-pad, a German-Italian dictionary, and a soap-dish. The note-pad was of a type not sold in Italy and was traced back to a shop in Münster, Germany, where a shopgirl confirmed that some scribbles on the back were in her handwriting. She also recalled that she had sold a pad like it to Horst Meyer, one of the Monster's victims, who had been studying art.

Inside the pad was some scribbling and notes with dates by Pacciani, which the defence said predated the murder of the German tourists, and thus the pad could not have belonged to them. The prosecution maintained that Pacciani had cunningly misdated the notes, which had been made after the murders. Not even graphologists could help there, although a whole morning was spent listening to three graphologists arguing the point.

Now came yet another anonymous letter. This time it also contained a piece of cloth wrapped around a rod from the barrel of a .22 Beretta. The anonymous informant pointed out that the scrap of cloth matched exactly a similar piece found in the farmhouse. What the letter proved was that its writer had access to the murder weapon, and could have been motivated by more than a wish to see justice done. But the police ignored this point. They were more excited about the cloth.

Other clues consisted of a pad on which Pacciani had written the number plate of a car which had parked under his window causing a nuisance. Police said this showed his obsession with parked cars. There were also crude drawings of nude women, with emphasis on the breasts and genital area. There were pornographic magazines found in the farmhouse as well, and a rubber dildo, which one daughter confirmed had been used on her. Incriminating as all these things might have been, they didn't constitute quality evidence.

Then there was Pacciani's hobby. He was an amateur taxidermist – and stuffing dead animals can sometimes conceal an interest in necrophilia.

Perhaps the most interesting point was that Pacciani seemed to have developed a fascination for the left breast which had stemmed from the episode with his fiancée in 1951. Pacciani also expressed horror at the idea of any woman exposing either breast – a fact Perugini later admitted convinced him that he had got the right man.

Pacciani's behaviour didn't help his case. He often told unnecessary lies. Asked why he had been seen driving near the spot where the French victims died two days before the event, he said he had taken a short-cut through the village because the main road was blocked for repairs. A simple check with the records showed that the main road had been open as usual on that day. And Pacciani had a habit of disappearing at weekends, nobody knew where...

But against all this was the evidence in Pacciani's defence. True, he had killed before, but his first murder – that of his fiancée's lover – was an impulsive and emotional act: a rage killing. The Monster murders were carried out with perfect self-control and coolness, by an efficient killing-machine which betrayed no emotion. Not the same sort of thing at all.

The Monster killings point to those of a sexually inadequate man, with the scalpel serving as a substitute for the penis. Almost certainly the Monster could not achieve erection by any normal means. But Pacciani had no sexual problem; he could achieve erections on demand – albeit with his own daughters.

The trial of Pacciani began in Florence on 19th April 1994. The small, stout defendant, with his white hair cut short in a crew-cut, his trousers help up by a piece of string, sat beside his lawyer, Signor Fioravanti, at a long table covered with 20,000 pages of notes. Signor Fioravanti was confident that the prosecution would not get a conviction on the evidence available.

On the opposite side of the room sat the prosecutor, Signor Canessa, and behind him sat four more advocates representing the victims of the Monster. The presiding judge sat at a half-moon table, with two judges either side of him and the members of the jury seated along the rest of the table. Over their shoulders they wore sashes bearing the colours of the Italian flag.

The Italian justice system is not bound by the strict discipline of many other countries. As Pacciani was led into the court reporters shoved camera and microphones into his face. He replied with peasant oaths, threatening obscenities upon those who persecuted him. He was fond of referring to himself as a "sweet little lamb" and played the part of a coarse court jester with aplomb. When a former girlfriend of his was called to testify about his sexual behaviour Pacciani muttered loudly: "She stinks like a buffalo."

As the trial progressed, however, his behaviour began to change. Soon Pacciani began sobbing. "What do they want with me?" he shouted loudly. "I am innocent. I am a scapegoat." He raged against the detective who had brought about his arrest, saying of Perugini: "God will cut him down to size one day, and like a snake he will have to slither across the earth without arms or legs." The Italians are good on insults.

The prosecution's case was not strong. Signor Canessa spent much of the opening weeks doing nothing more than trying to demonstrate that Pacciani was a man of bad character, saying of him: "He is a man of violent nature, unparalleled cruelty, fierce temperament, disproportionate reactions, crude and bestial instincts and extremely perverse character." Eventually even the President of the Court wearied of this tirade, telling the prosecutor: "Even if the public prosecutor succeeds in demonstrating that Pacciani's personality is identical to that of the maniac, he would still be light years away, from demonstrating that the maniac is indeed him."

By the end of October the case was virtually over. All that remained was for the jury to decide their verdict. It would be a close thing. Despite the prosecution's claim that their evidence was "compelling", the fact remained that it was all very circumstantial.

On the afternoon of 1st November 1994, after three full days of deliberation, the eight-man jury returned with its verdict. They found Pietro Pacciani guilty of the fourteen murders on which he was charged (because of a legal technicality the Lo Bianco and Locci murders were not included).

On hearing the jury's decision Pacciani, raised his arms to the heavens, then broke down in tears. He was given the maximum terms under law: fourteen life sentences and three months in solitary confinement.

The verdict brought an angry reaction from legal experts, who felt it was against all the evidence. "He is a simple peasant who has already paid his debt to society for the violence in his past," said one. "He has been offered up to the public as a convenient scapegoat, when he is certainly not the murderer," added Francesco Bruno, a criminologist and a witness for the defence.

The only real test of whether Pietro Pacciani was the Monster of Florence is a simple one. Will the murders cease or will they continue?

Chapter Sixteen
JACK UNTERWEGER
THE KILLING POET

Serial killers are by definition odd characters, with weird and warped personalities. But there can have been none stranger than Jack Unterweger. All the experts tell us that serial killers are inadequate, failed human beings. Typically, they suffer from low self-esteem, and are miserable and humiliated people who cannot achieve or sustain sexual relationships. Unterweger flies in the face of all that expert opinion, because he was a success. He had a large, admiring audience, money, fame, and all the women he could want. He was the epitome of the man who reinvented himself, rising from the gutter to be lionised in Vienna's literary circles. But he had one fatal flaw: a compulsion to kill prostitutes...

He was born in 1950, the illegitimate offspring of an American G. I. and an Austrian mother, both of whom abandoned him in his infancy, condemning him to a childhood spent in institutions or with relatives. Later Unterweger was to claim that his mother had been a prostitute; that the grandfather who raised him was an alcoholic who beat him savagely; that the aunt with whom he spent part of his formative years was a hooker who was later murdered by a psychopathic whore-hater. This, however, was something of an exaggeration, as was the claim made in his autobiography that he grew up in a hovel, surrounded by pimps and prostitutes, alcoholics and criminals. Unterweger's mother had no convictions for prostitution, and neither had the aunt – who was killed in a domestic dispute, not by a sex killer. And as for the wicked grandfather, neighbours remembered him as a gentle man "who had nothing but love for the boy." Still, Unterweger needed a fantasy to explain his behaviour.

In 1974 he killed Margret Schäfer, an eighteen-year-old German girl who lived next door, beating her with an iron bar before strangling her with her bra. At his trial in 1976 for this murder, Unterweger – then twenty-four – admitted the crime but pleaded for mercy, explaining that because his mother had been a prostitute he had developed a hatred of whores, and while having sex with his victim – whom he claimed was a prostitute – he had been seized with a sudden and irresistible impulse to kill her because he saw his mother's face flash before him.

He told the court about his deprived childhood, about how he had been abandoned at birth, shunted off to homes from which he always absconded, becoming a persistent offender who was locked away again and again. He spoke of his terrible relatives who so ill-treated him, and he said the thought of prostitutes tormented him. At night he strangled them in his dream...

The court was not impressed. The police gave evidence that the victim was not a prostitute, and a psychiatrist testified that Unterweger was a plain sadist. He was duly sentenced to life imprisonment.

Jack Unterweger made good use of his time in Stein Prison reading voraciously and seeming to channel the pain and anger of his childhood, such as it was, into writing rather than violence. In the years that followed the maladjusted brute became a sensitive and cultured man, producing a series of children's stories which were critically acclaimed, and a collection of poems which was equally applauded. He also became the founder-editor of the prison literary magazine.

Unterweger appeared to have undergone a miraculous metamorphosis, his raw and powerful autobiography *Purgatory or the Journey to Prison – Report of a Guilty Man* finding a publisher and bringing him instant fame, critics hailing it for its "deeply sensitive and authentic tone". Jack the killer had transformed himself into Jack the poet.

In that autobiographical novel he repeated his claim that the murder for which he was serving a life sentence had been inspired by hatred of his mother. It was a lie which he kept reiterating, until perhaps he came to believe it himself. In reality he was on friendly terms with his mother.

Such was the success of his writing that respected Austrian artists, prison reformers and the literary organisation PEN began campaigning for his release, claiming that he was fully rehabilitated, living proof that any criminal, no matter how bad, could reform and make something worthwhile of himself. He became the *cause célèbre* of the moment.

Unterweger was allowed out of jail to attend literary soirées and film festivals, the prison governor enjoying the poet's fame because it reflected favourably on him, suggesting that his liberal regime could reform any brute. He praised Unterweger, saying of him: "We will never find a prisoner so well prepared for freedom." But there was another, darker, hidden side to Unterweger. One only fellow-convicts saw...

A man who had been in Stein Prison at the same time as Unterweger, and who had known him well, told a reporter that his jail mate had been hated. "I didn't like him," the former convict said. "I wouldn't want to drink a beer with him." He claimed that despite Unterweger's lowly status as a sex offender, he had special privileges because his new role as a cult figure was as valuable to the governor as it was to Unterweger himself. His apparent rehabilitation was good for the prison's reputation.

"Jack was a bastard, a bad bastard," the former convict said. "He was detached and fantastically condescending. He was like a super-guard, much worse than the guards. Jack manipulated the whole prison. Remember, he was a pimp. Pimps manipulate. They control people – the hookers and the customers."

He said that Unterweger was allowed to wear many more gold chains than prisoners were usually permitted, along with an expensive watch. He had his own cell, with a cushy job in the laundry. He was a prison "baron", dealing in drugs, alcohol and even TV sets. He had a porn library he would loan out – at high prices. He also had a reputation as a grass. He would inform on his own customers so that when the illicit goods were confiscated they would eventually find their way back to him.

He had unheard-of visiting privileges, and several of the wealthy women who came to see him – attracted by his sudden fame – claimed to have had sex with him in jail. His fellow-prisoners reacted to his claim to literary distinction with derision. They considered him pompous and vain, with no credibility either as a hard man or as an intellectual. Many of his ideas had been picked up second-hand from the books he read.

"He behaved like a super-guard because he had to be better than the other prisoners," Unterweger's prison mate said. "Just as he believed himself to be better than any other poets or writers. Those intellectuals didn't know Jack from Adam. They were not his friends. Jack had no friends. I always thought Jack had only slaves or enemies. It was nonsense to see Jack as this angel. Jack learnt to be like that because he knew it would get him free."

It was certainly true that the prison governor at Stein accelerated Unterweger's release, avoiding the usual parole restrictions. Instead he was catapulted back into free society, where he immediately began dressing as either a pimp or a famous writer, depending on your point of view. He wore a white suit, like the American writer Tom Wolfe, with a red paper rose in the lapel, and a black shirt with a white tie. He sported snakeskin boots, and around his neck he had several thick gold chains.

He appeared to be urbane, with a cool intelligence. But beneath the clothing was the heavily muscled, heavily tattooed body of an ex-con. Beneath the façade of sophistication was the soul of a pimp. He bought himself a Ford Mustang Convertible, with the personalised number-plate W-JACK-1. His flat in Vienna was decorated in typical pimp fashion. Around the walls were framed soft-porn photographs of naked women wearing only high-heel shoes. There were many tacky ornaments, framed condoms, fluffy animals, and an ornamental sword.

It was the bedroom which was the real clue to Unterweger's personality. The door bore a sign: "JACK PARKING ONLY". Above the door was a huge red leather belt. Inside the bedroom were paintings and drawings of naked women being ravaged, or in the throes of sexual ecstasy. There was a framed certificate listing all the great events in sport, art and war that had occurred on Unterweger's birthday, 16th August. Yet this man was being fêted in Vienna, appearing on TV in discussion programmes as an expert on penal reform.

He was a regular television chat-show guest, as well as a writer, playwright, journalist and man about town. He was listened to with respect, his views courted. He gave public readings of his prison autobiography and was much sought after on Vienna's social circuit as the ultimate prize guest at parties.

Unterweger was released from prison on 23rd May 1990, officially on probation. In October a prostitute, Brunhilde Masser, disappeared from her usual patch. Three months later her body was found in woodland. She had been strangled with her underwear. Five weeks later another prostitute, Heide Hammerer, also vanished. She too had been strangled with her underwear and was not discovered until the following January.

More prostitutes began to disappear from Vienna and the southern Austrian town of Graz. They all turned up later, dead. The victims were named as Silvia Zagler, Sabine Moitzi, Regina Prem and Karin Sladke-Eroglu. On 7th March 1991 a 35-year-old prostitute, Elfriede Schrempf, vanished from Graz. That made seven women murdered in just eight months. They had obviously been murdered by the same man, since they all bore the distinctive signature of the unknown serial killer. All had come from Graz or Vienna, all were found dumped in woodland, all had been strangled with their underwear, usually the bra they were wearing, or their stockings.

In the early stages of the Graz prostitute-murders investigation, Unterweger covered the story for Austrian television and questioned Chief Inspector Edelbacher about the progress he was making with the case.

With the killing in the spring of 1991, however, the Graz police linked Unterweger to the murders. He was known to have been in the area at the time the victim was abducted, and he could not furnish a satisfactory alibi. The news of police suspicion about him was deliberately leaked, and it caused a sensation. The police reminded those who didn't know that Unterweger had always been obsessed with prostitutes and was a notorious ex-pimp – and hadn't he served a life sentence for killing a girl he called a prostitute, a girl who had died in exactly the same way as the victims in these new cases?

The problem was that there was no real evidence against Unterweger. There were no fingerprints, no witnesses, and the bodies of the victims were too decomposed to provide any forensic clues. There was just the fact that Unterweger had been in the area of all the killings at the relevant time. In leaking Unterweger's name, perhaps the police hoped to panic him into doing something rash.

Instead there was an angry backlash from Unterweger's influential supporters, who protested that he was being hounded by the police, harassed because of a past he had paid for, and now the police were trying to make him the scapegoat for their failure to catch the real killer. Some newspapers even took the line that, far from being the killer, Unterweger was the victim. And he agreed with them. He complained that he had been forced to change the personalised number plate on his car for fear of reprisals, and had already been attacked with a knife by an aggrieved relative of one of the murdered women.

During that same summer of 1991 Unterweger was busy researching Los Angeles's red-light districts for a magazine article which had been commissioned by an Austrian journal. He was driven around LA in patrol cars as a guest of the Los Angeles police, and was there for five weeks. During that period three prostitutes were found dead in scrubland around LA and Malibu. They had been strangled with their underwear. None had been killed in such a fashion prior to Unterweger's visit, and none since. Then Unterweger travelled to the Czech Republic in September, where another whore was strangled with her underwear.

At the beginning of that month the respected Vienna newspaper *Kurier* reported that the man police were looking for "could be a known murderer... Police have even given this monstrous killer the nickname 'Jack the Strangler'." All of Austria knew who they meant.

On 17th January, 1992, Unterweger went to Graz voluntarily to see the police. He was questioned for four hours, but was released without charge. He had given an alibi for 7th March 1991 – the night of the Schrempf murder – claiming he had been with his 18-year-old girl friend, Sabine, in Vienna. He was officially in the clear.

In fact, however, the story of his date with Sabine merely served to arouse detectives' suspicions further. They all knew that he could have given them a far better alibi – that he was giving a reading at a café in Koflach, half an hour's drive away from Graz. So why had he concocted a false one? The police now publicly linked him with the five murders in Vienna, although the chief prosecutor refused to issue a warrant for his arrest or to make any connection with the murders in Graz.

Unterweger was left in no doubt that his days were numbered. In the months that followed the police patiently gathered evidence. They questioned Unterweger several times, always letting him go. They learned of his trip to the Czech Republic, and of the prostitute murdered there. Finally, on 13th February 1992, a warrant was issued for his arrest – an event predicted in the newspapers the previous day. Graz police raided his Vienna flat – having invited the state TV channel to accompany them – but they found the apartment empty.

Unterweger was in Switzerland with a new girl friend, Bianca Moak. Then he vanished. The Austrian and Swiss police blamed each other for the bungling which had allowed him to slip through their fingers. And the liberals, artists and intellectuals who had championed Unterweger had to face the fact that he was back on the run from the law, the sole suspect in the murder of eight prostitutes.

"On the one hand, he just *can't* have done it," said one writer. "He was desperate to get out of prison and is really too intelligent and too afraid of prison to risk going back inside. He had been in prison too long, had achieved enormous success and respect outside prison; he had changed. And there is obvious evidence of police persecution against him... But on the other hand, it *must* have been him – he had no concrete alibis, his sexual habits and brutality are well known."

Others who had come to know him – artists, writers, film-makers – were equally ambivalent. One suggested that perhaps reading all those books in prison had made him go mad. Most agreed he had the potential to be a killer, but that did not make him the murderer the police were hunting. Willi Hengstler, who made a film of Unterweger's life story, said: "Jack is a freak, but not necessarily a killer."

Some even suggested that Unterweger had deliberately manipulated the whole scenario, implicating himself by his flight simply to revive his flagging fame, receive lots of publicity, and avenge himself on the police by loudly and publicly humiliating them when his innocence was finally established.

"It's one of Jack's games," Willi Hengstler claimed. "A kind of Russian roulette with the authorities – putting his head in the noose, only to emerge at the end triumphant, with an irrefutable alibi. Jack likes to be the victim." Extraordinary as this suggestion was, no one could dismiss it out of hand. Unterweger certainly had the intelligence to implement such a scheme.

He did not stay silent during this period as a fugitive. In fact he was in the newspapers practically every day, sending letters from his hide-out complaining about police persecution, and also claiming that two well known society women kept diaries which would provide him with further alibis. Rumour had it that one was the wife of a politician, and the other was married to a newspaper magnate.

Unterweger made cheeky phone calls to the police, and even gave a television interview, albeit by telephone, in which he told the newsreader that he couldn't cope psychologically with being kept in prison while he was being investigated, and that he would commit suicide rather than go back inside. The headline in the *Kurier* read: "HELLO, IT'S ME, THE MASS MURDERER."

But Unterweger's use of the media to enlist support backfired. The police could, and did, play the same game. Reminding readers of Unterweger's past, they revealed that a search of his flat had uncovered handcuffs, a tear-gas canister and pornographic photographs.

Moreover, in his book Unterweger had written about his sadistic sexual practices: "I wielded my steel rod among the prostitutes and pimps of Hamburg, Munich, and Marseilles." The police disclosed that the faces of some of the victims bore the marks of beatings with a steel rod and with whips. A collection of whips had been found in Unterweger's flat...

Furthermore, Unterweger had been a prime suspect not just for 12 months, but for almost twenty years. He had been suspected of murdering Marica Horvath, 23, whose strangled body was found dumped in a pond in Salzburg in April 1973 – a year before the murder which got Unterweger life. The detective who investigated that case had been August Schenner, who was now retired. But he had been so convinced of Unterweger's guilt that from the moment the bodies of Masser and Hammerer were found in January 1991 he had gone to the Graz police urging them to arrest Unterweger every time another prostitute's body was found.

Schenner, who had been dismissed by newspapers as an old fool, now became the hero of the tabloid press, which were now denouncing the prison system and raging against the authorities for releasing Unterweger into the world. They also warned of the danger facing Unterweger's new teenage girl friend, urging her to seek police protection.

The publicity became so intense that the Interior Minister imposed a news blackout on the case, fearing that Unterweger – if and when he was caught – would never get a fair trial. But it was too late. The public mood had swung against Unterweger. People were sick of intellectuals who were so easily taken in by cunning crooks.

One shopkeeper said: "When his clever friends tossed him aside, he gave up writing books and went back to what he did best – killing. Everyone goes on about what a terrible childhood he had. Everyone in Austria has a terrible childhood."

But where was Jack Unterweger? It was his former hosts, the American police, who finally caught up with him. Noting that credit card receipts placed him in Florida, they traced him to an address on Miami Beach. On 27th February 1992 Federal agents swooped. Unterweger was staying with Bianca Moak, the 18-year-old schoolgirl who had travelled with him from Austria to Switzerland, then from Paris to Miami. "He looked like a normal tourist," said one of the agents who arrested him. "Once we finally caught up with him he surrendered." He had been free for just 673 days since being paroled from Stein Prison.

Unterweger was held pending investigation of the murders of the three prostitutes in LA in the summer of 1991 and the killing in the Czech Republic.

The case against him looked slim. There were some circumstantial details. While in LA he had stayed in cheap motels close to the murdered women's regular patches, and a menu from a restaurant on the Pacific Coast Highway, close to where one of the bodies was found, had been found in his flat. But it was hardly damning evidence.

When investigators showed him photographs of the bodies he remarked coolly that the victims had not been beaten, and they did not have their bras or stockings around their necks – which, according to Austrian police, was his trademark. But a detective was reported as saying: "He's like a man with two faces. He was very cool at first, a real charmer. Then he lost his nerve and started whimpering like a child."

The authorities on both sides of the Atlantic had a problem. Neither the American nor the Austrian police had any real evidence against Unterweger. And, under immigration rules, after 90 days the American police would have to charge him or release him.

Meanwhile, in an interview Unterweger complained about not being allowed to return to Vienna to defend himself, adding: "How many unsolved murders are there in Los Angeles? One victim is supposed to have been found in the vicinity of a housing estate. I wouldn't be so crazy as to kill one in front of a house. That would be to mock the intelligence that people grant me." He added that the dead American prostitutes "were not my type" and said he had two hopes: "Either they find the murderer, or he will strike again while I am in jail."

The Austrian authorities were not actively seeking his extradition. Lacking evidence, they were hoping the Americans might convict him. For his part the American district attorney – running for office – was pressing for Unterweger to be extradited: he didn't want it on his record that he had let a serial killer go free.

Unterweger had agreed to give blood and hair samples. These were being matched against blood and semen samples found at one of the LA murder sites. The tests would take about six weeks – and it was now 9th May. The Americans, it seemed would have to release Unterweger on the expiry of the 90-day period, on 24th May.

In Vienna Jack Unterweger's lawyer, George Zanger, gave an interview in which he said that Unterweger had volunteered to take a DNA test – it wasn't compulsory. Zanger had advised him against taking it. He said there was no evidence to link his client with the death of eleven prostitutes, and when asked why that first murder – for which Unterweger had served life – seemed to match these latest murders so well, he explained that the first murder of Margret Schäfer had nothing to do with prostitution or even sexual frenzy. Unterweger had killed her because she had witnessed a robbery he had just committed. He had strangled her with her bra to make it look like a sex crime and confuse the police.

Zanger insisted that his client would have to be released on 24th May, pointing out that no evidence had been presented in any court in America or Austria, and no charges had been brought against his client.

Bianca Moak had returned to Vienna and had sold her story to a tabloid newspaper. She said that in Miami, because Unterweger couldn't work for fear of being recognised, she had taken a job as a topless dancer for $1500 a week. She insisted that her lover was innocent of any murders.

At the expiry of that 90-day period the police presented new evidence to the court in Miami. Scientists had found a slim DNA match linking Unterweger with one of the Austrian murders, and a forensic clue linking him to the murder of a Prague prostitute, Blanka Bockova. There were long courtroom rows over whether the evidence was strong enough to warrant extradition, but eventually the American judge ruled that Unterweger should be returned to Austria. It was one way of getting rid of an embarrassing problem...

What followed in a Graz court was one of Austria's most sensational murder trials in post-war years.

Beginning on 20th April 1994, it lasted two months, with forensic scientists and criminologists from the FBI being flown in to testify.

Unterweger looked distinctly ill at ease when the charges were read out in the packed courtroom. His lawyer immediately applied to have the case thrown out, claiming that a "hate campaign" against his client in the Austrian media had precluded the possibility of a fair trial. The court dismissed the application.

The prosecution's case, even after two years of preparation, proved to be highly circumstantial, although there were two items of hard evidence. The clothing of one of the victims had been found to contain 142 threads from a red scarf owned by Unterweger, and a hair found in his car was "almost certainly" from the murdered Prague prostitute. Richard Dirnhofer, the DNA analyst who presented the hair evidence, said it was "highly probable" that Unterweger had murdered all eleven victims.

The Los Angeles police, who presented evidence, said that the three US victims had all been murdered by the same person. Gregg McCrarry, an FBI psychologist and expert in serial killings, said that all eleven were murdered by the same hand.

The circumstantial evidence against Unterweger was that all the victims were picked up in red-light districts, taken to remote locations, strangled with items of their underwear, and dumped in forests. In each case, it was claimed, Unterweger was in the area when the crime was committed. The prosecution suggested that on his release after nearly 15 years confinement Unterweger had gone on a nine-month killing spree.

A psychiatrist who had spent two days interviewing Unterweger in prison testified that he found him to be "profoundly sadistic."

For one murder Unterweger had given his mother as an alibi, but she testified that she could not recall whether he had been with her on the critical date.

The trial concentrated on reconstructing the murders of Schrempf and Hammerer in particular. Heide Hammerer, 31, had disappeared from her patch on 7th December 1990. Unterweger had spent the night in a hotel in the vicinity. The next morning he attended a meeting to discuss the radio recording of one of his plays, and told police that he travelled to the meeting with two of the actors by train. However, the actors maintained that Unterweger had arrived the previous night in his white Ford Mustang convertible. The director of the play said that Unterweger had arrived at the 9 a.m. meeting in his white car "fresh and eager to work".

The defence made much of this. Would a man who had killed a prostitute that night have looked "fresh and eager" the following morning? Would a man who had already been convicted of murdering one prostitute have gone out and picked up another prostitute to murder in his distinctive white car? And how could he not have been noticed with his personalised number plate?

Elfriede Schrempf had been murdered on the evening that Unterweger gave a poetry reading in Koflach, half an hour's drive away. Graz CID placed her disappearance at between 10 and 10.30 p.m. When fans confirmed that Unterweger had still been at the poetry reading at that time, signing autographs, the police changed their story. Schrempf could have been murdered later than 10.30, if she had returned to her patch when all other prostitutes had gone…

In his closing speech state prosecutor Karl Gasser made an extraordinary plea to the jury for a conviction even if they were not sure of Unterweger's guilt. He warned them: "If Unterweger is acquitted he will walk out of the court a free man." As he spoke a bomb exploded outside the courthouse, causing extensive damage but not delaying the trial.

Defence counsel protested at the prosecutor's demand for a guilty verdict even if the jury were unsure, and asked to have the trial declared void. But the judge allowed the proceedings to continue. When both sides had made their closing speeches Unterweger was allowed to address the jury before they retired to consider their verdict. In a long and emotional speech he told them: "I was a greedy, ravenous individual, hungry for life and determined to rise in life from the bottom."

Speaking of his time prior to going to prison, he said: "I was a rat, a primitive criminal who grunted rather than talked, an inveterate liar." Admitting that the years since he had left prison had not been well spent, he said: "The prosecutor is right. I consumed women rather than loved them. But how can you have feelings after fifteen years in jail?"

Referring to the hair found in his car, he commented that it was odd that investigators had not found a single dog hair, because his German shepherd, Joy, was his constant companion.

He concluded: "It wasn't me. I'm innocent. I implore you, even if you are disgusted by Jack Unterweger's way of life, to think whether that is enough to say, 'He doesn't deserve to live in freedom.'"

On June 29th, after almost nine hours' deliberation, the jury convicted him on nine counts of murder and one charge of causing grievous bodily harm. He was found guilty of the three Los Angeles murders and the one in Czechoslovakia. Even then the jury were not entirely convinced, since the eight members voted six to two to convict, and five to three to clear him of two further charges of murdering Austrian prostitutes.

The court sentenced Unterweger to life imprisonment, to be spent in an institution for mentally disturbed criminals.

He appeared to take the verdicts calmly, but in the early hours of the following day he committed suicide in his cell, hanging himself with his shoelaces and elastic from his tracksuit trousers.

The public were outraged that a man so clearly disturbed had been left with the means and time to commit suicide after being sentenced to life imprisonment. Why hadn't there been better supervision?

A rattled Austrian Justice Minister said it was routine for warders to patrol and check the cells every forty minutes. During one inspection 43-year-old Unterweger had been seen lying on his bed. On the next round he was discovered dead. But one of the defence counsel said that he had asked the authorities to keep a close eye on Unterweger, who had told him that if he was found guilty he would kill himself.

Some people thought that perhaps Unterweger had been innocent after all, but a journalist on Vienna's *Die Presse* summed up the feeling of most people when he said: "He became a star of the literary scene. It became chic to go and listen to this convicted murderer who had turned good, giving his readings in cafés. Not many of those who supported him then like to talk about it now. And many Austrians are convinced that the decision to set him free was a big mistake.

"In the soul of Unterweger there resided both the poet and the killer. The tragedy is that it was the killer who triumphed."

Chapter Seventeen
COLIN IRELAND
KILLING FOR FAME

Whether one should define Colin Ireland as a sex killer is a debatable point. It certainly was not sex in any normal sense of the word that drove him to his crimes. But he followed the methods of the typical sex killer to the letter. Only his motivation, twisted and dark as it was, set him apart.

Seldom has so much hatred for mankind been concentrated in one person as it was in Ireland. He had set himself one target: to become a serial killer. That way he could achieve some dubious fame in an otherwise undistinguished life – even if it meant a lifetime in prison. He thought it was a price worth paying. A poet once wrote: "One crowded hour of glorious life is worth an age without a name." There was nothing glorious about Colin Ireland.

Born illegitimate to a newsagent's assistant in Dartford, Kent, in 1954, he never knew his real father. He lived with his mother and his grandparents in a council house in the town, and neighbours in Myrtle Road remember him as being a "very ordinary boy".

Ireland attended a local school until, when he was 12, his family moved to the Isle of Sheppey. It was then that his mother met a man and got married. But the new husband and the stepson never got on, and there were frequent rows – mainly because the stepfather was a strict disciplinarian who beat young Colin for any breach of his rules.

Whether this caused his later problems is not known, but Ireland became a difficult child and had to attend a special school for the maladjusted – a school from which he was expelled for starting a fire. Those who are familiar with the patterns of the early life of serial killers will know that there is often a history of childhood arson as well as bed-wetting and cruelty to animals. There is also almost always a history of minor law-breaking. Serial killers also tend to be police "groupies", or attracted to uniforms. It is thus perhaps significant that Ireland was a member of the Sea Cadets, the Scouts, and even worked as a volunteer fireman at one stage.

Three months after his sixteenth birthday Ireland appeared in Sheerness Juvenile Court, charged with stealing £4. He was placed in local authority care. After that there followed a string of court appearances for petty thefts which resulted in probation orders and finally borstal. Then, in 1975, Ireland was again convicted of theft and sent to prison for 18 months. It was his first time behind bars.

In 1977 he was released from prison and moved in with a young woman and her child in Swindon. Unable to find work, he turned again to crime and soon appeared before Swindon magistrates for theft. In view of his past record, he was lucky. He got a three-month sentence, suspended.

The leniency of the court was not appreciated by the young man, who did nothing to change his ways. By November he was in trouble again. This time it was for blackmail as well as theft. He was returned to prison.

It was a few months after serving this last term that Ireland decided to move to pastures new. He headed for the capital. Swindon's loss was London's catastrophe.

In 1979 he was convicted of possessing an offensive weapon – a truncheon. Soon afterwards he stole £750 and was sent to prison for two years.

Those who knew him at this time describe him as a loner who was extremely secretive. One friend said, "He would never discuss his past life. But on one occasion he went with us to see a lady who read Tarot cards. She looked at his cards and said, 'You've either been in prison or you're going there for killing someone.' His face went white and he never wanted to discuss the matter again after that."

Ireland developed an interest in outdoor survival training, often dressing in combat gear and spending days alone on the marshes and cliffs near Southend. He claimed to be able to exist on soup made from tree bark, cooking and eating snakes, and watching birds to see which berries were good to eat. He was often seen with a rucksack on his back, and at one stage he went to France and tried to enlist in the Foreign Legion, but he was rejected.

Those who knew him at this time said that Ireland, a non-smoker who drank very little, was interested in current affairs, liked to sit up all night listening to music, and had a talent for drawing caricatures of people. He appeared to them to be '"highly intelligent," but others remember him as being foul-mouthed and obsessed with schoolboy humour. The police described him as having the ability to be "all things to all men."

In 1989 Ireland, 6ft 3in and weighing 15 stone, turned up at the Globe Inn at Buckfastleigh, on the southern edge of Dartmoor. Within weeks he had swept the landlady off her feet. She was a jolly woman, then 42, who had moved to Devon in the late 1980s with her two children after her first marriage had foundered. She was entranced by the stranger.

One villager said: "She was besotted by him. None of us ever thought she would marry such a thickhead. They were like chalk and cheese. She just didn't seem to care what other people thought."

Speaking of Ireland, another regular said: "I wouldn't say he was handsome, but he was a big, fit-looking bloke who obviously looked after himself. He looked like a bouncer from a night-club. But when he opened his mouth the bricks fell out. He gave the impression of not being very bright."

A second Globe customer recalled: "It was strange. One minute he was just another customer drinking in the bar who had arrived with a few clothes in a suitcase. Then it was as if he'd moved in, taken over and was part of the furniture. I remember him telling us he used to bath the kiddies upstairs and put them to bed. But he never lifted a finger in the bar to help. When he wanted a drink he just used to help himself."

The couple were married at Newton Abbot Register Office on 2nd January, 1990. There was a reception afterwards at the pub, with free champagne. Then the couple went off on their honeymoon. Ireland returned alone, saying he was off on another of his survival training trips. Instead he took what money there was in the till, loaded the television set and video into his new wife's Ford Escort, and vanished with about £5,000 of her money. When she returned and found what had happened she called the police, but they were unable to trace Ireland. Eventually she was forced to quit the pub. She never heard from her husband again.

What she didn't know was that the scruffily dressed Ireland had had a string of girlfriends before her, as well as a wife. In 1980 he met and married a woman who had spent ten years in a wheelchair, left paralysed from the waist down by a hit-and-run driver. This had not prevented her from winning a gold medal in the paraplegic Olympics. When they married Ireland was 27 and working as a restaurant chef. She was nine years his senior and had a six-year-old daughter from a previous marriage. After Ireland had been arrested she said: "There were good times and bad. He would hit me occasionally, but then he could be very kind. He was a Jekyll and Hyde type character. He was battling between the good and evil forces within him. He felt it was such a powerful force, the evil force. He would talk and talk about it."

He told her that he hated gay men. "He never went into detail about it," she said, "but it was something that stemmed from a long time ago. I don't know why. I just assumed something might have happened when he was younger."

Ireland was in and out of prison throughout the course of this marriage, and had a succession of affairs. The couple were divorced in 1987, but Ireland soon met another woman through a lonely hearts advertisement. She later described Ireland as being a "gentle lover," but he killed her pet cat. One day she asked him where Fluffy was. He replied coldly, "You won't have any more vets' bills for that cat. I've killed it."

Eventually he ended up in Southend helping run a night shelter for down-and-outs. His boss there recalled that Ireland once told him, "I hate queers."

It is believed that a row with a homosexual at the night shelter shortly before Christmas, 1992 was the trigger which set Ireland off. He lost his job as a result of that row, and apparently resolved to take his revenge on gay men in general.

Now 39, Colin Ireland began buying books on serial killers. Before he could be considered one himself, he concluded, he would have to claim at least five victims. His copy of the FBI handbook *The Crime Classification*

Manual suggested that only those who killed at least five times qualified for the serial killer label. Ireland also carried around with him a copy of Brian Masters's book about Dennis Nilsen, *Killing For Company*.

Although he decided to choose his victims from the gay community, the police never accepted that he killed gays because he hated them. Homosexuals were simply convenient targets. Ireland picked on those who were into sado-masochism because they would willingly allow themselves to be tied up, and thus could not put up any resistance when he began to kill them.

Ireland was later to say that he had initially thought of choosing women as his victims, but had decided on homosexuals because he did not think the public would have much sympathy with them.

Following his arrest, he remained mute for three weeks, telling the police: "You've got me, but I'm not saying anything." But then he crumpled. On August 19th 1993 he decided to make a full confession. Sitting in a London police station with his solicitor at his side, he began to recount his murders in a matter-of-fact tone, speaking without emotion as he detailed the tortures he inflicted on his victims prior to death. From time to time he broke off to crack jokes.

Describing his decision to become a serial killer, he said he chose as his venue for victims a well-known pub, the Coleherne in Earls Court, west London. Here the gay community held court. Whenever Ireland went into the Coleherne he was careful to avoid the security video camera which he knew was trained on the main door. He entered by a side door instead.

The first victim was Peter Walker, 45, a theatre director who lived in Battersea, south-west London. He was found naked under a duvet at his home with rope-burns on his wrists and ankles. On 8th March 1993

Ireland had left his bedsit in Southend with murder in mind. He had his rucksack on his back containing his "murder kit": a knife, gloves, nylon cord and a change of clothing. He caught a train to London and made his way to the Coleherne.

He told detectives, "I went to the Coleherne that evening and I felt that if I was approached by one of the group that tended to trigger feelings in me – masochistic men – I felt there was a likelihood I would kill."

The would-be victim, who never made a secret of his homosexuality, must have liked the look of Ireland, the burly man who had once worked as a bouncer at a gay club. In the crush around the bar Walker accidentally spilled his drink on Ireland's coat. Later, as Ireland stood near the toilet door, Walker brushed against him. That was the signal. Within minutes, after a brief chat, the two were in a taxi heading for Walker's flat. Even as they walked towards the building, Ireland was carefully pulling on a pair of gloves.

Once inside the flat, and after the victim had locked his two dogs away in the kitchen, Ireland began tying Walker to the bed. It was what Walker wanted.

With his victim helpless, Ireland beat him with a gloved fist and whipped him with a dog leash before suffocating him. Ireland's confession went on: "I tied him... there was a four-poster bed... four posts with knobs on the top and I tied him by his fists with cord. Specially made cord."

With Walker lying helpless on the bed, Ireland got a plastic bag from the kitchen and pretended to suffocate him with it by placing it over his head, taking it away at the last minute as the victim gasped for air.

Ireland told the police: "I took the bag away and told him how easy it was to end it all."

It was at this point that Walker realised that his new "friend" intended to kill him. Ireland said: "It was a fate thing and he said to me, 'I'm going to die.' And I said, 'Yes, you are.' I think in a way he wanted to die. There was a lack of desire to carry on. I think he knew he was going to die – he was quite controlled about it. In the end I killed him with a plastic bag. I put that over his head and killed him with that."

Ireland then took £200 from his victim.

He also singed the dead man's pubic hair – to see what it smelt like – and stayed with the body for four hours, searching the flat, watching television, and then reading Walker's letters. From these he discovered that his victim had been suffering from AIDS. He marked his disgust by making a grotesque display of the body with condoms and teddy bears.

Afterwards, Ireland said, the enormity of what he had done suddenly struck him. "I remember after killing Walker I looked at myself in the mirror. Then I walked down the road and thought that anyone who looked at my face would be able to see I had just murdered somebody. I thought they would be able to tell by just looking at me. I remember losing my virginity and I remembered the same feeling. You're always buzzing."

Two days after the murder he rang the Samaritans to express concern for Walker's two dogs which had been locked up in the flat, and claimed responsibility for the killing. He also rang the *Sun* newspaper, telling a reporter, "It was my New Year's resolution to murder a human being. He was a homosexual and into kinky sex. You like that sort of stuff, don't you?"

Despite this telephone confession, the police could not be sure it was a case of murder. There was the possibility it had been a bondage accident. Investigation was difficult because homosexuals had a historic mistrust of the police. If they admitted to bizarre practices, how could they be sure they wouldn't be prosecuted?

Nearly two months passed before Colin Ireland returned to his killing-ground at the Coleherne. This time he decided that, as murder was costing him money, he should make it self-financing. He had the expense of travel and purchasing such items as handcuffs and gloves, all of which had to be disposed of after each murder. He would make his victims pay for their own deaths in future. He had gone to a yachting shop to buy special nylon cord, and from another shop he bought a pair of handcuffs. For someone on the dole it was quite an outlay.

Once at the Coleherne, on the night of 28th May, he got into conversation with Christopher Dunn, 37, who worked at the Harlesden Library in Brent. Like most gays, Dunn tended to live a double life. By day he was a quiet librarian in a smart suit and spectacles. But at night he dressed in black leather and wore an earring. The spectacles were put away, and around his neck he wore a studded dog collar. An extremely pleasant man, Dunn was noted for his talent for telling children stories which held them enthralled.

After he had told Ireland that he enjoyed being dominated, the two left the pub together for Dunn's flat in Wealdstone, north-west London. They had drinks and watched a S&M video together, and then it was time for action. Ireland was ruthless. He told the police, "I had gone out quite prepared to kill the man and I was going to have him."

Once Dunn was handcuffed to the bed, with his feet trussed and expecting rough sex – wearing a black leather harness and other sexual equipment to heighten his enjoyment – Ireland first went through his wallet and took his victim's cash and also his bank card. He told Dunn that he had better cooperate, "if you want to hear the birds singing tomorrow morning." He demanded Dunn's PIN number. Dunn, thinking that Ireland was simply a thief, refused to give him the number until Ireland began burning his testicles with a cigarette lighter.

After noting the number, Ireland strangled Dunn with a nylon cord, leaving his body sprawled on the bed. He then searched the flat by torchlight. "I was tempted to steal more from Dunn," he said, "because of his collection of old Dinky toys and Matchbox toys. They're quite valuable and collectable. But I didn't in the end. I didn't want anything later on to be used as a pointer to me." But he used Dunn's bank card to withdraw £200 from his account.

He had stolen a Walkman radio cassette from Walker, but later he threw it away. Now he was refining his technique. "After that killing I never took anything in case it could be traced to me," he said.

Ireland described how he always cleaned his "murder kit" afterwards, remembering to throw away the torch batteries he had used after carefully wiping off any fingerprints. "I had got that idea after watching *The Bill* ," he told detectives. "You know, you ought to ban that programme. It gave me lots of ideas."

But he didn't need television to give him all his notions. He had decided for himself that returning home in the early hours after each killing was too risky. He might be stopped by a beat bobby and asked to explain the thin leather gloves in his plastic carrier bag, so he sat with the corpses of his victims all night, until it was safe to leave in the morning, mingling with people on their way to work.

Talking of what he had learned during those lonely hours with the bodies, he said: "It's strange, but I now remember overwhelming things... death and what it smells like. When people have been strangled they break wind. That's what it smells like. There's nothing dramatic or even wonderful about it. It's almost like a base thing... that's just what comes to my memory. I think that affected me mentally to a degree. I think if I had just killed these people and gone, I wouldn't have been affected mentally so much. But sitting with these bodies like five or six hours on some occasions, watching them sort of gradually blotch as they go cold... it wasn't something I think I could cope with, quite honestly."

After each murder he would throw the handcuffs he had used into the Thames, at the same time discarding any incriminating items such as gloves. He was to boast of being methodical and meticulous about his murders.

The second killing was not recognised as such. When Dunn's body was found by a friend, bound and gagged, it was thought that he might have died from accidental suffocation. One bizarre sexual practice – known as auto-erotic asphyxia – involves the individual almost hanging himself to achieve a more acute orgasm. The obvious risk is of going too far, and there have been many cases of accidental death as a result. There seemed to be no obvious link between Dunn's death and the first murder – apart from phone calls from Ireland, who was demanding recognition for his acts.

The next victim was a thirty-five-year-old American sales director, Perry Bradley III. From Sulphur Springs, Texas, Bradley lived in Kensington but worked in Slough for an American adhesives firm. He was the son of a US Congressman, and few of his friends knew he was gay. Ireland met him at the Coleherne on 4th June, and after a brief flirtatious chat, both men went to Bradley's flat.

Bradley was a little dubious about allowing himself to be tied up, but he agreed when Ireland told him that he could not respond sexually unless there was sado-masochism. And so, like the previous two victims, Bradley allowed himself to be bound, expecting sado-masochistic sex. Ireland had now become so proficient at killing that once he had the victim in his own home there could be no escape. He had also refined his methods to leave as few clues as possible, including wiping down surfaces to remove fingerprints and taking away any items he might have touched.

He told his trussed victim that he was a thief, and that he intended to torture him to get his PIN number. Bradley accepted the situation philosophically, saying, "I'm quite happy to give you anything you want to know." He even offered to accompany Ireland to a cash machine but was told that "wouldn't be allowed".

Whether from compassion or to lull his victim into believing that he might be permitted to live, Ireland told him, "It's going to be a long night. I suggest you get some sleep if you can." Ireland told the police: "I just sat and listened to the radio and he actually went to sleep."

Once the American was soundly slumbering, face down on the bed with his hands tied behind him and a ligature around his neck, Ireland killed him. He said: "I put a noose around his neck and tied it to something. I sat there thinking and at one point I was thinking of letting him go. Then I thought, 'It's easier to kill him.' When he was asleep there was no way I could allow that man to wake up. That wasn't part of my plan anyway. My plan was to kill. While he was asleep I went round to his side of the bed and just pulled the noose. He hardly struggled."

Ireland then went through the dead man's wallet, and it was at this point that he thought he had been trapped. He heard a police siren outside the flat, but when he looked through the window he saw that the police were checking on a disturbance further down the street. He took £100 in cash from Bradley's wallet and later used his bank card to withdraw £200.

Before leaving the flat the next morning – after having spent the night listening to the radio – he went through his ultra-careful routine of cleaning up behind him. He told the police: "Anything I touched I put in a plastic bag. In his flat there was a wine glass I had touched. I made a point, for instance, of disposing of any footwear I was wearing. I always disposed of the gloves I had worn. In the case of the shoes I would rip them apart and then buy another pair." He could afford to: murder was becoming lucrative.

Even at this point the police could not link the three murders, although in each instance money had been taken from the bank accounts of the victims through their cashpoint cards. Each case was being investigated by different local teams of detectives, and there was no coordination. But Ireland was still making telephone calls to the newspapers and the police to brag about his slayings and to taunt them with threats of more to come.

By now the gay community had become terrified by news of the third murder. There was speculation that the unknown killer might have AIDS, and might be taking revenge for his own HIV infection on other gays. But they were not yet frightened enough to stop their activities. The fourth victim was also taken from the Coleherne.

Ireland went there on the evening of 7th June – just three days after his previous murder. He was becoming more proficient, and much quicker. He was in a hurry to qualify as a serial killer. The fourth victim was Andrew Collier, 33, from Dalston, east London. He was warden of a block of sheltered housing, and the elderly people he looked after had a high regard for him. What they didn't know was that he was gay. What Ireland didn't know was that he was also HIV positive.

At Collier's flat both men went to the window at one point when they heard a noise outside. It was this which caused Ireland to accidentally leave his fingerprints on a window grille. After strangling Collier, he went through his wallet and discovered a document notifying the victim that he was HIV positive. Ireland was to tell the police: "I think Collier was the only one I was angry with. In a funny way I suppose I felt angry with him because he thought there was going to be a normal sexual encounter – which there wasn't going to be."

As a result of his fury Ireland did something which was to puzzle the investigating detectives – something which didn't fit his pattern. He hanged Collier's pet cat, using a rope thrown over a door in Collier's flat. Then he left the dead animal draped obscenely over Collier's body. The cat's tail was in Collier's mouth, and its own mouth covered the end of Collier's penis; both the tail and the penis wore condoms. Although the similarities to Walker's death were obvious, it took the police several days to make the connection.

His ritual with the cat, Ireland told detectives: "was part anger. It was part of an increase in the thrill of killing. I wanted to know how you would react when you came across the scene. You're not thinking normally when you do something like this. But it was almost like a signature – to let you know I'd been there. I was reaching that point... you know, where you feel you have to step up a stage each time."

He added that by now the murders were "building up" inside him: "I was reaching a point where I was just accelerating. It was just speeding up, getting far worse. It wasn't just him making me angry, it was like a roller-coaster effect, and I felt that roller-coaster feeling more the more I killed."

Another reason for killing the cat might have been his reaction to press speculation that the unknown killer was an animal lover, because of the call he had made to the Samaritans. It had begun to annoy him.

After the murder of Collier, Ireland realised he had forgotten to ask the victim for his cash card PIN number, but in searching the flat he found £70 in cash. He also remembered that he had forgotten about a couple of things he had used, and he was anxious not to leave any fingerprints.

His confession went on: "There was a mug I had used, so I put that in the carrier bag and got rid of it later. I made a big search of his belongings – all his papers – trying to find his PIN number." As usual he remained with the body all that night before slipping away in the morning rush hour crowd.

The next day he telephoned the police at Kensington to claim responsibility for all four murders. "If you don't stop me," he said, "it will be one a week. I pissed myself when I read I was an animal lover. I thought I would give you lot something to think about so I killed the cat." Later the same day he telephoned Battersea police station and asked: "Are you still interested in the death of Peter Walker? Why have you stopped the investigation? Doesn't the death of a homosexual man mean anything? I will do another. I have always dreamed of doing the perfect murder."

Five days later – on 12th June – Ireland set out to select his fifth and final victim. He was Emmanuel Spiteri who worked as a chef. Maltese-born, he lived in Catford, south-east London, and made no secret of his sexual tastes. Ireland described him as being the "leather type".

Unlike the previous victims, Spiteri knew Ireland in a casual way. They had often exchanged glances in the Coleherne. Spiteri was described by his friends as being "joyful, with a nice personality and a pretty face." Ireland later commented on the resemblance between Spiteri and the actor James Dean. Within minutes, in Ireland's own words, "we then went from the Coleherne – via a couple of trains – to his flat."

At Spiteri's flat in Hither Green, Ireland handcuffed his victim and then tied his feet together before placing a noose around his neck.

"I bound him, but he was becoming suspicious," he said. "The word had got around about the gay murders and he was getting a bit worried. By then it was too late. But he was a very brave man. I told him I wanted his PIN number. He refused to give it to me, even after I threatened to kill him. He said, 'Do whatever you are going to do. You will just have to kill me.' It wasn't my primary motivation to kill him. It was more finance, money really. He was a very brave, strong-minded man, but I couldn't allow him to stick around and recognise me so I killed him with a noose again."

With the previous murder he had changed his pattern by hanging the cat; now he did something different again. After a night in the flat watching television and eating, he set the apartment ablaze before leaving it at dawn. The fire went out. When he was later asked why he had lit it, he told the police that he had once been a fireman, adding: "There's a bit of arsonist in all firemen. There's an element in me that's highly destructive, very cold. In some moods I'd be quite happy to burn the world down."

In less than four months he had killed five men and had achieved his ambition. In his own words: "That makes me a serial killer, doesn't it?"

In a telephone call made on 13th June, shortly before Spiteri's body was found, he told the police: "I have read a lot of books on serial killers. I think it is from five people that the FBI classify as serial, so I may stop now I have done five. I just wanted to see if it could be done – I will probably stop now and never reoffend."

The police had by now mounted extensive surveillance on the Coleherne pub, realising it was the common link with the victims. Gay police officers had infiltrated "the scene". They had the fingerprints of the likely killer, but as yet had no suspect. Fearing that the murderer would

357

strike again within days, Detective Chief Superintendent Ken John decided to appeal to him directly, appearing on television to say: "I need to speak to you. Enough is enough. Enough pain, enough anxiety, enough tragedy. Give yourself up."

Back-tracking on the victim's last known movements had given the police an extraordinary piece of luck. Having established that Spiteri and another man had travelled by train to Catford on the Saturday night, the police began an exhaustive search of British Rail security camera video films. At Charing Cross station they found several frames of the victim – with his killer close behind. Although blurred and partly out of the frame, now they had a face to put on the wanted posters. It was enough to make Ireland panic. He had made himself a suspect.

Realising that he might be identified from the picture, on 19th July, after a couple of days pondering, he walked into a solicitor's office in Southend and said he was the man pictured with Spiteri, and that he had indeed been with him on the night he died. But Ireland claimed that Spiteri had been alive when he left him at his home with another man. That other man must have killed him.

The police knew they had their man as soon as they began interviewing Ireland. He had told his boss a detail about the Collier killing which had never been released to the press – that a cat had been left on the dead man's body. And, of course, there was that fingerprint.

Once Ireland's fingerprints were taken and matched with those found at the Collier murder scene he was charged with that crime. The police believe he had gone to a solicitor because "he wanted the publicity but not punishment." It was the action of a man craving the limelight, demanding some recognition. Following his confession, he was charged with all five murders.

Detectives involved in the case rejected suggestions that

Ireland had given himself up because after killing five victims his mission was now accomplished. Detective Superintendent Albert Patrick was to say after the case: "Ireland didn't want to get caught. As an experienced criminal he knew that once the picture of him caught on a security video was published he might be recognised.

"He decided to go to a solicitor with a cover story, hoping that we would not have enough to pin it on him. Before he did, he cleared his digs of every shred of anything that might link him to his crimes. He got rid of his books on serial killers and anything else that might point to him. But he had forgotten that he had slipped up just once and left one damning fingerprint at the home of his fourth victim, Andrew Collier. From then on he was finished. If he hadn't been caught then he would probably have gone on killing."

Detective Chief Superintendent Ken John, who led the investigation, rejected criticism from gay activists that the fifth murder could have been prevented if the police had realised earlier the links between the first four killings. But although Ireland had claimed responsibility in his telephone calls to the police, they had to wait for scientific confirmation of any link. Ireland could simply have been a crank.

On 20th December 1993 he had his brief moment of fame when he appeared at the Old Bailey to be sentenced for five murders to which he had pleaded guilty.

In his first interview, prefacing his confession, Ireland had said that he wanted whoever judged him to send him to prison for life. He explained: "For what I have done I should be locked up for thirty years. I feel there is a side to my personality that can only be controlled by my being restricted by a prison regime. I think long-term prison establishments are humane and they take good care of you. I feel that I am okay within that restricted environment. But I feel that there are certain sides to my character – especially within the group that I was targeting – that mean I may offend again. I want to remove that possibility. I feel there is a certain side of my character – not all of it by any means – but I'm probably sixty to seventy per cent quite a reasonable human being most of the time. However, there is a side of my character that is quite cold and calculating. I feel that because of the confession I am going to make I face an extensive prison sentence and that will restrict me. That will stop me harming other people."

He added: "When my case comes to trial any judge worth his salt is going to find me guilty and will imprison me and by doing so allow me not to offend again for some time. That's all I really wanted to say."

During his two-hour appearance in the famous No 1 Court at the Old Bailey, Ireland, his steel-grey hair closely cropped, spent part of the time gazing around the court-room, delighting in watching reporters scribbling down the details of his killings. At other times he looked bored, yawning and staring stonily at the prosecuting counsel.

Waiting for this moment in prison, Ireland had sent Christmas cards to his friends, telling them to put the date of his trial in their diaries. To one he wrote: "Health and Happiness for 1994. P.S. Watch the news on December 20."

Opening for the prosecution, Mr John Nutting QC told the court of how Ireland had begun the New Year with a resolution to become a serial killer, of his attention to detail in carrying out his five murders, and how he tortured some of his victims for their PIN numbers.

Mr Nutting revealed that after he discovered that his first victim had AIDS, Ireland got some condoms and put one in the victim's mouth and another in his nostril. "As a further humiliation, he put two teddy bears on the bed in a 'sixty-nine' position."

Ireland, Mr Nutting continued, had been very keen to emphasise three points after his arrest. He told detectives that he had not been influenced by drink or drugs. Although he had worked as a bouncer at a gay nightclub in Soho he was not himself homosexual, had not undressed or had sex during his crimes or become sexually excited. He also denied being bisexual, but he did admit that he had a sadistic side and had engaged in sado-masochism with women.

Asked by baffled detectives about the motive for his crimes, Ireland said that he had been bullied at school "as a thin, lanky runt – always getting the worst of it. It was building up in me – a general dislike of people." He said that after losing his job at a night shelter in Southend – where he felt he had been badly treated: "I just went over the top... just a rapid deterioration speeded up. I cannot explain it any other way."

Ireland's defence counsel, Mr Andrew Trollope QC, told the court: "I can advance no mitigation for this series of truly dreadful crimes."

Ireland had made no excuses for what he had done, and two psychiatrists had declared him sane and well aware of what he was doing. Ireland accepted that he was a sadist. But there was also a "good, gentle, caring side to him." He cared for his paraplegic wife, rescued a boy from drowning in a quarry, and had worked with the disadvantaged.

Imposing five life sentences on the prisoner, Mr Justice Sachs addressed him directly:"By any standards you are an exceptionally frightening and dangerous man. In cold blood and with great deliberation you killed five of your fellow-human beings in grotesque and cruel circumstances. The fear, brutality and indignity to which you subject your victims are almost unspeakable. To take one human life is outrageous. To take five is carnage. You expressed the desire to be regarded as a serial killer – that must be matched by your detention for life. In my view it is absolutely clear you should never be released."

When the sentences were announced, Ireland's mother sobbed inconsolably in court. His stepfather described the five life terms as "justified."

With regard to the collection of books on serial killers which Ireland claimed to own, former FBI agent Robert Ressler, interviewed on radio, said in defence of his own volume, *Whoever Fights Monsters*, "It is a professionally designed book to aid society. In my many years working in criminality and law enforcement I have seen people who have used medical text books, law books, all sorts of things to support their deviant criminal behaviour. That is unfortunate. It is one of the prices we pay in a free society. If one deviant person abuses that in a free society we cannot close down the publication of books."

He also pointed out that the police had made use of his expertise in tracking down Ireland; the detective in charge of the investigation having "read all three of my books and gained material which helped him in his work."

What Robert Ressler said is true. Even in the last century there were deviants who got their sexual kicks from reading such Christian books as Foxe's *Book Of Martyrs*, with its detailed description of the tortures various saints suffered. Almost anything can be used as an aid to sexual fantasy by those so disposed – even "Little Red Riding Hood."

Books which tell us how to catch serial killers can only be useful. They tell us much about the psychology of such types.

Chapter Eighteen
ANDREI CHIKATILO
THE ROSTOV RIPPER

All was going well with the family picnic in the woods near Rostov, 500 miles from Moscow. It was a fine day in the summer of 1978, just right for such an outing. It was also a day the family would never forget: a holiday of horror. Awaiting them in those woods was a young girl's body, sexually assaulted, brutally mutilated.

As soon as they made the discovery the picnickers called the police. Stay put and wait, they were told. Before long a mustard-yellow *pobedas* (police car) arrived. Out stepped a senior investigator, straightening his cap. One look at the body sent him back to the car to radio for assistance. The savagery of the mutilation told him this was no ordinary murder. It was the work of a maniac. Unwittingly, the picnickers had raised the curtain on the career of the Rostov Ripper.

The *Militsiya* – or civil police – carried out a formal murder inquiry as best they could, given limited resources and a vast area to cover. A pathologist examined the body, after it had first been photographed *in situ*, and various samples were taken away for analysis. Semen found on the victim enabled the police to determine the blood group of the killer. Suspicion fell on a local man with a history of child-molesting and rape convictions. When a similar murder occurred – this time of a young boy – the suspect was arrested, and under interrogation he confessed. He was duly tried, found guilty, and executed. But the murders continued...

The police were stunned when the next killing took place, followed by another. Clearly the executed man had not been the murderer they had thought him to be. Detectives resumed their investigation. The police were largely immune from criticism because, for the most part, the public was kept in ignorance about the presence of a serial killer among them. No newspaper was allowed to print details of the murders, for such publicity would have been bad for the image of the Soviet Union. But among local people the news was spreading.

Within two years the unknown killer's tally of victims had risen to a dozen or more, and top investigators were sent for from Moscow. They too scratched their heads when confronted with the evidence. They had never seen anything like it.

Since the murders usually occurred in the narrow strips of forest which ran beside railway lines, the police had dubbed the wanted man "The Forest Strip Killer." They knew that he usually killed around Rostov, although he had possibly killed in the Ukraine and elsewhere. So he travelled. Possibly he owned a car, more likely he used the railway system. They knew his blood group. They knew his pattern. He was a sexual sadist. He did not seem to seek out a particular type, but killed girls, boys and women at random. All that mattered was that they were alone and could be tortured.

The ages of his prey ranged from eight to the mid-fifties. The victims were usually found with their hands bound behind their backs with thick twine. Many had been stabbed dozens of times with a knife, or had been attacked with a hammer. It appeared that the killer prolonged the death agonies to obtain the maximum pleasure. He cut off body parts, including the sexual organs, which he ate.

He made incisions into the eyes to blind his victims, biting off their tongues to stifle their screams. After perhaps hours of rape and torture, he would leave the victim disembowelled.

As the murders continued, the rumours began. Some believed the killings to be the work of a satanic sect; others whispered of a gang killing to obtain body organs to sell for transplants. The police knew better. No particular organs were removed, and certainly nothing suitable for transplant. The killer cut and mutilated as if experimenting, but always focusing on the sexual organs of his victims, who tended to be waifs and strays.

Similar murders, undoubtedly the work of the same man, now started to be reported in Leningrad, Moscow and in Central Asia. Whoever the killer was, he had an occupation which allowed him extensive travel. A rumour rife among the police was that the killer might be a top party man, a member of Russia's ruling élite.

The search for the Rostov Ripper had now become the biggest manhunt in Soviet history, with hundreds of officers involved in the hunt. But what still hampered the investigators – and was to do so for years to come – was the fact that there had been no press coverage of the case for fear it might be viewed as anti-Soviet propaganda. Had the public been warned that a serial killer was loose, he might have been caught much earlier.

In fact, in 1979 – just a year after the murders began – a militiaman apprehended a man called Andrei Chikatilo near the scene of one of the murders. But the gentle, middle-aged ex-schoolteacher was able to convince the officer that he was a nature lover, out collecting samples of the local flora and fauna. Besides, a grandfather in his mid-fifties did not fit the police impression of a killer so savage that some of his victims had been found with their windpipes bitten through.

And so the murders continued, victims being found almost every week. Once there were eight in a single month, and on another occasion there was the double-murder of a mother and daughter. Fifty investigators were now working on the case, along with five hundred policemen. News of the murders had begun leaking out, with critical reports in local Rostov newspapers. But slowly the police were making progress. From the American FBI they had borrowed "psychological profiling," a technique of building up a portrait of the killer from his method of operation and from clues left at the crime scene.

A leading psychiatrist, Alexander Bukhanovsky, was given the task of drawing up this profile, and he concluded that the killer was perhaps a sexually impotent teacher suffering from an inferiority complex who might seem respectable and dull to his neighbours. He put the killer at the top end of the age-scale. Killers of this type tend to be aged from 18 to 40. By 40 they will have either gone mad or have been imprisoned. The killer was *organised*, which meant he could function 95 per cent of the time in ordinary social settings and would appear quite normal to those around him. It was only in five per cent of his waking life that he turned into a fiend.

This profile fitted Andrei Chikatilo almost exactly. In 1984 he was again arrested near the scene of one of the murders, this time with a knife in his attaché case. Once again, however, he talked his way out of the situation by claiming to have been out in the woods studying nature.

Chief prosecutor Vitaly Kalyukhin was in charge of the massive investigation, and at his instigation hidden cameras photographed hundreds of men seen walking with teenagers, while women police officers acted as decoys. Twenty-five thousand men had been questioned, and 163,000 had been forced to give blood samples. The police believed they were seeking a man with a specific blood group – any man not of that group was dismissed from the inquiry. It was accepted that a man's sperm and blood shared the same group, and police had samples of the killer's sperm, found in the bodies of his victims. But in 1990 scientists discovered that one man in a million has sperm and blood samples which don't match. Chikatilo, it later transpired, was that one man in a million.

Meanwhile one suspect who was questioned many times became so depressed by it all that he committed suicide. After his death the police thought that the killings would stop. They did not. They continued with increased ferocity. Some officers became frightened, convinced that they were seeking a devil in human form. Superstition still lingers in primitive parts of Russia.

The murders of the Rostov Ripper had topped fifty, making him Russia's most prolific serial killer of all time, and his crude butchery displayed a growing frenzy. He had begun bursting his victims' eardrums with a screwdriver and gouging out their eyes *while they were still alive*. He would finally achieve sexual gratification – indicated by semen on the victims' bodies – by carrying out bizarre "operations". The boys had their testicles removed, the girls their wombs. Thus rumour had it that the killer was a doctor.

Children in every school in the region were given questionnaires to fill in. Had they ever been approached by a strange man? Had any of their friends reported such a contact? The scope of the investigation beamed so wide that in the 12 years it spanned the police solved more than a thousand unrelated crimes, including 95 murders.

The arrest of the Rostov Ripper came about through routine police work. Seven days after burying his last victim in the woods – on 6th November 1990 – Andrei Chikatilo was stopped for a routine check by a policeman who asked to see his papers. The officer noticed a speck of blood on his cheek and made a note of it in his report. When the body was discovered a few days later Chikatilo was put under surveillance.

Vitaly Kalyukhin explained later: "By that time we knew that the killer picked up many of his victims in suburban trains, and we had people in every wagon of every train out of Rostov."

On 20th November the watching detectives saw Chikatilo approach two boys, both of whom backed away from him. The decision was taken to arrest Chikatilo immediately. He was too dangerous to be allowed to run free any longer in the hope of catching him in the act.

The gentle-looking Chikatilo was taken to police headquarters for questioning. It didn't take him long to talk, and soon he was taking officers to sites in the forest where he had hidden even more bodies: corpses of people not known to be dead, but simply names on the missing persons' register. Chikatilo was proud of his excellent memory for places, names and dates. He talked calmly, almost indifferently, of every murder he had committed.

The softly spoken man, of obvious intelligence and good education, told of how he had killed a mother and her daughter by inviting them to come and see his non-existent country house. He planned his crimes too, reconnoitring the thick woods around Rostov to find good burial sites, and even changing his job so that he could travel and cast his net for victims wider.

How many people had he killed? Perhaps fifty-three, he told his horrified listeners. His *modus operandi* was to approach children on their way home from school and begin chatting to them, persuading them to take a walk in the woods to see some exotic plants or animals. As a former schoolteacher, he was charming and plausible. Other victims were lured with chewing gum, a meal, or the promise of watching a film on his video.

Describing his irresistible compulsion to kill, Chikatilo said: "As soon as I saw a lonely person I would have to drag them off to the woods. I paid no attention to age or sex. I would walk for a couple of hours or so through the woods, and then I would be seized by a terrible shaking sensation." Detectives wrote down his every word. Never had the former university graduate and teacher had such attentive students – and he appeared to revel in it.

He explained that he usually killed his victims with a single knife thrust between the eyes, although some had been strangled with a rope and some had their windpipes bitten through.

Chikatilo had grown up in the town of Novocherkassk, some 25 miles north-east of Rostov. By the time he reached puberty women loomed large in his fantasy life, but he was shy and inept. He wanted his women to be meek and submissive, but the reality was far different. He found great difficulty in establishing relationships with girls, who tended to laugh at his clumsy attempts to woo them. In his anger he began to blame women for his impotence.

To compensate for his lack of sexual prowess – he remained a virgin until well into his twenties – Chikatilo turned to self-improvement through education, graduating from Rostov University with a good degree in Russian literature. Even during his compulsory army service he was studying at the Lenin Library while his comrades were out chasing girls.

Chikatilo was a committed Communist, determined to succeed in life through his dedication to the Party. But knowledge of his sexual inadequacy was eating away at him, and the Communist Party of the Soviet Union did not recognise the existence of sex. Even if he had wanted to seek advice about his sexual problems, there was no one to turn to.

Marrying in 1966, when he was twenty-eight, he had managed to father a son and a daughter by 1969. Although he was becoming increasingly impotent, his wife did not complain. And he had other interests, for by now he was chairman of the local sports committee and was rewarded with a second-floor flat in a shabby block in his home town.

A few years later he moved to a new job, teaching literature at a boarding school in nearby Novoshaktinsk. Here he witnessed sexual encounters between boys and girls – encounters he had missed out on in his own youth. He became frustrated and bitter, consumed with rage. It was not long after this that children around Rostov began to disappear. The 12-year-long nightmare had begun. Yet during this same period, while he was killing, he was also writing articles for local newspapers about bringing up children in a proper Communist spirit.

In 1984, however, Chikatilo was arrested for the theft of "government property" – three rolls of linoleum – and was jailed for three months. He was also expelled from the Party, which meant the loss of his privileges. This confirmed his belief that the world was against him – even his beloved Party – and after his release, as if in revenge, he killed eight people in a month.

He had originally sought his victims in lonely forest strips, but he changed his methods when he got a factory job which meant he had to travel extensively. Then, in 1989, he was appointed head of supplies at Rostov's Lenin locomotive repair plant. This gave him the excuse and opportunity to hang around trains and stations looking for his young prey, often picking them up in railway carriages or buses.

Later chief prosecutor, Vitaly Kalyukhin, was to tell reporters: "Not one of the victims appears to have shown any sign that they went unwillingly to the woods with him, despite the fact that everyone in Rostov knew there was a cannibal on the loose who always took his prey into the woods. Chikatilo made contact with people very easily. I would say he had an amazing talent for it. He could join a bus queue and say to the person in front: 'Hey, where did you buy those beautiful mushrooms?' and before you knew it he would have the whole crowd chatting."

The police had quickly revealed the news that they had the Rostov Ripper in custody, and the *Tass* news agency reported how at least one innocent man had been executed for Chikatilo's crimes and another suspect had committed suicide. The authorities promised a posthumous pardon for the executed man, and officially cleared the suspect who had killed himself. In general, the Soviet press treated the case as a splendid example of good police work, although the leader writer of one Rostov newspaper commented: "It is not such a triumph to have caught a criminal after leaving him on the loose for twelve years."

Fearing reprisals from relatives of the victims' Chikatilo's wife and adult children fled the area following his arrest. They began life anew under assumed identities. In an interview before the trial the judge, Leonid Akubzhanov, told reporters: "This case is the only one of its kind in the whole world. There has never been anything like this anywhere."

Chikatilo had undergone a thorough psychiatric examination by doctors from Moscow's Serbsky Institute, who found him to be fully responsible for his actions. But he was to behave bizarrely throughout his trial, at first shaving his head and at times stripping naked inside his cage.

When he was first led into court spectators began wailing in anguish and shouting abuse, baying for his blood. An elderly woman began sobbing hysterically, shouting at him: "You are a damned soul – an evil sadist! How could this be allowed?" Chikatilo merely grinned at her. Another two sobbing women tried to break through the police cordon to attack him. Chikatilo removed his jacket and sat on the floor, grinning crazily and rolling his eyes, looking more like an inmate of a mental ward than one of the world's most ferocious killers.

The judge tried to calm the angry crowd, saying: "I understand your feelings, but we must have due process of law." But one plump, middle-aged woman shouted back: "We won't calm down. How can we calm down?" Her own young son had been one of Chikatilo's victims. The trial was delayed for 30 minutes while first-aid workers revived spectators who had fainted.

After the charges were read out by the prosecutor – a process which took several days – the court was told something of the history of the man, described by friends as a "kindly, retiring and respected grandfather," but who had confessed to having killed twenty-one boys and thirty-two girls and young women. And then the killer himself gave evidence.

From within his steel cage, Chikatilo described constant business trips during which he was forced to stay at dirty railway stations and miserable hotels. He complained that his bosses were rude to him.

Telling of how he had killed his victims with a knife, a rope, or even his teeth, Chikatilo said that he could not be sure of how many people he had murdered. "Possibly fifty-five, maybe more," he told the judge in a matter-of-fact tone. Although he raped most of his victims before killing them, he admitted to having had sex with at least one corpse.

He described his "joy and satisfaction" in eating the sexual organs of his teenage victims. One of his relatives had been eaten by starving peasants in the thirties, he said, and this had preyed on his mind, making him determined to exact revenge.

Chikatilo also complained that he was a victim of a totalitarian system, having been a graduate of the Marxist-Leninist Institute. In short, he blamed the Party for his crimes. But he also shouted: "I am a freak of nature, a mad beast, a mistake of nature!'"

The psychiatrist Alexander Bukhanovsky, who had examined Chikatilo in prison, told the court that the killer had inhabited a fantasy world since childhood, and by the time he reached 40 he was so deep in it that the only way he could achieve sexual satisfaction was through the cannibalistic atrocities which had shocked the nation – and indeed the world.

Treating Chikatilo in prison, taking the killer his breakfast every morning and chatting to him in the hope of learning more about his strange psychological make-up, the psychiatrist found he was far more intelligent and more sensitive than he appeared to be in the court. "He was a great theatre-goer. He could sit in on a performance of something by Chekhov and be moved to tears – but then go out and murder someone," said the doctor, who also revealed: "He is very interested in the American presidents; he can reel off the names and dates and biographies of every one of them."

On 14th October, 1992, the court formally found Andrei Chikatilo guilty of the murders of 52 people. As the judge said, "He ruthlessly and cold-bloodedly cut up his victims, literally tearing apart women and children while they were still alive."

The prisoner stood unshaven and without socks in his cage, a pathetic figure as he listened to the judge's condemnation.

The following day he was sentenced to death by a bullet to the brain.

An appeal for clemency was made, but President Yeltsin refused it. Chikatilo was executed on Valentine's Day, 14th February 1994. His death was mercifully swift. Scientists had hoped to study the killer's brain to see if it might give up any grisly secrets. Unfortunately, the bullet to the base of the brain is likely to have caused too much damage for any useful studies.

Chikatilo is likely to become one of the last Russian murderers to be executed. In the first six months of its existence, a presidential commission made up of writers and human rights activists commuted 45 death sentences and backed only one. The death penalty is not as popular as it used to be.

But it may enjoy a revival.

Even as Chikatilo's trial was in progress, the press reported the existence of a strangler, operating not far from Rostov, in the town of Taganrog. This killer selected young women who wore black tights, throttling them before leaving their bodies naked save for those tights. And, while Chikatilo was being tried, the death sentence was passed on a man known as Russia's "Jack the Ripper". Alexander Timofeyev, a former shepherd, had been convicted of raping nine women and murdering two of them. The *Tass* news agency reported that Timofeyev told the court that he "lost his head"' whenever he heard the clatter of his victims' high-heel shoes.

One sex killer is caught, another emerges.

As we try penetrate the icy madness of these killers' minds, we have to ask ourselves one question. How many others are there like them?

Conclusion
INSIDE THE MIND OF
THE SEX KILLER

This entire book has been an attempt to look inside the soul of the sex criminal, and now it is perhaps appropriate to ask ourselves what we have learned about the inner workings of his mind. At first glance the answer might seem to be: not very much. But in fact we now know a great deal, and we owe that knowledge to the pioneering work of Professor David Canter in England and the more celebrated FBI "Mind-Hunters" in the United States, and before them, to such people as Dr James Brussel, and even fiction writers like G.K. Chesterton, who was pointing the way forward in his Father Brown stories.

In *The Secret of Father Brown*, (1927) a rather curious American asks him how he had been able to solve so many murders. Had he used occult means? What was his secret? Father Brown replies, "You see, it was I who killed all those people... I murdered them all myself.... I had planned out each of the crimes very carefully, I had thought out exactly how a thing like that could be done and in what style or state of mind a man could really do it. And when I was quite sure that I felt exactly like the murderer myself, of course I knew who he was."

Father Brown describes his technique as being "a religious exercise" recommended to him by a friend of the Pope. But in fact Chesterton was describing how a detective could get inside the mind of a killer and by thinking like him, capture him. Such ideas were quickly followed up in real life.

Dr James Brussel was formerly the Assistant Commissioner of Mental Hygiene for the State of New York and psychiatric consultant to various police forces. It comes as no surprise to learn that he once worked for the CIA. The Press have described him as the "Sherlock Holmes of the couch", and his fascinating account of the criminal cases in which he has been involved, *Casebook of a Criminal Psychiatrist* (1968), certainly bears this out.

The police first consulted Dr Brussel about the case of the "Mad Bomber" who planted twenty-eight explosive devices around New York City over a sixteen-year period, beginning in 1940. With the bombs came letters blaming "Con Edison", the company which supplies the city with its electricity. In December 1956 a bomb planted in the back of a cinema seat injured six people, forcing the police to mount a major hunt for the bomber.

Inspector Howard Finney of the New York Police Crime Laboratory visited Dr Brussel, giving him copies of the letters from the bomber and the files on the case. After studying the documents for some time, Dr Brussel told the detective: "It's a man. Paranoiac. He's middle-aged – forty-five to fifty. Well-proportioned in build. He's single, a loner, perhaps living with an older female relative. He is very tidy, neat and clean-shaven. Well-educated but of foreign extraction. He's a Slav. Probably lives in Bridgeport, Connecticut. (Bridgeport has a large Polish community.) He has had a bad disease – possibly heart trouble. When you catch him he'll be wearing a double-breasted suit. Buttoned."

When he was arrested at his home in Bridgeport, Connecticut, George Metesky, the "Mad Bomber", was found to be well-proportioned, aged fifty-one years, of

Polish extraction, unmarried, living in a house with two older sisters, and was wearing a double-breasted suit. Buttoned.

Why had Dr Brussel's profile been so accurate? Because it was based on solid deductive reasoning, experience, and playing the averages. Paranoia takes a long time to develop – say ten years before that first bomb in 1940 – which meant he had started to become ill in 1930, making him middle-aged in 1956. Paranoiacs tend to feel intellectually superior, are neat and obsessive, tidy to a fault. Hence the neat lettering on the notes and the double-breasted suit. The words in the notes were those of an educated man, but had no American slang and read as if they had been translated into English. The wildly Victorian "dastardly deeds" in one note hinted at a foreigner. Why a Slav? Because historically bombs have been favoured in Central Europe. Well-proportioned? Because research had shown that 85 per cent of paranoiacs have an athletic build. Why a paranoiac? Because they are the champion grudge-holders. Why single? Because of all the neatly printed capital letters in the notes, only the "W" was odd: it was shaped like two U's joined together – the shape of a woman's breasts. This suggested that the Mad Bomber had sexual problems... It all sounds far-fetched, but it actually worked, and Dr Brussel went on to solve many other cases using the same techniques. And, of course, the FBI's "psychological profiling" owes much to his pioneering approach.

We can sum up the data gained to date by saying that the typical sex killer is usually young – probably under thirty-five years old – and fantasises about killing long before he actually turns to murder. He tends to be a quiet, withdrawn person – witness Sutcliffe and Dennis Nilsen – and in most cases kills not for sexual needs, but to service power needs.

There is usually some history of early abnormal behaviour, graphically seen in the case of Kürten and in Patrick Byrne's peeping-Tom activities. There may be bed-wetting, arson, cruelty to animals. There is usually some trace of necrophilia present in the killings, and more often than not a latent homosexual streak in the killer. Most have rich fantasy lives.

Currently there is great disquiet about cannibal cases. Jeffrey Dahmer's seventeen cannibal murders in Milwaukee highlighted the problem, but there are many others to choose from. There are the Russian cannibal killers, Nikolai Dzhumagallev, nicknamed "Metal Fang", who butchered dozens of women, serving their barbecued flesh to his unsuspecting neighbours and Andre Chikatilo, "The Rostov Ripper", whose crimes were perhaps even more gruesome. Then there is the case of Issei Sagawa, the Japanese killer who raped, murdered and devoured the flesh of a Dutch student, Renée Hartewelt, in Paris in 1981. And there are the disgusting crimes of Albert Fish in the 1920s... The American psychologist Joel Norris has written four books on three hundred separate serial killers, and claims that about one in three experiments with cannibalism, often saving portions of their victims as a talisman. Christie, of course, saved pubic hairs...

Does it help to try to see what these killers have in common? They do not look alike, for example, or even have the same or similar domestic situations. Albert DeSalvo committed thirteen murders and 1,300 sex crimes but was young and good-looking and his wife complained that he was sexually insatiable. Ted Bundy had an active sex life, and Norman Collins dated two or three times a week. Paul Knowles was an attractive man who had normal relations with many women. Gary Heidnik had enough money to employ all the prostitutes he wanted. For the most part these were all intelligent, dominant men who wore what Dr Norris calls a "mask of sanity". On the other hand, Dennis Nilsen was miserably alone, as was Michael Dowdall and Edward Gein. Intellectually the killers range from idiots like Kenneth Erskine to able, and perhaps even brilliant characters like Jack Unterweger. They can be obviously vicious like Colin Ireland and Peter Sutcliffe, or ostensibly placid like Christopher Wilder and Andre Chikatilo...

In other words, we cannot detect sex-killers by their appearance, domestic situations or day-to-day behaviour. *Nor should we expect to.* The sexual impulse is primarily a mental process. It begins inside the head. So too does sex murder. It germinates within a closed, secret interior universe. We only get the chance to look inside the head of a sex killer after he has been caught, and only then, with the benefit of hindsight, will some of his early behaviour take on significance and reveal a pattern. That is the value of compiling cases like these: every new case provides us with that much more data, so that we can begin profiling the sex killer as a type, and hopefully we may quickly identify him.

We are now in a position to make some statements about the nature of sex killers, even though in most cases they are merely broad generalizations. It is a fact that sex killing is a specifically male activity motivated by a lust for power, or as a means of expressing intense anger. Adler would seem to have been nearer the mark than Freud in this respect.

Generally, the sex killer will belong to one of three broad types, the characteristics of which may overlap in some cases. First we have the "biological" killer, whose crimes are triggered by a physical defect of some sort. A surprising number of such killers have a history of head injuries in early youth. Albert DeSalvo might be considered to have been born with an over-active sex-drive, perhaps an organic brain defect.

The second type of killer is psychologically predisposed to kill. Perhaps there was a trauma in early childhood, or the child grew up in an all-female environment, or was rejected by females. Many sex killers were brought up within a dysfunctional family unit of one sort of another and these individuals are more likely to be motivated by a power-needs complex, and to kill compulsively over and over again to release some internal psychic pressure. Both Bundy and Sutcliffe were of this type.

The third type might be termed the sociological, for want of a better word. They are "made" killers, born into a grim environment, the typical deprived-child syndrome. This type may feel that he has been cheated, that life owes him more, that he is being brutalized by his job, marriage, or life in general. He would welcome imprisonment, since prison imposes a structure on life and gives meaning and order to existence. Hence Heirens's note: "For Heaven's sake catch me before I kill again." To such a miserably alienated person only the act of murder can bring a sense of being alive to his torpid sense of reality. To him murder is therapeutic: murder as psychodrama.

Norris warns us that demands for capital punishment are counter-productive because: "Perversely, he wishes for death, and the threat of the gas-chamber and the electric chair or lethal injection is only an inducement to keep committing murders until he is caught and put to death... The serial killer can no more stop killing than a heroin addict can kick the habit."

And so finally, what use is all this information to us? Here we must admit that, on a purely practical level, the answer must be "very little". It may be possible in the future to devise a diagnostic test to detect serial killers *before* they begin to kill. But not yet.

However, the situation is not as bleak as it appears,

and there is good reason to feel optimistic about the future. Technical advances alone will help to make the detection of sex killers that much easier.

But the most exciting and promising developments have been in the field of behavioural science. The detective is no longer expected merely to sleuth; he must also be a psychologist. The new type of "psychological detectives" will prove to be far more successful than the old type of man-hunters. You simply cannot hope to catch a sexual serial killer by the same means that you would employ to catch a bicycle thief. You need to become a mind-hunter. And in a very real sense, every reader of this book has now become just that...

INDEX